# Voices from the Digital Classroom

UNIVERSITY OF CALGARY
LCR Publishing Services

# Voices from the Digital Classroom

25 Interviews about Teaching and Learning in the Face of a Global Pandemic

Edited by Sandra Abegglen, Fabian Neuhaus, & Kylie Wilson

LCR Publishing Services
An imprint of University of Calgary Press
2500 University Drive NW
Calgary, Alberta
Canada T2N 1N4
press.ucalgary.ca



LIBRARY AND ARCHIVES CANADA CATALOGUING IN PUBLICATION

Title: Voices from the digital classroom : 25 interviews about teaching and learning in the face of a global pandemic / edited by Sandra Abegglen, Fabian Neuhaus, Kylie Wilson.
Names: Abegglen, Sandra, editor. | Neuhaus, Fabian, editor. | Wilson, Kylie (Researcher), editor.
Identifiers: Canadiana (print) 20220223068 | Canadiana (ebook) 20220223076 | ISBN 9781773852782 (softcover) | ISBN 9781773852799 (open access PDF) | ISBN 9781773852805 (PDF) | ISBN 9781773852812 (EPUB)
Subjects: LCSH: Web-based instruction. | LCSH: College teachers—Interviews. | LCSH: College students—Interviews. | LCGFT: Interviews.
Classification: LCC LB1028.57 .V65 2022 | DDC 378.1/7344678—dc23

The University of Calgary Press acknowledges the support of the Government of Alberta through the Alberta Media Fund for our publications. We acknowledge the financial support of the Government of Canada. We acknowledge the financial support of the Canada Council for the Arts for our publishing program.

Printed and bound in Canada by Friesens
♻ This book is printed on 57lb Rolland Enviro Opaque FSC

Copyediting by Peter Midgley
Cover design, page design, and typesetting by Frances Motta

# Contents

*Interviews included represent a selection.

INTERVIEWS

# Foreword: Technology-Enhanced Learning in COVID Times

Alex Spiers, Eden Centre, London School of Economics and Political Science, United Kingdom

From 2018 to 2020, I worked at the Liverpool Institute for Performing Arts (LIPA) as the technology-enhanced learning (TEL) manager, leading the digital transformation strand of a Higher Education Funding Council for England (HEFCE) funded Catalyst project, an ambitious program of research and change aimed at transforming the physical learning environment, developing new curricula with industry partners, as well as instigating a program of digital education innovations to support enhanced teaching and learning practice at the school.

What follows is a collection of actions, reflections and activity as a TEL manager looking back over the fog of those first COVID-19 months in Spring 2020, which coincided with the ending of the digital education strand of Catalyst. Not being a diligent blogger, the writing for this foreword has been pulled together from tweets, **Evernote** documents, scribbles snatched at odd hours of the day and night, and photos. My reflection on events and activities starts in January 2020, just before COVID-19 appeared in the news media, and governments started implementing rules and regulations to curb the spread of the virus. It encompasses the United Kingdom (UK) national COVID-19 lockdown in March 2020, through to my departure from LIPA at the end of June 2020, when it became clear that technology-enhanced learning and teaching would be the "next big thing."

### Institutional Project Context

LIPA opened in 1996 to forge a new approach to performing arts training (LIPA, 2022). As one may expect from a relatively new institution, LIPA's implementation and adoption of technologies to support blended learning was at an early stage of development prior to 2018, although technology-enhanced learning had existed since the beginning. This first included the use of analog technologies such as land-line telephones, audio tapes and photocopiers and then, more recently, digital technologies, electronic tools, systems, devices, and resources that generate, store and/or process data. However, the blended approach, combining face-to-face learning activities with online learning components, was still in its infancy more than two decades later, when I joined the institution.

In January 2018, LIPA was awarded £3.87m by HEFCE for a project to expand its curriculum and transform its learning facilities (LIPA 2018). The Catalyst funding aim was twofold: 1) to help the institution address the changing nature of the performing arts industries by developing graduates' understanding of the new ways in which performance is created and help them develop the skillsets that are required for this; and 2) to embed "modern" teaching methods and practices to ensure an effective digital learning experience and expand the technological provision for students.

LIPA had been using a single VLE (Virtual Learning Environment) for twelve years but much of its practice had an emphasis on administrative rather than pedagogic functions. Furthermore, there was neither limited technical support available, nor someone who could train faculty or students to make the best use of the system. Anecdotal feedback about the system was negative, focusing on its unreliability, basic functionality, and difficulty of use. To move forward with a technology-enhanced curriculum and teaching approach, it was therefore key to remove this prejudice, reduce the barriers to its adoption and effective use, and provide highly visible, expanded guidance and support. The TEL team was tasked with mitigating the issues associated with large-scale digital transformation and developing solutions for accessible and student-focused technology and pedagogy.

## Adapting Learning and Teaching: An Attempt

The Catalyst project was well underway by January 2020 with the adoption of new learning technologies and the subsequent creation of new facilities for film, TV, green screen work and motion capture, alongside the development of a bespoke virtual learning and performance space that would enable students to access, record and publish digital material. Additionally, TEL developed a newsletter that kept staff and students informed about the project and engaged them in a wider discussion about digital teaching and learning. While the project started slowly, many new technologies were introduced, and the existing ones were updated and relaunched.

While everything got off to a good start, COVID-19 then entered the stage, dominating more and more meetings and hallway discussions, and management decisions. On 23 March 2020, the UK government legally enforced a stay-at-home order, or lockdown, meaning the final face-to-face project meeting that we had was on 6 March 2020. At that time, we did not know that this would be our final in-person get-together but everyone attending sensed that COVID-19 would transform not only our project and work, but higher education more generally.

The first few weeks in lockdown were hectic and stressful for a variety of reasons. As a TEL manager, I had to deal with various questions and issues, ranging from the prevention of "Zoombombing" to the rapid rollout of MS Teams as the synchronous learning platform for the institution, and ad-hoc IT support and teaching advice. Invaluable at that time was the help of the wider TEL community on Twitter but also regional support groups such as Digi Learn Sector. Still, working from home put pressure on the family because of the collapse of home and workplace, and private and professional live. Like many in support roles in higher education, I was often working early in the morning and late at night to meet tight deadlines and minimize, as much as was possible, any detrimental impact to the staff and student experience.

The TEL work continued like this throughout April, with a short but desperately needed intermission because of Easter. During this time, we adapted a range of final assessments from in-person face-to-face, to wholly online. The Dance department, who, by their own admission, "used very little TEL in their teaching," responded to this challenge most flexibly. For example, building on their pre-pandemic work of filming a range of ballet steps for revision, senior lecturer, Anna Hall, with support from the TEL team, introduced a novel method of assessment during the lockdown to ensure that students were still able to learn, receive feedback and meet assessment requirements (Spiers et al. 2021). Students were provided with access to the institutional digital video platform, where they could use the Panopto app to record themselves demonstrating the range of steps they were being assessed on. These were done in a variety of different locations, including at home, in the garden, in the kitchen or wherever they had space. Once uploaded, the tutor was able to view them in Moodle, the learning management system, and provide feedback on their work. Both students and staff found this to be a useful approach to a difficult situation.

Finally, in May 2020, the stay-at-home order was lifted, allowing for an initial reflection on the situation. This coincided with the confirmation that my TEL manager contract would not be extended because the digital transformation strand of the project had come to an end. Luckily, at that time, there was an increase in learning technologist vacancies across the higher education sector, with organizations expanding their teams in preparation for the future. This allowed me to apply for new positions and, a short while later, take on a new role at a different university.

**Reflection and Discussion**

The COVID-19 pandemic has accelerated the demand for educational technology and learning technologists in a way never seen before (Morris 2020). Most universities and educational institutions were at one point or another forced to deliver all or part of their programs online. Yet, as my example shows, even with the heightened demand for online education specialists, my TEL contract was not extended. This was disappointing and, to some extent, it seemed that there was no rational explanation for it.

Looking at national statistics of employment at that time, however, I was not the only one to lose my job at that time. As outlined in the *Coronavirus: Impact on the Labour Market* report by Powell and Francis-Devine (2021, 9), "The recorded level of redundancies in September–November 2020 was the highest in any quarter since the records began in 1995, at 402,000." In addition, many institutions announced "faculty hiring freezes" in response to the uncertainty caused by the pandemic (Flaherty 2020).

So, although the opportunities to develop educational technology and expand online education increased with the emergence of the COVID-19 pandemic, these were not without contradiction. While there was a lot of enthusiasm for new tools and software, and a heightened demand for support and guidance, there was an equal amount of pressure and stress that academic and professional services staff as well as students were under and had to deal with. This tension becomes visible in the conversations presented in this book, together with the creative solutions that individuals found to deal with the unprecedent situation.

As time progressed, people certainly got more "secure" and confident. They began experimenting with existing technology, tried out new software and tools, started discussions around sustainable educational practice, and formed support networks to co-create and invent. Yet, at the time of writing, the pandemic is ongoing, demanding flexibility from everyone involved in higher education. The future is uncertain, but technology has entered the educational arena for good. A big question remains: How can we maintain the increased adoption of educational software and tools, and make good use on the promise of TEL to create the education and education system we want, rather than reverting back to the way it has always been done?

### Acknowledgements

Thanks go to Vaiva Adamonyte and Carol Maynard for their hard work and unerring support.

ABOUT

**Alex Spiers** is currently a senior learning technologist and part of the Eden Centre for educational enhancement at the London School of Economics and Political Science. He has been working in UK higher education for seventeen years at a range of institutions that include research intensive Russel Group to small specialist schools. He has significant knowledge in blended learning, Electronic Management of Assessment (EMA), Virtual Learning Environment (VLE) administration, effective use of digital media for feedback, and the use of social media in higher education. He regularly presents at national and international conferences and has contributed to writing and research within his field. He is a keen collaborator and active participant in a wide range of technology focused user groups and online open education courses such as #CreativeHE, BYOD4L and MELSIG (Media-Enhanced Learning Special Interest Group). He was co-founder of Association for Learning Technology North West England SIG and an event organizer for the Heads of eLearning Forum steering group.

# Introduction

TALON, the Teaching and Learning Online Network

> *"It is not about the technology; it's about sharing knowledge and information, communicating efficiently, building learning communities and creating a culture of professionalism ... "*
>
> Marion Ginapolis, Superintendent of Lake Orion Community Schools, US

In March 2020, higher education experienced a monumental shift as COVID-19 forced universities across the world to move their teaching online. Driven to capture this pivotal moment in history, TALON, the Teaching and Learning Online Network, spoke with faculty, education professionals and students about their experiences. *Voices from the Digital Classroom: 25 interviews about teaching and learning in the face of a global pandemic* showcases the voices collected. The collection presents a time capsule of the early days of the pandemic; a period of rapid change where bedrooms were turned into makeshift offices, kitchen cabinets became Zoom backgrounds and FlappyBird advanced to the 'go-to' icebreaker game.

Most of us working from home wrestled with similar experiences, trying to embrace the 'new normal' while juggling distractions, and a never-ending flood of emails and online meeting requests. Two years later, it is already hard to remember these early days of emergency remote working and instruction. Revisiting the void that opened overnight and the scramble to fill it with structure is a treasure trove of great intentions desperately trying to find a foothold on a slippery slope flooding with new tech to build a foundation for learning and teaching to continue.

The voices presented in this book highlight how instructors and students alike navigate the emerging and rapidly changing educational landscape. This makes the book an interesting read for all those who have had similar experiences as well as those interested in education who want to find out more about teaching and learning in pandemic times.

## The TALON voices

The voices included in this book were collected between July and December 2020. They were conducted by TALON team members, mainly the Graduate Assistant Researchers. In total, 27 interviews were held, of which 25 are included in this book.

The interviews conducted at the beginning of the COVID-19 pandemic, between July and September 2020 Series 01 Voices, focused on the following questions:

- The biggest challenge experienced when moving to remote teaching?
- The opportunities created by digital education?
- Your most used software/tool?
- Your favorite resource for teaching online?
- What do you expect Higher Education to look like in 10 years?

The later interviews, Series 02 Voices, conducted between September and December 2020, expanded on these questions and prompted interviewees to further reflect on the changes experienced as well as the benefits and challenges of remote education:

- How has your teaching changed in 2020/21?
- What are the opportunities created by digital education?
- Are you seeing challenges with remote teaching?
- Which is your most used tool for remote teaching?
- Can you point out your favorite resource for remote teaching?
- What do you expect Higher Education to look like in 10 years?

All voice interviews were transcribed and edited for this book, presented in the order in which they were conducted. Each interview is presented as it unfolded, structured according to the questions posed. With the themes of the conversation emerging and experiences being 'raw' at the time, it means there are moments of inaccuracy due to a literal lack of terminology, and an overwhelming number of new directives, protocols, and tools. For example, some of the interviewees had difficulties recalling exact names of software and tools that were introduced rapidly and in vast number. Others misremembered names of IT support services and technology resources that were created on the fly by institutions to support faculty and students. It was a conscious decision to leave these inaccuracies in the text to capture the atmosphere at the time.

In a short epilogue each interviewee has revisited the conversation a year later adding an update or extension to the original discussion. There are many moments in these personal reflections that provide deep insights on 'what worked'—and 'what didn't'—providing an overview of what can be learned from the time when higher education was turned digital overnight.

## Additional Voices

Included in the book are additional voices to complement the stories told. These include a *Foreword* by Alex Spiers, Senior Learning Technologist at The London School of Economics and Political Science, in the United Kingdom, and an *Afterword* by Richard Parker, Honorary Fellow at the University of Calgary. Spiers, in the vein of the TALON Voices, provides reflections on digital learning based on his role as Technology Enhanced

Learning Manager leading the digital transformation strand of a project aimed at transforming education delivery with and through digital innovations. He poses important questions about the role of technology in education while advocating for a conscious use of technology to create the education system we want rather than the one we think we need. Parker, similarly to Spiers, takes his personal experience as a starting point to explore the possibilities of digital technology, not just in academia but also in other institutional settings. He outlines how a center for seniors adapted its offerings and how this has created new opportunities and connections, prompting questions about what might be possible regarding technology-enhanced learning for different age groups and across generations.

Julian Salinas, Photographer, and Frances Motta, Graphic Designer, outline how they have 'translated' the digital material into print format. Salinas describes how the recorded Zoom interview videos became portrait stills that capture the moment of the interview as well as the personality of the interviewee. Motta outlines how she developed the design for a book that discusses the struggle with virtuality to support the translation of digital content into print format. Their voices highlight the challenges and opportunities of projects where digital information needs to be transformed for long-term preservation and expanded discussion hinting at the new hybrid era we are about to enter.

**Concluding Outlook**

Developed from the TALON voices interviews conducted at the beginning of the COVID-19 pandemic, *Voices from the Digital Classroom: 25 interviews about the teaching and learning in the face of a global pandemic* outlines online education experiences by faculty, education professionals and students. The voice contributors bring forth unique, international perspectives on software, technology-enhanced teaching, online learning and remote classrooms. This makes the book a historic cache of information to delve into.

The aim of the book is to provide you, the reader, with a platform for critical thought, resources and inspiration as well as a sense of connectedness to the challenges, successes and perspectives in the arena of digital higher education.

We hope that the voices provided transform into wider conversations about the areas of online education that have been accelerated by the pandemic, and raise questions about access, connectivity, equity and diversity, testing and evaluation, wellbeing and many more. TALON advocates for a future of higher education that considers the many and not the few—in the spirit of the continuing heightened sense hybridity across academia. Thus, it is important that we learn from the past because we are truly all in this together. As Lisa Silver (S02:E11) said:

*"... I think there's always an opportunity to do things better."*

# Acknowledgements

**The Land**

TALON has mainly unfolded online; while apart in separate makeshift settings we were all on the land somewhere and therefore connected. We would like to acknowledge the land on which the TALON team works, the traditional territories of the people of the Treaty 7 region in Southern Alberta, which include the Tsuut'ina First Nation, as well as the Stoney Nakoda (including the Chiniki, Bearspaw, and Wesley First Nations), and the Blackfoot Confederacy (comprising the Siksika, Piikani, and Kainai First Nations). The City of Calgary is also home to Métis Nation of Alberta, Region 3.

**Thanks**

TALON would like to thank the Richard Parker Initiative for its generous support. Special thanks go to all the Voice Series contributors for taking the time to share with us and speak about their experiences in the digital classroom, and Alex Spiers and Richard Parker for their framing thoughts.

Additional thanks go to Julian Salinas for the photographs and Frances Motta for the book design.

We would also like to mention Clare Sandford who did the initial proof-reading and helped us frame the interview transcriptions.

The TLN editorial team
Sandra Abegglen, Fabian Neuhaus, & Kylie Wilson

# Series One

July - December 2020

# Gregory Tweedie

Associate Professor, Werklund School of Education,
University of Calgary, Canada

Interviewed July 2020 by *Martina MacFarlane*

*MM Greg, why don't you start by telling us a bit about what you do?*

GT I'm an associate professor at the Werklund School of Education. My particular interest is to do with language teaching English as an additional language. I do a lot of online teaching, in particular teacher development for those who are language specialists.

*MM You recently won a University of Calgary teaching award. Can you tell us more about that, and about what led to that accomplishment and recognition?*

GT I was lucky enough to receive the Teaching in Online Environments Award. The application was due before we heard of COVID-19, and I have been involved in, and have really enjoyed, online teaching for quite some time before that. The award recognizes that earlier work. The students that nominated me, humbled me with their response about the engagement that they had experienced during my courses. That was the greatest compliment I could have received, to be recognized for that formally. The timing was quite coincidental, as then we switched the whole university to online learning.

*MM Clearly, you've come into this current COVID situation with a wealth of prior knowledge and experience in online teaching. What, for you, has been the biggest challenge experienced when moving to remote or online teaching?*

GT I think the biggest challenge in any online teaching is presence, enhancing the sense of presence. We all need human contact. I've learned through the school of hard knocks that it's not enough to post an article up on to the course platform—**D2L** or whatever platform—and then just give instructions—in written form—for students to read it.

One of the students wrote in one of my USRIs (Universal Student Ratings of Instruction) that sometimes they experience online learning as a nebulous concept, that someone just posts an article, and then there's a written discussion. There is no sense of person-to-person contact. And so, using video, the affordances that video gives us, the video technology that's built into D2L (the learning platform we have at the University of Calgary), it is an enormously beneficial tool for meeting that challenge of presence, instructor to student, and student to student.

*MM In trying to tackle this challenge of presence and jumping full force into the online world, what are some of the opportunities created by digital education?*

GT There's something called the SAMR (Substitution, Augmentation, Modification, and Redefinition) model. It's a hierarchy of the affordances of technology for education. At the bottom of the hierarchy are the technological tools that don't actually do anything different than traditional classroom methods. For example, a keyboard really is a pen and paper. It has the same functionality. At the top end of the hierarchy are things that technology actually brings to education, to learning, that are not available in a typical classroom. For example, the ability to write on a **Google document** simultaneously, of having people co-composing a Google Doc—you can't really imagine that in a blackboard scenario at the front of the classroom, with people leaning over each other to co-compose. So that's one of the opportunities the tools of technology provide. There are other tools like that. We tend to use those tools that we're comfortable with, so a lot of those tools are the same as a traditional classroom, like posting an article and reading it, and then writing about it. So, things that enhance presence—technology affords us some of those—we just have to put them to work.

*MM* *I apologize, Greg. You may have heard my dog barking in the background, and I guess that's one of these added challenges of remote learning or collaboration of any kind, especially when it comes to things like Zoom meetings. You're suddenly transported to my living room, and you're hearing sounds around me as well.*

GT Yes, but having said that, when you're managing a group of junior high boys with the windows open, and people are passing in the hallways, and people can't find their books, or their pencil breaks, or are asking to go to the bathroom—these distractions are, in a way, more easily managed online. On **Zoom** I can mute a distracting student, but I can't press harder to mute them in a junior high classroom.

*MM* *That makes a lot of sense. You do have a lot more control in some ways over your students, or co-collaborators, and how they participate along the way. That's a plus! So what would you say is your most-used software tool?*

GT So, an assumption you could make about me is that because of winning the online teaching award, I am the ultimate tech geek; and I'm actually not. There are a lot of people who are more tech savvy than me. What I have learned to do is to use the D2L platform, which we're provided at the university, to the max. I do my best not to have students needing to access other software tools. I'm really interested in containing the course within the software provided by the university. So I've learned to use lots of tools in D2L—not all of them, I'm still learning—to maximize the teaching and learning. That way, students don't have to sign up for a tool just for this course, get a password, and give their e-mail and contact information to who knows what, or where. Everything is self-contained. So I work almost exclusively with the university-provided course platform, D2L.

*MM* *Working with D2L, there are lots of built-in features and different tools that you can use. So what are some of your favourite resources, within D2L, for online teaching?*

GT The best feedback I've received from students is about the use of video in D2L. I generally don't do written discussions. I ask students to read and respond to a prompt by video, and I use the D2L-only feature for video. It's called **Video Assignments**. They click a button, the program accesses their camera and mic on their computer, and records. And so, my discussions on D2L are student-to-student video discussions. Although many students are nervous at first, in the course evaluations that's often what they list as the strongest feature of the course. They're producing videos themselves. I do my lecture content and recorded screencast videos in video, but here I am talking about student-produced videos using D2L itself. Another feature that I use

*"... I think the success of teaching and learning will always be that element of presence."*

is that I put everything that a student needs on the course landing page and use links so I don't have them searching around looking for what they need to do each week. It's all a click away: A new window opens to that task. So, those are a couple of the D2L features that I really use a lot.

MM *It sounds like a lot of what you do in your teaching is working to bring that human element back into the platform by aligning how you would approach any regular in-person class, and then using features that can leverage that human connection in the class. Is that right?*

GT The online research literature uses the term "presence"—instructor presence, student presence. How I make decisions about technology and which technology to use is to ask, "Does it enhance learner-teacher presence?"

MM *As always, new tools are emerging and quick shifts to the online world are happening. What do you expect that higher education might look like in ten years' time?*

GT It's so difficult to predict. COVID has punctured internationalization in a way, and it's very difficult for me to predict. I think there will be micro-credentialing. I think universities worldwide will have to do a lot of work around recognizing each others' credentials. Yeah, it's a very confusing world at present. I expect that the key issue for successful teaching and learning, no matter how advanced the technology is, is going to be presence. To what extent does it humanize it? I guess that's a belief that I have about education—that knowledge and values are transmitted from person to person, and that they are taken on board as people share with people. And so I don't expect that will change. The means by which we do it might get better, faster, more complex. But I think the success of teaching and learning will always be that element of presence.

MM *I think that message is both simple and really quite profound. The goal of knowledge sharing is very much the same as ever, but the tools are rapidly changing. Do you have any last thoughts, or additional tips and tricks that you'd like to share?*

GT If there were two things that I would pass on to encourage instructors who are thrown into emergency online remote teaching, the first would be that you don't have to be a tech geek to pull it off. D2L provides a lot of the tools that you need, and you don't have to be a computer whiz. Most of the instructors I know who are struggling with the idea of online teaching in my small circle are already doing the basic functions that are required to pull off an online course—they're emailing, they're uploading and posting and sharing. So really, you don't have to be a super tech geek.

The second piece of advice I'd have, and I say this because I'm not as IT savvy as other people, is to stick with a platform. In this case, stick with the university-prescribed one and learn it well. Rather than pull things from here, there and everywhere, I encourage instructors, especially if they're beginning this process, to work within the system you have as far as possible.

I would say that this third piece of free advice probably reflects my learning style. I've never read an owner's manual for a computer, or a car, or the desk I bought from IKEA. I just don't work that way. When I have a question, I go find the answer. I don't like to read the manual from start to finish, because a lot of the information is not relevant. But when there's a fuse that I can't identify, I go looking for it in the owner's manual. So, too, much of what's offered is one-size-fits-all workshops. And I think that freaks people out, when you have things like a workshop on how to use D2L, or a workshop on how to use **YuJa**. I attended an excellent workshop on YuJa, but ten percent of it was relevant to me. The presenters were outstanding, but they were trying to give a whole overview. I had a specific question about something to do in YuJa, and that's what I needed the answer to. So, I really prefer tech drop-in sessions to workshops.

*MM* *These technologies can be really overwhelming at first when there's so much information to take in. As you're picking and choosing which tools you'll use for instruction, are there ways that you help your students to navigate using the technology itself?*

GT Yeah. So, for example, I create how-to do videos in D2L for students. But Zoom is a game-changer. To be able to say to a student who's really struggling with tech, "As long as you can get into Zoom" Most people have been dragged kicking and screaming into it. It's like when my grandmother first saw touch-tone phones, but she got it. She had to. The other one, the rotary phone disappeared on her. So, again, people have been dragged into Zoom.

The screen share feature is also a game-changer. Now I can say to the student, "You share your screen. I'll make you co-host, and I'll talk you through where to click and how to do it." What a tool. Amazing. That's one of those ones that is high on the hierarchy of the SAMR model—something we couldn't do in a normal classroom.

## REFLECTION

My own experiences with remote learning began before the word "online" was in anyone's lexicon, as a high school student in correspondence school. Course textbooks and learning materials were packaged up and sent to my rural post office box, and I returned essays, short answer responses, and quizzes for grading to my teacher in a self-addressed, stamped envelope. It must have taken weeks to get feedback on the assignments, but there was no need to identify this method as "snail mail"—there was no other kind. Despite these long lag times, I began to be cognizant, even back then, about instructor presence. Though I didn't use the term then, I was keenly aware that some teachers marked up my written work with stars, circles, underlining and smiley faces that prefigured today's emojis. Some told me how I could improve future assignments, indicated specifically what was good about my work, and added personal notes like remarking on the weather where they lived, or the names of their pets. Other teachers returned my work devoid of comments with only a letter grade at the top. Sometimes certain words were circled in red. Unless the circled words were obviously misspelled, I had no idea what these circles meant. You can probably guess which instructor practices led me toward more engagement with the course content, and which ones led me toward less.

I took some correspondence courses to supplement my undergraduate studies as well, and it was more of the same: some instructors would add personal touches to the reams of boxed materials, and others must have felt it was outside their brief as a "serious" university lecturer. In one exceptionally dry undergraduate course that contained an uninteresting title and equally uninteresting content, both of which I've forgotten, an instructor's "presence" changed my life trajectory. The instructor saw something in my work that no one else had and took the time to write a lengthy note on my paper about the potential he saw in me for graduate level research and writing. The comments stuck with me, calling out what I couldn't see in myself, and provided a seed of confidence that would take root in future. Now, many years later, as I myself mark up papers for undergraduate students, I try to draw out the latent potential I see in their work. I still wish for the life of me that I'd kept that page of comments from that instructor, and even more I still wish I knew how to contact that instructor to tell him how his comments shaped my life path.

All this is to say: We don't need to be up on the latest technological gadgetry to have presence as instructors. We just need to be present.

ABOUT

**Gregory Tweedie** is an associate professor at the Werklund School of Education, University of Calgary, Canada. He is a recipient of the Teaching in Online Environments Award 2020 from the University of Calgary. Gregory holds a PhD in education (applied linguistics focus) from the University of Queensland, Australia. His teaching and research draw heavily upon his experiences as a language teacher and trainer in East, Southeast, and Central Asia, the Middle East, Canada, and his native Australia. He has been involved in remote learning since it was just called "learning."

# Patrick Kelly

Manager of Learning and Instructional Design, Taylor Institute for Teaching and Learning, University of Calgary, Canada

*Self-recorded interview* July 2020

Q *Can you tell us a little bit about yourself and about what you do?*

PK I work as an instructional designer with the Taylor Institute for Teaching and Learning at the University of Calgary. In my role, I support instructors in course design and teaching in different environments, including both in the classroom and online.

Q *What is the biggest challenge you've experienced when moving to remote teaching?*

PK Although I have experienced many years of teaching online, the move to emergency remote teaching was eye-opening in terms of the many challenges and opportunities that came with it. The biggest challenge for me was how quick the move was, with courses going online in a matter of days or weeks. A well-planned online course typically takes months to design and develop, and instructors gather evidence-informed best practices to promote student engagement and meaningful learning. With the quick move to online, we did not have all the answers, and the university community had to come together to create the many online resources and supports for instructors who were transitioning to online teaching in a short time period.

Q *What are the opportunities that are created by digital education?*

PK The biggest opportunity that I saw in moving to digital education was the meaningful conversations about what good online learning is. Good education practices transcend the different learning environments, from the classroom to online, and these practices opened up discussions on topics like student engagement, quality, good assessment, and teaching and learning in general.

Q *What software or tool do you use the most?*

PK I spend most of my time on **Zoom**, **D2L**, and **Microsoft Teams**. Like the rest of the University of Calgary campus, I had to move all my workshops and programs online and rely on Zoom most of the time. With the mix of audio, video, and chat interactions, I find the patterns of engagement fascinating. When I have an activity or question in my lesson, I get responses in all these ways, which at first I found challenging. Now I plan for these methods. I'm still getting used to the silence in the Zoom sessions—unlike in a classroom, where I can wait comfortably for someone to speak up.

Q *What is your favourite resource for teaching online?*

PK My favourite resource is learning from the campus community. Hearing the experiences, reflections, and questions from across the campus helps to direct my work and interest in online learning. Everyone is willing to share their resources and experiences to help others, and the Taylor Institute is compiling many of these on the Teaching Continuity website.

Q *What do you expect higher education to look like in ten years' time?*

*"Good education practices transcend the different learning environments, from the classroom to online, and these practices opened up discussions on topics like student engagement, quality, good assessment, and teaching and learning in general."*

PK With so many external factors shaping the landscape of higher education today, I see trends in the workplace experience becoming more accessible and playing a key role in a degree. Furthermore, more research experience can be incorporated at the undergraduate level. Micro-credentialing is another area for growth, which could impact the pathway by which students earn degrees with more flexibility and options. What is certain is that online learning is going to have a major role to play in how we work toward creating the most meaningful learning experiences possible.

REFLECTION

What an adventurous year 2020 was. It was a year full of challenges, emotions, opportunities, problem solving, and deep discussions as we continue to voyage into unknown times. The initial response to the pandemic through emergency remote teaching wasn't ideal, yet it sparked many discussions around teaching and learning, such as academic equity and good student assessment. Moving all courses online for the 2020/2021 academic year was a huge achievement from everyone, and it taught us some important lessons. Those who had already begun using alternate pedagogies such as blended or flipped learning before the pandemic found themselves being able to reuse online material and were able to stick with much of their original course design. Some of our earlier best practices for online learning were challenged as both students and instructors faced the reality of the workload anxiety, instruction and learning as entire course loads and programs went online for the very first time. Although there was a mix of greatness and struggles during the pandemic, I for one will hold onto those lessons and experiences as we move forward so I can continue to adapt in a changing environment.

As I reflect on the past year and think toward the future, a key issue for me is to intentionally plan for disruptions and uncertainty. Education will continue to need to be flexible and adaptable as we will be faced with a variety of external pressures, including the pandemic. When faced with challenging situations in higher education, my default response was always "use good pedagogy" and many of the strategies for adaptable and flexible learning are based on good pedagogy, with the caveat that it depends on the context, such as large enrolment courses.

This brings me to adaptable course design, which is a relatively unexplored approach to designing and teaching a course. Adaptable course design is all about planning ahead and identifying course elements that can be transitioned to the online environment when faced with disruptions. It is about the ability to maintain continuity for students and the instructor, using assessment strategies that can be completed in different modalities, and leveraging active learning strategies that can engage students, whether in the classroom or in online sessions. And since many of us have already created online content, activities, and assessments during this past year, why not leverage those and take advantage of the opportunities that online learning provides us to be intentionally adaptable as we move forward.

I look forward to the continued discussions around good pedagogy and how the pandemic has shaped higher education and brought to light some of the traditional elements that we were holding on to out of habit. Looking to the future, we have opportunities to rediscover the nature of teaching and learning in higher education.

ABOUT

**Patrick Kelly** is a part of the learning technology & design team and the manager of learning and instructional design at the Taylor Institute for Teaching and Learning, University of Calgary, Canada.

His role is to coordinate the instructional design group, collaborating with instructors to design online and face-to-face courses that engage students and promote deep and meaningful learning experiences. He facilitates the Teaching Online Program, and Course Design Program, and coordinates pedagogical support for educational technology.

Patrick's career at the University of Calgary spans more than fifteen years and includes extensive experience with classroom and online learning. He holds a bachelor's degree in biomechanics and a master's degree in education technology.

# Anthony Seto

Intro to Clinical Practice Course Chair, Cumming School of Medicine, University of Calgary, Canada

*Self-recorded interview* July 2020

Q *Please introduce yourself and tell us a bit about what you do.*

AS I am the course chair for Intro to Clinical Practice, a course at the Cumming School of Medicine, University of Calgary. The course is intended to train second-year medical students in the foundational knowledge and skills they need to help them succeed in their clinical rotations and future clinical practice.

Q *What is the biggest challenge you experienced when moving to remote teaching?*

AS For me, it was the preparation time. Prep time includes brainstorming; designing and piloting; recording and editing; and recruiting and training. Brainstorming includes thinking about how to transform interactive sessions that are typically held in-person into an online interactive session. I ask myself:

- What type of mechanism can I use that will help recreate the type of feel that students would have in the regular in person learning environment?

- How can I connect that offline feel to the online experience?

Often, the solution is a video. With videos, I can get creative and consider my lectures as show productions. Another mechanism for achieving interactive learning is **Google Forms**, where learners can type in answers and get instantaneous feedback. Through Google Forms, I can create "games with aims." Finally, before launching into the design and creation aspects of my lessons, I connect with other educators and learners to pitch my ideas.

The next preparatory task is the actual design and piloting of the online interactive sessions. I try to think of ways to design online delivery mechanisms that I myself would enjoy as a learner. I then run it by many, many people to get feedback, and continually revise the design after multiple pilots with different learner levels.

Next is recording and editing the lectures. I didn't realize how picky I was with recording and editing until I started doing online teaching. I'm now able to edit out all the "uhs," "ums," and pauses that I and my colleagues would put in. By stripping away all of these verbal distractions, I feel that learners are able to hear the messages more clearly.

Another element of online teaching preparation requires the recruitment and training of facilitators. When we moved to remote teaching, I had to take additional time to create written manuals for facilitators to review, as well as schedule online **Zoom** sessions to train facilitators in the online platform that we were going to use to deliver our lessons. Often, the facilitators would identify technological glitches or have additional insights that could help improve the quality of online delivery.

Q *What are the opportunities created by digital education?*

AS One of them, for me, would be a push toward creativity and innovation. Digital education has really pushed me to think of creative ways in which I can still connect and engage with my learners, but

> *"I try to think of ways to design online delivery mechanisms that I myself would enjoy as a learner."*

through digital means. Another opportunity that I think is great in digital education is the ability and drive to connect with other educators and experts outside of your hometown. When we're hosting in-person lectures, workshops, and activities, I feel we often recruit local teachers and expertise. But with digital education, we're able to connect with anyone around the world. For example, I've connected with out-of-town instructors and learners to help me create and give feedback to my course content. Another opportunity presented by digital education is that it helps keep messages clear and succinct. The traditional university lecture is often one hour long. With digital education, lectures and sessions can be edited to take less time. I can literally cut out all of the extraneous information so that we can connect learners to the key pieces of information to minimize their cognitive strain.

*Q* *What is your most-used software or tool?*

AS I use a lot of different varieties of software and tools for online teaching. For example, I use Zoom in combination with Google Forms. I use my cell phone to film videos. I use **Final Cut Pro** as my video editing software, and I use **PowerPoint** for slides. Using Zoom in combination with Google Forms has allowed me to host and facilitate interactive sessions. I've used this in online simulations and even in online escape games for teamwork skills training.

How it works for teamwork skills training is that I have two sets of Google Forms. One is called Side A and the other is called Side B. Students are placed in either Side A or Side B, and they are not allowed to look at each other's forms. They have to communicate what they see on screen to help solve the other side's corresponding puzzles. It requires a lot of communication, collaboration, and teamwork to be able to go through all the puzzles that they are presented with.

In terms of cell phones for filming, I have pretty much transitioned to using my cell phone to film all my videos. I feel that it's easy to navigate angles, to upload clips to your computer, and to delete files if you do not need them anymore.

Using Final Cut Pro, I edit my videos and create course trailers to connect learners and instructors before the course starts and to get them to engage with each other. I feel that course trailers paint the mood and flavour of the overall course, and then throughout the course I maintain the same energy through the course material and ways of facilitation.

Although I do use PowerPoint to create slides for my lectures, I also use PowerPoint to send e-mails. I call them my video e-mails. Rather than sending a black and white written e-mail to the students at the beginning of the course, I like to create a video PowerPoint message. I simply use a single-slide PowerPoint presentation, and then I do a voiceover to talk about its contents, and that becomes the video e-mail that I send out to the students before the course.

*Q* *What is your favourite resource for teaching online?*

AS My favourite resource for teaching online is using videos. This is because it offers a lot of flexibility. I can control the information delivered, the duration of the session, and the tone of the session. For example, some of my sessions may be a bit more formal, while others are a bit sillier, including a game show style. And mistakes can be removed. I also like videos because they evoke emotion. Emotional responses help memories form. So, facilitation through videos, I think, may connect with learners more.

*Q* *What do you expect higher education to look like in ten years' time?*

AS In ten years, I think more online education will occur. What resonates with me for online learning is that it's convenient, and it allows people to learn at their own pace. I myself recently signed up for some online DJing and movie-making courses to help me improve my own practice in these skills. I would also say that there will be more opportunities for collaboration and facilitation by experts from out of town, since you can do that online. We can't fly people here and there all the time. And finally, I think the traditional one-hour lecture may be dissolved. We can move to a less-is-more approach, literally by chopping down and editing down the sessions to just the key messages so that students can have more time to do active hands-on practice and study at their own pace, and we can create more opportunities and time for interaction and connection.

## REFLECTION

The COVID-19 pandemic has sparked the necessity of online learning and blended learning options. I've seen lots of organizations and companies that teach life support courses transition into offering their curriculum in a blended format, where students learn cognitive knowledge online first and then come into the classroom to practice and demonstrate hands-on skills.

For my own future medical education courses, I think this is how I will be approaching the design of my curriculum.

I'll have cognitive knowledge pre-recorded into on-demand podcasts and then deliver in-person sessions that focus on hands-on practice, with opportunities to reflect and debrief. The pandemic has really jumpstarted blended learning. Now, I can re-direct my focus and energy toward crafting solid in-person educational experiences. I don't have to worry about rehearsing my lectures to deliver them live, as they can all be pre-recorded.

Most people would consider blended learning to mean reviewing online preparatory material and then attending an offline, in-person class. I'd like to put out a challenge to educators to consider adopting a blended model *within* electronic materials, as well as *within* in-person sessions. For example, let's think about how we can blend different items into our online podcasts to vary the pace—blend in pop quizzes, and blend in something unexpected like a random surprise (e.g., a musical number, a cameo, etc.) to keep viewers engaged and to offer intermittent mental breaks. As for blending during in-person sessions, one consideration is blending in videos, games, skits, and other surprises to maintain audience interest and engagement.

ABOUT

**Anthony Seto** is a clinical assistant professor and course chair for Intro to Clinical Practice. In this medical school course, escape games, simulations, and exciting audiovisual experiences are the norm.

Anthony has experience in creating and facilitating various online educational experiences, including medical simulations, an escape game for teamwork skills training, an oral clinical case presentation workshop, and a faculty development workshop on "gamification and education games."

Outside of medical education, he enjoys participating in 48-hour movie challenges, learning how to DJ, and working at electronic dance music festivals as part of the medical team. Clinically, he practices as an urgent care and rural emergency physician.

# Isadora Mok-Kulakova & Laura Perissinotti

Isadora Mok-Kulakova: Online Learning Environment Lead, Taylor Institute for Teaching and Learning, University of Calgary, Canada

Laura Perissinotti: Learning Technologies Specialist, Taylor Institute for Teaching and Learning, University of Calgary, Canada

*Self-moderated discussion* conducted July 2020

Q *Isadora and Laura can you please introduce yourself, tell us a little bit about the work you do?*

IM My name is Isadora Mok-Kulakova and I am the online learning environment lead at the Taylor Institute for Teaching and Learning. I'm originally from Hong Kong, and I used to be a student here at the University of Calgary where I obtained degrees in psychology and education. I taught elementary school for a little bit before I decided to go back to school and get my master's in education, specializing in educational technology. After that, I worked at the IT support centre, supporting e-learning tools such as **Elluminate** and **Blackboard**. A few years ago, I started in my position as the online learning environment lead at the Taylor Institute. Now, I'm supporting tools like **YuJa**, **Zoom** and **D2L**.

LP My name is Laura Perissinotti and I am a learning technology specialist at the Taylor Institute for Teaching and Learning. I have a PhD in physical chemistry. I'm originally from Argentina and I love technology and teaching. I came to Canada to do a postdoc in biophysics at University of Calgary and during the program, I started working as a learning technology coach for the Faculty of Science. I joined the Taylor Institute two years ago and began my current role. I provide assistance to instructors in a range of different technologies that are institutionally supported; I explore new options and how to implement them.

Q *What do you think is the biggest challenge experienced when moving to remote teaching?*

LP One of the biggest challenges, I would say, is presence. Remote teaching is difficult because you don't see your audience, you don't see their expressions, and you lack that instant feedback. Another challenge is that it is difficult to keep constantly updated and informed on the rapid changes in technology. The features are changing all the time, for example the way they look, and new features are being introduced. For this reason, we need to continually revise our slides to make sure that all of the information that we are sharing is accurate. There have been some unexpected challenges while we have been presenting.

IM I know there were times when there were power outages or we lost the Internet connection at home, so every time we do a workshop, we have to make sure we have multiple devices. If I'm using Zoom and I'm sharing my screen, I need to have at least one other mobile device beside me. Sometimes, that may not even work. I may see something shown on the screen on my end, but Laura and all the other participants are seeing a black screen. When you're working with technology, you have to expect those things. If we're taking time to switch screens when it's online, sometimes it feels like it takes longer. When it's in-person, it seems that people could be a bit more patient as we're going through the transitions because they can see what we're actually doing in the classroom.

The other thing is just to give you an example. Last year in the summer of 2019, we implemented YuJa, the video hosting platform. Our workshops weren't that well attended. At one point we had maybe three or four participants, and only half of them were actually facilitators. We didn't have that much participation, but when the whole

> *"When you have more time to explore and experiment with the tools, go ahead, but don't try to overwhelm yourself with trying to use all the bells and whistles."*

Isadora Mok-Kulakova

COVID situation happened and everything was switched online, all of a sudden we had forty participants, and we've never had that many participants in a face-to-face workshop. Just having that extra pressure of more bodies posed a lot of challenges.

As Laura said, the vendors come up with changes all the time, mostly because there might be bug fixes or a new feature. Sometimes when they come up with these updates, it's not something we can control. All of a sudden, something new gets presented while we're in the middle of the workshop. That can be a little bit scary and embarrassing sometimes, to be honest, but we always try to do test sessions prior to our workshops.

LP I would say the other challenge is in the format that we offer for training. Sometimes we're offering different workshops focused on different technologies and they are an hour to an hour and a half long. We have participants who are looking to find out a particular thing about the platform, but they have to sign up for the entire workshop to just learn what they want to learn. It's difficult to offer that balance in training. You can offer drop-ins where some people attend to just ask their questions, but sometimes they will end up taking the whole workshop because they don't have a particular question or they don't know what to ask. It's difficult to find that balance.

IM Prior to COVID, we were supporting a smaller number of instructors, faculty members, grad students and postdocs online and we were doing face-to-face consultations and workshops too. From March 2020, when everything moved online, Spring and Summer courses were all offered remotely and there were a lot more instructors that we needed to interact with. All the work that we do has grown exponentially. The good thing is that we now have some additional resources and learning technology coaches who are able to help out with faculty members.

Q *What are the opportunities created by digital education?*

IM Working from home really makes our work situation authentic. Everything is done online, so we're meeting instructors on Zoom or via a phone call and through remote sessions, so we can still assist them even if they're just working from home.

LP I would add that in terms of tools, there are so many out there that you can use. If you're an instructor and you've just switched to remote teaching, I would start simple with a technology that is institutionally supported. Just stick to one, get comfortable with it, and then you can start exploring all the other options that you can find out there, because there are so many. There are a lot of things that you can do, for example, with D2L. You don't have to go out there to find a tool.

IM Laura and I always speak in our workshops; our role is not to sell a particular product, learning management system or particular tool. Our job is to let you know what's out there and what options are available. We say to always start simple, start small. When you have more time to explore and experiment with the tools, go ahead,

*"If you think about digital education, it gives students a lot of control over their learning by giving them access, choice and control in terms of how they navigate the different content that you are sharing with them."*

Laura Perissinotti

but don't try to overwhelm yourself with trying to use all the bells and whistles. And we're happy to experiment with you. That's part of our job—to experiment, play, and test. There are so many different tools that allow you to do the same thing. So sometimes you just have to make the decision, "Why would I choose this and not the other tool?"

We want to make our tools accessible and user-friendly, but at the same time we need to think of security. So part of our job is to work with IT and make sure that the right settings are in place. Let's say, if your students need to join a Zoom session, how can we make that secure and easy so that the students don't have to download too many things or use one specific browser.

LP If you think about digital education, it gives students a lot of control over their learning by giving them access, choice, and control in terms of how they navigate the different content that you are sharing with them.

*Q What tools do you use most for teaching online?*

LP Well, my most commonly used tools are D2L and Zoom right now. And I have to say, Zoom is really useful. It has changed the way we teach online a lot. The ability to share your screen and also give participants the ability to share back is so important. It makes it more interactive. Also, Zoom provides a lot of features that help you make your sessions interactive and more engaging.

If I have to name a favourite resource for teaching online, I like those resources that are interactive, to which you can add some sort of interactivity, and I have a few favourites. For example, I love one called **H5P**. That is easy to use. It's free, open-source and you can create resources and then you can put those resources into D2L. I love **Google Apps**; I use a lot of them. Yes, I would say those are my favourite ones. I love to have interactivity. I think interactivity is very important when you're teaching online because it can be very isolating and thus passive. Adding that interactivity to the resources that you are sharing with your students is important to keep them engaged with the content.

IM So the ones that I use most would be D2L, and Zoom and YuJa. These are the ones we do workshops with. Part of our job is also to troubleshoot, so if instructors are having an issue with these platforms and it gets escalated past the IT support centre, they can be referred to us at the Taylor Institute. If it is something that we cannot address, we will refer the instructors to our educational development consultant or to our instructional designers. If it's a bug, then we will report it on behalf of the instructor or the client. So really, when we are working with these main tools, we do a little bit of everything.

Another tool that I like is **Snagit**, which, if you're an instructor or member of staff at the University of Calgary, you should be able to get off the IT software distribution site. What Snagit allows you to do is to take screenshots or quick recordings of your screen. I personally find that very useful, because a lot of the time instructors will contact us with an issue with D2L or they will ask a question about how to do a particular thing, and instead of sending an e-mail of two or three pages of instructions and including screenshots, you can just take a video that's less than a minute long and that shows the whole process. That speeds up how quickly we can do our job. I also want to give a shoutout to the University of Arizona because they have a lot of good materials on how to use D2L. We always go to their site to get ideas and then see how other institutions have provided their documentation.

*Q* *What do you expect higher education to look like in ten years' time?*

IM I think that with more courses being offered online, we don't want students to be just passive receivers of information. We don't want them to just go into the D2L site at the University of Calgary, download information and do an online exam. We want students to be able to show their work, collaborate with their peers, and build a relationship with their instructors. Maybe they can show their experience by creating videos on their mobile devices, because it's so easy to do these types of things now. Students can easily upload them to the D2L site or YuJa and share the experience with their colleagues and peers. And of course, with Zoom students can collaborate with each other and do group work, have group discussions, and do something together.

LP So I'm thinking about micro-credentials, and I would like to see **Blockchain** being implemented more widely, especially when concepts like trust, value, privacy, and identity are all coming into question as we go into this new suite of technologies. However, that would imply that we need to rethink and reimagine many aspects of traditional systems of education. So I also imagine a lot more of virtual reality and augmented reality. I know a number of institutions have already implemented those technologies in their courses. Those technologies provide a higher level of interaction, allowing the students to visualize things in 3D and even interact with them. This is happening so fast, and I think it's really amazing—the things you can transport to different places and through time. I think, and I hope, that will be something that becomes more common in the next few years.

## REFLECTION

It's been well over a year since we started working from home. It's beginning to feel like a normal summer again where we can actually take some time off before the Fall term. At the same time, we can't help but wonder why instructors aren't reaching out to us as often anymore. Is it because the COVID restrictions have been lifted and they can finally enjoy some downtime? Is it because the university has announced its return-to-campus plan for the Fall and many classes will be delivered in-person once again? Is it because instructors have become so proficient in the use of D2L, Zoom and YuJa that they don't need our support anymore? Or perhaps they have just been accessing other resources at the University, such as UService (IT), the learning technology coaches, our vendors or the eLearn site? Does our department need to increase its promotion so that the community is reminded of the different services and resources that the Taylor Institute for Teaching and Learning is offering? We'll never know the answer, but we suspect it's a combination of all these reasons.

To give you an idea of how things have changed during the pandemic in terms of teaching and learning technology usage and support at the university, here are some statistics and anecdotes:

1. This table highlights assessment tool usage in D2L @ UCalgary between 2019 and 2021. You will notice a steady, if not significant, increase in the use of online assessment tools within our LMS (Learning Management System), especially during/after the Winter 2020 semester.

| SEMESTER | # OF COURSES USING | | |
|---|---|---|---|
| | Quizzes | Dropbox | Grades |
| Winter 2019 | 203 | 1092 | 1468 |
| Winter 2020 | 542 | 1534 | 1498 |
| Winter 2021 | 767 | 1645 | 1587 |
| Spring/Summer 2019 | 97 | 373 | 521 |
| Spring/Summer 2020 | 284 | 529 | 540 |
| Spring/Summer 2021* | 218 | 438 | 441 |
| Fall 2019 | 273 | 1165 | 1548 |
| Fall 2020 | 834 | 1678 | 1567 |

*Ongoing

2. 1,005,522 Zoom meetings were held between 1 July 2020 and 1 July 2021, though not all of them were course-related, as many units were also using this tool for business or administrative purposes.

3. YuJa usage has significantly increased over the course of the pandemic. The tool allows instructors to pre-record their lessons, edit their videos and incorporate accessibility features such as captioning. Students may also use it to share their experiences and submit assignments in the form of a video. As of July 2021, more than 49,225 media and captures objects had been hosted on YuJa (these include video and audio files that have been uploaded directly to the user's My Media page, as well as videos that were created using the YuJa software station on both **PCs** and **Macs**).

4. Since June 2020, the Taylor Institute's eLearn site has received more than 312,194 views. The site was redesigned, and we have also added more videos and included accessibility features such as closed caption

and bookmarking. Recently, we launched a blog section to provide monthly updates about core campus online learning platforms.

5. It's just a personal observation, but the average consultation time spent with instructors has decreased this year. We can usually cover all the questions or resolve issues in less than an hour now or we can send a quick e-mail so that they can complete the steps at their end. Thinking back to 2020, there were so many occasions when our one-on-one time on Zoom would last up to two hours. Isadora remembers how she once ended up having a four-hour Zoom call with an instructor. Initially, they were exploring the D2L and Zoom functionalities, but then it snowballed into a conversation about video production and an e-mail/authentication troubleshooting session. Though it was physically and mentally exhausting, it's an experience that she will always remember. These sort of experiences helped us appreciate:

   - The time, care, and hard work that instructors put into designing their courses and creating the best learning experiences for their students, even in the midst of a pandemic;

   - The interconnectedness of our campus platforms and how we need to be very careful when making system changes (take for example, in the case above, the instructor was not able to log into Zoom to pre-record a lesson for his class because he was having trouble with his IT account. Resetting the password led to e-mail and MFA (Multi-Factor Authentication) issues on multiple devices);

   - The collaboration between the Learning Technologies Group at the Taylor Institute and the IT department at the university as we make decisions together and support each other while serving the University of Calgary community; and

   - The roles of online learning environment leads and learning technologies specialists because they get to work with both human beings and machines.

There are still many uncertainties. To help support our community, the learning technology and design team at the Taylor Institute is currently developing a learning module on adaptive/adaptable course design. Keep an eye on https://taylorinstitute.ucalgary.ca/resources/learning-modules!

## ABOUT

**Isadora Mok-Kulakova** holds a BA in psychology and a Bed from the University of Calgary, Canada. Her interest in adult training led her to complete a master's degree in education, specializing in educational technology. She was the IT department's e-learning specialist for seven years before transferring to the Teaching and Learning Centre, now the Taylor Institute for Teaching and Learning, University of Calgary, in April 2014.

As the online learning environment lead, Isadora facilitates the use of technologies to enhance learning and teaching. Her role entails working collaboratively with faculty, students, staff, and administrators at the University of Calgary to enrich learning experiences. Isadora supports the use of university technology platforms such as D2L and **Adobe Connect**, through consultation, training, and troubleshooting.

**Laura Perissinotti** holds a PhD in physical chemistry and completed a postdoc at the University of Calgary, Canada in the field of biophysics (Centre for Molecular Simulation, Department of Biological Sciences, Faculty of Science). Laura worked as a learning technology coach for the Faculty of Science during her time as a postdoctoral scholar.

As a learning technologies specialist at the Taylor Institute for Teaching and Learning, Laura provides a range of support and resources around technology integration. She supports faculty and staff who are interested in using technology to help transform students' learning experience. She organizes and runs workshops and one-on-one consultations with interested faculty and staff members on a wide range of projects involving technology to support their teaching—everything from using D2L more completely, to teaching online using technology, or producing videos.

# Kris Hans & Erik Christiansen

Kris Hans: Instructor; University of Calgary and Mount Royal University; Canada and Co-Founder of Market Grade

Erik Christiansen: Assistant Professor/Librarian, Mount Royal University, Canada

Kris and Erik: Creators, co-hosts EdTech Examined Podcast

S01 E05

Interviewed August 2020 by *Mac McGinn*

MM *Kris and Erik, why don't we start by having you introduce yourselves and telling us a little bit about what you do.*

KH I've been teaching since 2005. I teach at both Mount Royal University and the University of Calgary. I have taught over 100 courses, about half via online delivery. In consultation with my program manager, I took professional development courses in 2013 on both learning and teaching online as I anticipated the tremendous potential for online course delivery and with the pandemic we've all been thrown into online delivery without any preparation. For my day job, I co-founded Market Grade, an interdisciplinary consultancy focused on design, innovation, marketing, and strategy. Recently, Erik and I launched a podcast series called EdTech Examined. In Summer 2020, we produced weekly episodes to help people prepare for online remote delivery in the Fall.

EC I am an academic librarian at Mount Royal University. Prior to getting into this position, I worked at the University of Alberta's Faculty of Education where I was in the unit that focuses on education technology, online learning, and instructional design. At Mount Royal, we are instructional librarians, so most of my time is dedicated to teaching the nuts and bolts of research, including creating good research questions, logically thinking through how to answer these questions, where to find information, and the kinds of resources that are available. Our team do a huge amount of library instruction. That's primarily what I do, as well as the service and scholarship that's required from most faculty members. Outside of work, I am a long-time technology enthusiast with interests in computer hardware and software development.

MM *What are some of the biggest challenges you experienced when moving toward online teaching?*

KH I was fortunate that most of my classroom student interactions and deliverables had already been addressed in March, so when we had to go to emergency remote, the only outstanding assignment was the need to adapt the final group presentations. However, to move courses that were supposed to be face-to-face to online delivery in a short span of time certainly does pose a challenge. On average, I would estimate it takes six to nine months to prepare an online course. Even then, I've been teaching an online course where we have a full team of instructional designers we work with, and we've evolved the course over the years and are constantly iterating. It's no easy task. For this reason, I highlight the difference between emergency remote delivery and online teaching. Online teaching takes a great deal of time and care. You also have to take into consideration your pedagogical approaches while teaching online.

I saw the pandemic and emergency remote delivery as an opportunity. I began investigating some of the technology that might help facilitate a better student and course experience. For instance, I came across whiteboarding technology, specifically **Miro, MURAL** and **Jamboard.** Likewise, I was able to consider guest speakers from all over the world. In the past I would limit myself to guest speakers in the Calgary area; for my design thinking course I brought in guest speakers from Amsterdam, Kansas City, New York, and even Silicon Valley.

EC Kris makes a good point. There's a big difference between emergency online instruction and preparing for instruction online. For some context, it's a bit different for me because I'm a librarian. I don't teach credit courses; rather, I support credit programs, which is very different. My instruction is prepared but also somewhat reactionary to what the assignments and the objectives are that are laid out in the curriculum of a program. I'm the librarian for psychology, health and physical education, and I also do liaison work around the collections for health, wellness and our music conservatory.

In terms of challenges faced in moving to online instruction, I think I experienced these less than a lot of other credit instructors. Creating online resources is my job. If you Google "Erik Christiansen MRU," the first page you'll see is my faculty profile and a link to the library guides, which, especially if you look at psychology, are very extensive. In my profession, creating online asynchronous learning materials for reuse is very common. That said, it was a big challenge to transition some of the face-to face sessions and appointments. For instance, my library instruction largely went asynchronous except for dedicated time where people could ask questions. The challenge there is that it requires a lot more preparation. Now I've done this before because I worked in EdTech and I've worked in remote learning, so I know what to do when there's a problem, but it still requires a large amount of time. I started recording very short videos for students on how to create a mind map for a research question, how to break down a research question into its essentials, and how to narrow it down and pick it apart. I did an iPad Pro stylus annotation and then uploaded all the videos onto **YouTube**. Initially, that was a huge amount of preparation but now I can reuse those videos.

The other big piece for the classes is the communication because when I do synchronous instruction online I don't do a lecture like I would for a face-to-face class; I don't try to recreate that experience. I give students an abundance of materials in advance with very clear instructions on what they need to read. I tell them to watch these videos, go through the process, and try to create a mind map to start. I let them know that I will check in at our live class to see how they're doing, and that I'm going to answer questions about where they're struggling and then provide some guidance for moving forward. That all sounds easy, but again that requires a huge amount of preparation. Especially in an emergency situation, you are trying to create materials quickly to give enough lead time so people can use them in a thoughtful fashion and allow for time where they can follow up. If you just say "here are the resources and I'll check back in next week," that's not going to work. It's not specific enough. I think that's the biggest challenge: the creation and the lead time. In an emergency situation, you're really under a time limitation.

MM *Do you find that this presents opportunities for each of you in terms of digital education and creating a different type of learning atmosphere compared to what it would be in the classroom?*

EC Definitely. Kris probably has some things on his mind, but I think there's an opportunity in this strategy for creating a database of online teaching resources for yourself; but there is also a fear. In instruction, if you release everything to the world in an online environment, you're giving away your "secret sauce" so to speak. That's the impression. But I think the opportunity is that if you take the time to create reusable materials, that's a sunk cost in the beginning but then it pays for itself in the long run. I think it's worth it.

I also would say there's another opportunity, which is that in addition to creating resources that you can reuse, students have a chance to rewatch and relisten over and over again, and there's a really good chance that next time I see them they'll understand the concept better and their questions for me will be more interesting. The better I prepare the students, the more advanced their questions become. It's more of a conversation, and it's more satisfying because I get to see their growth.

I think that's where having a blended approach within a face-to-face environment is a good example. You can come to class, get that real-time social interaction, but then there's something to rewatch. Concepts are difficult, especially in content-heavy disciplines. They require a huge amount of consideration. Listen to any philosopher academic do a podcast; I have to listen to them more than once. That's why Joe Rogan's interviews are so successful because he has deep conversations. If you can create materials where your students have an opportunity to reconsider a concept multiple times, perhaps from different perspectives, they're not only going to come to class more prepared and more engaged, but they're also going to ask much more interesting questions—which I'm always thirsty to get.

KH We did an interview with Mohammad Keyhani, associate professor of entrepreneurship and strategy at the Haskayne School of Business, and he mentioned this exact point of not seeing the potential opportunities. It's a great deal of work to prepare course materials in advance, but once you create the resources, you can reuse them over and over. The fear among educators is more around putting your course content into the world and the uncertainty of the unintended consequences of having your course materials in cyberspace. For instance, other people may come across your content and use it. Likewise, students may find some way to use these materials to cheat and there are other concerns around academic misconduct. With regard to tests and quizzes, educators may have to reconsider making the evaluations open book or instituting other constraints for student examinations.

Going back to the question of challenges, we also need to consider Internet etiquette. One suggestion for synchronous sessions is to have everyone muted so we don't experience external noise or distractions. I've had some students ask about whether they should have their webcam on. I leave the use of webcams to their discretion as it's not mandatory. I don't want to create a situation where webcams are required because of uncertainty around their personal situation at home. For example, a student may have a child in the background that they're looking after. I don't want to put any student on the spot. In terms of netiquette, I suggest setting up video conference sessions with everyone's mics and webcams turned off by default and leave it up to them to make the decision if they feel comfortable enough to engage in this way. I don't know if having webcams on adds much value with faces in this Brady Bunch or Hollywood Squares-type of grid.

*MM The idea of "netiquette" was the focus in the TALON newsletter of 4 August 2020 (Issue 6). It's the idea of privacy, and how you're being transferred to somebody's home or private workspace, and how to go about making a space for people to participate comfortably. What is your most-used software tool for communication or meeting with people online in an education setting?*

> *"Constraints breed creativity."*
>
> Erik Christiansen

EC In terms of collaboration, the biggest software tool for video conferencing is whichever one is institutionally supported. If I were to distill library instruction, I'd say that it is supporting an existing curriculum and helping people find and understand what they don't know. That's primarily what library instruction is for, and that is the basis of library science. In terms of tools that facilitate that, we are a **Google** campus. I have set up Google collaboration docs and put students in groups in this online environment. If they have a group project, I will set it all up for them and say, "I want you to come up with a pitch for what you're going to cover in this presentation" or "Develop and answer to this research question." I want them to start with a broad topic (or research question), then I want them to narrow it down, and then I want them to narrow it down again, and so on and so forth. You can collaborate in **Google Docs**. Sometimes I'll set up **Google Suite** in a way that is similar to breakout rooms. All the people have to do is just click the link, go in, and do their stuff.

There are other collaboration tools that work well too, depending on the privacy level and things like that. There is one called **Padlet**, and it's really useful because it's like a virtual pinboard. I am interested in any virtual collaboration tool where I can put people together and get their ideas down, because one of the issues in library instruction is that if it's not face-to-face and you're not documenting it, it can be quite ephemeral as it's that "one shot" style of instruction. To mitigate some of that in a face-to-face session, if I write a bunch of stuff on a whiteboard, I take a photo and upload it to the guide that I send out. That way, people have something to reflect on. When doing work in either an online or face-to-face library session, I think you should have something to show for it. Students can leave with something they've accomplished on what their assignment is. Evidence of your collaboration is very helpful for the instructor too.

KH We interviewed Dr. Tom O'Neill, associate professor in the Department of Psychology at the University of Calgary, and he's developed a system called **ITP Metrics**. I think ITP (Individual and Team Performance) Metrics could be very beneficial for people when putting together teams remotely for students. The platform can also be useful for the students themselves to reflect on their own personality and their strengths and weaknesses.

It's funny, in 2016 when I returned to Mount Royal University to teach, I didn't know much about the Google Suite with my experience being mainly with the **Microsoft** and **Apple** suite of products. I gave my students an in-class exercise and some started working away on their computers, and I wasn't entirely sure what they were really working on their laptops. When we were ready to debrief and discuss the class exercise, the students asked if I wanted them to come up to the front of the classroom and present their slides. I was a bit blown away and inquired, "what do you mean"? They explained how they had created a presentation in **Google Slides** during the class exercise and were collaborating while on their computers. This real-time collaboration took in-class exercises to a whole new level.

As a side note, I mentored a student—probably about ten years ago—who was in a senior role at ATB Financial. This student explained how ATB had switched everything over from Microsoft to Google Suite. The ATB senior management made this decision assuming it would appeal to the millennials, but they actually pushed back. The student mentioned how all these years in school they had to learn Microsoft products, and now ATB had implemented the Google Suite, and **Google Sheets** is crap compared to **Microsoft Excel**. This is especially the case if they need to run high-level calculations, macros, and so on. Ultimately, the technology that is used comes down to organizational culture.

I have tried using a variety of different tools for course delivery in my design thinking course, and one piece of feedback I received from my students is that they were getting overwhelmed because I was using multiple tools. I didn't consider this at first because I was scrambling to figure out how I was going to transition from in-class to online delivery. Students had three tools to choose from and we only had so much time for course delivery in addition to the learning curve for each tool. I realized the learning curve should always be considered. In our interview with Mohammad, he pointed out that we should not put in the technology just for technology's sake and overdo it. The technological tools should be used for a specific purpose.

EC In terms of all the technology available, there are diminishing marginal returns. I've tested a lot of tools at a surface level to get an idea of what their potential is, but I'm not going to go down that rabbit hole unless it offers something really quite profound and different. In my previous position at the University of Alberta, I took the Google Suite and **Webmaster Tools** certification. It's probably expired now, but I did it because I wanted to maximize what I could get from those tools. There is an advantage to working within the tools that you're comfortable with and within what you know well. Constraints breed creativity. I've actually given students that challenge. For instance, students must work in Google Suite and find out how to create a Gantt chart or a spreadsheet. Is there an existing template? Can you find a website that expands your ability to use the tools we already have, rather than constantly adding new things?

To see how the students navigate the instructions within the constraints of one tool makes things interesting. Obviously, the instructor can't be like, "here's a tool that I saw video on that I've never used" because they won't be able to provide any support. As an instructor you have to know the tools to a certain level, but maybe there's a template or a strategy that I didn't know about, and the students can then show me. Now that's an incredible learning experience. That's the benefit of open educational practices where the instructor has some crystallized and tacit knowledge that they are teaching, but there is a back and forth in terms of process. I think that makes it much more interesting to students. When I can learn something new from students ... I think that's brilliant.

MM *I completely agree. Similar to what the TALON project is doing with creating a collection of resources, you discuss various online resources on the EdTech Examined podcast. Other than what's institutionally supported, are there certain ones that you lean on?*

KH Even though I have several years of online teaching experience, I pushed myself to attend professional development sessions at the Taylor Institute for Teaching and Learning and also at the Academic Development Centre at Mount Royal. I find in Alberta, perhaps even in the wider Canadian context, that we're very open-minded and open-hearted in the way we share. If we take "Six Degrees" of Kevin Bacon approach, in Alberta the degrees of separation in our tightknit community are quite often two or three at most. It's much more of a neighbourly or pioneering culture. For instance, if we look back to challenging circumstances with the Fort McMurray fires or the 2013 flood here in Calgary, people came out in droves to help one another out. I have this saying, start locally but act globally. We have many resources locally with many people being unaware they even exist. EdTech Examined is our attempt with our podcast to start locally to see what we have through our initial network, and then assemble this information and resources to act in a global manner. We have the potential for global reach with the power of the Internet.

MM *We took a similar approach with TALON, documenting what approved technologies or resources are available within the University of Calgary, providing access to instructors, staff, and students, and then branching out nationally and internationally to find out what other institutions are using and what other kinds of resources are out there.*

EC Yeah, and I would agree with Kris that it's great to take on opportunities for academic development. I haven't done any of the seminars at the University of Calgary, but it has an excellent reputation. I've done it at the University of Alberta and through the Academic Development Centre at Mount Royal University, and they have a fantastic and wide-ranging series on instructional methods. I am almost certain that teaching online will be the focus for the next year or more.

Internally, we do some great things through the library at Mount Royal. We have instruction roundtables, which are very informal discussions where we encourage our colleagues to share what kinds of instructional sessions they're doing, and what problems they're trying to solve, and we give feedback. Sometimes people want to borrow from each other, and I think that is really good.

For me, I follow a lot of **Listservs**. I've cut them down over the years because it starts to clog up my inbox up, but I've been interested in ISSOTL—the acronym, SoTL, stands for the Scholarship of Teaching and Learning. That's a discipline, and ISSOTL is the International Society for the Scholarship of Teaching and Learning. They have some really interesting Listservs. Of course, it's good to go to SoTL conferences and explore any online things that they provide. The library network for Listservs and online instruction through CARL (Consortium of Academic Research Libraries) is pretty good. So, these are ways that I get my instruction strategies, but in terms of the learning about the tools, I actually don't get that from a lot of education sources. I'm more interested in what the tools are and then figuring out how they could be useful in an education context.

I listen to probably twenty-five hours of podcasts a week. A lot of them are on productivity and technology, not specifically on education. I curate this list of technologies that could potentially be useful, and then I choose the ones I think may have an educational application and start investigating them. There are many podcasts out there that talk about higher education, but in the EdTech realm, that's where Kris and I felt that we could contribute something, and we're very proud of that.

KH In terms of other things we do, Erik has set up a Google news alert, so we get alerts about any EdTech news. For the most part, we both have an interest in technology, so we come across information in our regular reading. I usually start off my day reading Fast Company. I look for my interests, not only in tech, but in business, design, innovation, and strategy. I find Fast Company is one of the best publications and one of my go-to resources.

*MM Thank you for sharing these resources with us. We have come to the final question: what do you expect higher education to look like in ten years' time?*

KH In the future people are going to probably—hopefully—re-evaluate. Going beyond even what's happened with COVID, people are questioning the value of higher education in the first place. Google recently came out with its own certifications, and I believe they're giving them out to around 100,000 people for free on a scholarship basis. If you have Google certifications and with these credentials can get a job with Google, why would you as a student pursue a computer science degree at the University of Calgary?

When I start off my first lecture of any course, I always ask the students. "What should you be getting out of school?" In my opinion, it comes down to three things. The first is developing your critical analysis and skills. This is especially important today. I never would have thought that fake news would exist. You should be equipped with the skills to go and gauge for yourself whether the actual topic or facts you see are legitimate. You can go to a technical school and get what you need in just two years, but that's the value in taking all these other optional and elective courses. It's a matter of being able to develop your experience on philosophy, humanities, science, business, and a whole variety of disciplines, and that's why postsecondary undergraduate degree programs typically take four years. These soft skills are not going to be replaced by artificial intelligence or other technologies.

The second thing that people should be getting out of university is research skills. You need to be equipped with the skills to figure things out for yourselves. University libraries spend millions of dollars getting you access to all this information. Students should take full advantage of access to these research databases because when you're working in industry, accessing these resources and materials can be very expensive.

The final thing is the development of communication skills, and particularly writing. I teach business communications, and our textbook mentions that 30 percent of your time is spent writing or communicating in some way. If you take a 60,000-dollar salary, this equates to about $18,000 a year that a company is paying for their staff to write e-mails, and prepare reports, presentations, etc. This helps to answer the question of why students have to write these essays and answer certain questions, and so on.

These three major skills combined is what students should take away from university; they are considered soft skills. If we look at someone like Stewart Butterfield, co-founder and CEO of **Slack**, he didn't even have technical skills. Butterfield has both a bachelor and a master in philosophy. He created his first start-up **Flickr** and sold it to **Yahoo!** Both Slack and Flickr were actually developed as video game concepts that were transformed to meet an unmet need and become commercially viable. Likewise, Ben Silverman, Founder of **Pinterest**, is also a non-technical founder, and so you might wonder.

I recall reading that Silicon Valley tech companies have stopped hiring people with technical expertise and are looking for those with a background in liberal arts because they have those critical analysis and critical thinking skills. They're thinking, as they say, outside the box. They're adding another dimension to the organizational culture. Especially when you're dealing with users, you need to have an understanding and development of soft skills. In the future we're going to have to rethink what value students are taking away from school.

EC Kris' analysis is pretty interesting. I would agree with what he said. My belief is that universities are going to go back to the state that they were in during their inception. So let's think about skills for a second. If you look at the research, RBC (Royal Bank of Canada) has done research on desired skills and outcomes—"twenty-first century skills." It feels like every ten years there's a new name attributed to the same set of skills, which I find infuriating to be perfectly honest. They are all, like Kris said, soft skills such as communication, logic, critical thinking, etc. and it's very difficult to teach critical thinking. That is a massive challenge, and in many ways we don't do a very good job of it. But I think one of the best approaches is to give people real-world problems to solve. First of all, it gives you a goal, which is really important and that's why we're moving toward more active learning methods.

You can take all the degrees that you want, but if you're faced with a problem it's only then that you are really confronted with what you don't know. In this case, "I can't actually solve this until I've learned X." Nobody who has a PhD would tell you "Well, I figured out everything I needed to know and then I just applied it to my research." That's impossible. It doesn't work like that. For this reason, those soft skills are going to be increasingly important. They're going to be largely problem-based, team-based classes, so that you're developing your problem-solving skills, thinking outside the box, plus having to work with other people.

I have to be careful how I say this, but I think you're also going to see a shrinking perhaps—a shrinking of the disciplines or a more interdisciplinary approach. I'm not sure how that's going to work. I didn't take a specific discipline in my undergrad. I have an undergraduate arts degree in international relations, so I had to take economics, international trade, political philosophy, philosophy of logic, political science, a variety of history courses, languages, and things like that. The idea is that you use all these skills in tandem to write papers, answer questions and solve problems. So I think university is going to go more general, more interdisciplinary and more problem based, active learning based. If you were to look at where universities—I don't want to say lose, because it's not necessarily a zero-sum game—but where they're maybe going to shift their focus away from is from the highly specialized areas. I think places like engineering are in good shape because they're basically what I've described. They are applied sciences and interdisciplinary in many regards. But I think you're going to see a growth in non-accredited micro learning, such as **LinkedIn Learning. LinkedIn** bought **Lynda**, and LinkedIn was bought by Microsoft. Microsoft owns the largest online learning platform in the world. It is very good. If you talk to a web developer, somebody who works for Google, or somebody who does their own contracting, I do not believe they would say that a computer science degree is a necessity to be a successful person in that field. Like Kris said, these fields are not solely technical fields. If you studied the philosophy of logic, you're probably a very good programmer because it's about arguments and consistency. If you want to be a web developer, yeah, go take a computer science degree, but I think that the curriculum should mandate that people take math and statistics and philosophy. Then they can go and specialize through micro learning, and that's probably outside the academy. I think that's the better investment.

I have these pie in the sky ideas of what I'd like to see education look like. For instance, if I were in charge of a program, let's say psychology, you would have general courses that are supposed to give you well-rounded, interdisciplinary skills. Many of the skills that you get from a psychology degree, a political science degree, a history degree, or perhaps a biology degree, involve a lot of writing, presentation, critical thinking, plus concepts that you just have to learn. I think in our programs there should be regular intervals for reflection where people compare themselves, not to others, but to where they were the previous year and figure out how they can translate those general skills into solving a problem in the workforce. It doesn't have to be a specific position in the workforce because I think that the advice to "follow your passion" is misguided. People become passionate because they become good at things. Reflecting on your skills and how to apply them helps when having to explain to an employer what you can do for them. That's very, very difficult if you've just been in academic mode. Ask any student who's graduated and become demoralized because they didn't get a job right away. That is a difficult transition. It doesn't mean people can't do it, but I think that we can build that into the curriculum. If we built that into the curriculum, we'd give people a lot more confidence.

MM *Yes, bridging the gap between education and entering the workforce.*

KH It's interesting what you said about following your passion. It reminds me of when I was asked to do the keynote talk at the dean's list in 2018 for Haskayne School of Business and that was one of the things that I mentioned, following your passion. I gave this anecdote: My business partner was raised by his grandmother, and she would tell him that if you go and chase money, you're running after your shadow and you'll keep going around in a circle. You may get close and then it'll slip through your hands. Instead, she advised him to follow the sun, the sun being your passion, and then the sunlight will shine on you. Consequently, the shadow will be cast behind you and the shadow will follow. Everybody loved it! They ate it up. I said the same thing at a Mount Royal event as well.

After about a year of reflection, I was wrong to say that to the student audience. It's important to follow your passion, but you should also determine your superpower. If we were all to follow our passion, especially growing up in Canada, we'd probably all be hockey players. I don't know about you, but I'm not the best skater and wouldn't have any shot at making it to any kind of league. So, it's really important to figure out your core strengths and try to build upon that foundation.

Going back to the question of what the future holds for higher education, I would hope we would use technology for the betterment of society. Some really exciting things are developing, especially in the area of **AR** (Augmented Reality) and **VR** (Virtual Reality). Imagine, before you had to take a field trip out to someplace, and now you can just put on goggles and get a virtual lecture from Socrates. You're able to actually see some of the ruins in Greece or something along those lines depending on the course you're taking. Ultimately, we've got to find a reason to go and get a higher education. I do think it's important. My parents always told me that a degree is something that nobody can ever take away from you.

EC That's what I was told too. Did our parents all go to the same seminar?

KH In a field like computer science, look at people like Mark Zuckerberg. He dropped out of Harvard. He's one of the richest people in the world and he didn't bother to graduate. In many ways, we're idolizing—and especially in business where I come from and apply my lens. It almost feels as though we're so desperate to find a new Steve Jobs, whether it's an Elon Musk or a Jeff Bezos. In becoming very successful, a combination of factors exist, and it isn't about having the most genius IQ. In many cases, it's about finding the right people at the right time and capitalizing on the right trend when it comes along.

If dystopic movies are any indication or reflection of our culture, it certainly feels we're heading in this direction where rich individuals such as Elon and Jeff are creating space companies. I'd feel much better with NASA heading up the space program, but this gives you an indication of the lack of innovation. Every time you send up a shuttle, you lose rockets, and it takes someone like Elon to push back and ask, why don't we reuse the rockets? You need to have people to challenge the status quo, because the same old "what's been happening" isn't going to solve our problems in the future. We have to think outside the box. I hate to even use that phrase, because in some ways going to university is almost like getting the box put on your head and getting pushed into the world. Hopefully students have developed their soft skills to become more well-rounded skills along the way.

EC I agree with Kris. I think what education is supposed to do is to make people less dependent. It's meant to empower people to take risks. If you're twenty-two and you've finished a degree, you're like, "Yeah, I'm

*"It's important to follow your passion, but you should also determine your superpower."*

Kris Hans

going to start a business," part of the issue is that it is harder now than it was in say 1965 because of the cost. There's not a lot of risk-taking you can do if there's such a big cost. That's why we see a vacuum in education. As costs in higher education go up, market forces are going to come in and they're going to produce, perhaps, more non-accredited micro learning. Then industry may start to say, "Well, we can't really tell the difference." I think this could be true for some things. Definitely for technical skills. For example, if you want to be a web developer, it doesn't mean that a computer science degree isn't valuable. Perhaps it gives you a better foundation, but then you have to do additional learning to specialize. I think that is the reality. University is considerably more expensive, so if you want people to take risks, empower them to think outside the box and do problem solving, you have to allow for that.

To build on something else that Kris said about passion and projects, I'd also say that we should encourage students to take on projects that they're interested in. Universities could do better at this, and it's not impossible to achieve, but it's perhaps a bit out of the bounds that they might otherwise recognize. I had never done a podcast before, and I tweeted that I really want to do an EdTech podcast, and Kris responded. We've never actually met in person. This is all remote and we're learning a lot. I could have taken a course in creating an audio empire, but I don't think it would have been as good a learning experience as taking on a project like this. I think that if you build that into the curriculum, when people leave the institution they're more likely to continue taking those risks. People have to be taking risks in class so that they can take risks outside when they've graduated.

MM *As we wrap up, are there any final thoughts or pieces of advice you would like to add?*

KH We're getting down to about a month until the semester starts. Don't get into this perfectionism standpoint. Looking at it for our podcast, maybe this is a very opportune time. For instance, celebrities such as Trevor Noah have increased their following and he's just broadcasting out of his apartment. All of a sudden, our expectations as a society have changed. So, again, don't be afraid, and push forward. I think even for students themselves, they should endeavour to push through and break out of their comfort zone. There isn't anything wrong with dropping an e-mail to your instructor or professor and talking to them after class. This is something everybody is going to have their own take on and their own approach to. But really, we've just got to be humble. Especially now that we're entering an era where it's all online, all remote, and we're not all comfortable with it. Acknowledge that this is all a learning process for all of us.

EC I realize that TALON has more of an educator audience, but I received a great piece of advice as an undergraduate student from a faculty member who is someone I greatly respect. He said, "Make a nuisance of yourself." Go ask questions. We're supposed to be smart people at an institution where you learn, so maximize the value. Get to know people. It not only builds tacit knowledge that you're not necessarily going to get in class. You're out building a network and finding potential mentors, and this is hugely valuable. That's the biggest thing I ever got out of university. That's my advice for students.

For faculty, as the late Christopher Hitchens (and many others) said, "Do not let perfection be the enemy of good." I think there's two ways to do that. One of my research areas is in open education and part of that is pedagogy and practices—meaning being forthright with your students about where you're an expert and what you can bring them, while also being honest when you're trying new things. If we're in an online environment and you've never taught online or have minimal experience, you should say, here are the best practices I know, but I'm going to do some experiments and it's a two-way street because I want and value your feedback. Nobody knows everything. If you're honest with the students about that and you give them the agency to provide feedback, then you're building leeway for experimentation in your course to try new things. I think that's very valuable.

Universities have really receded from the public eye, and I think that's coming about because of the vacuum left by what universities are not providing. Universities used to do a lot more public lecture series and interactions with the public. We used to get a lot more news articles where a real expert on a topic would provide a context, and you still get that on television news, but that's not the same thing as say, a public lecture series. There is a deep interest in long-form academic discussion on current issues. People are smart and interested. Joe Rogan would never be successful doing three-hour podcasts with some of the highest-sighted professors ever if people did not have an attention span of more than ten minutes. Now, attention span does matter in a lecture but that's very different from a conversation. Public conversation, public interaction, that back and forth, leads to longer discussions that are more interesting than me delivering a lecture to an empty vessel. There's a difference between best practices for lectures versus public debates and public interaction. So, I would tell instructors who have something to offer the world, whether it's their open educational practices or their expertise, that they should go public. There are some really well-respected academics doing this. Kris pointed out Scott Galloway. I'd also point out Cal Newport, who's a computer scientist at Georgetown University. He wrote some great books about productivity and deep work, and he has a whole podcast about it. He is a public intellectual as well as a university professor, and we need more of those people.

As we recede from the public eye, we're going to become less relevant because we're not going to be on people's minds. People who've done cool things should be highlighted, and that's what Kris and I are trying to do on EdTech Examined. That's what TALON is trying to do. People should be bold and be as public as they can about the unique things that they have to share.

## REFLECTION

**Erik:** Since our interview with TALON, I have continued to reflect on my teaching practices and consider the impact of the pandemic and, subsequently, the move to remote instruction. After our collective twelve-month crash course on education technology, I'm seeing my colleagues exude a little more confidence with these tools. I have many thoughts, but I want to share two themes that I've observed since March 2020.

*Being intentional when implementing technology into your class*
Online teaching, as scary as it was for first timers, is an exciting opportunity for experimentation. Teaching in a digital environment forces us to rethink how we will create engagement in the classroom. There is a "wow factor"—a feeling of endless possibilities—when we find a technological solution that fits with our teaching style. Kris and I have spent much of the past year highlighting the pros and cons of specific tools in our podcast. We evaluate technologies based on personal experience and find solutions to questions submitted by listeners. We've examined digital whiteboarding platforms, notes apps, data backup solutions, and project management suites—just to name a few categories. Consider the following when selecting an EdTech tool. Will this actually help students develop a better product? Based on your experience, how long will it take your students to learn this tool? Do you need to build more lead time into the assignment?

Following some discussions with colleagues at my institution, instructors seemed to have the most success when they A) chose tools that helped students meet class objectives, and B) gained some mastery over that tool. Implementing fewer technologies and giving space for students to master those technologies is more valuable than introducing a smorgasbord of tech into your course. Instructors can more confidently answer student's questions beyond a surface level. I've also witnessed the pride and satisfaction that my colleagues display when they show me how they've used a tool to its maximum capability. Some of my colleagues are true masters of these technologies, and they're more confident to share their expertise with their peers.

*Going public*
The pivot to "emergency remote instruction" took its toll on educators at every level. You might assume that to counteract this exhaustion, instructors should invest in more self-care and mindfulness meditation. Although this may be true, for some instructors the solution to their lack of energy was to give more. Specifically, they gave back to their local and professional communities. For example, some of my colleagues have meticulously documented their approach to managing digital breakout rooms or their video production techniques. Some have leveraged their teaching into new scholarly endeavours or contributed to open textbook projects (OER). Others are partnering with students and educational developers to present at education conferences. I've always suspected that documenting your own practices pays dividends in the long term, but I only had limited evidence to support my claim. Now, the evidence is ample. Sharing your newfound online teaching skills and practices within your department meetings, learning communities, and online communities will benefit you and your colleagues. While the pivot to remote instruction wasn't easy, the experience has created

a sense of solidarity among instructors—particularly those who leaned into the opportunity to share their successes and failures.

**Kris:** Over the past year, we've all had adapted to a rapidly changing environment. If technology has transformed the limitations of what is possible, the COVID-19 pandemic has transformed how we imagine it. As we plan to return to campus, work, and life as what we used to know, it's important to acknowledge the hardships of the past year that have taken their mental, physical, and emotional toll. With emergency remote online delivery, educators took on the challenge to evolve their courses to successfully deliver to their students. Let's celebrate what we've accomplished this past year and bring with us the best of online teaching back into the classroom.

As I reflect over the past year and our TALON interview, the following are three themes I trust educators remember as we return to the classroom:

1. The future is hybrid
   The pandemic gave everyone the opportunity to experience first-hand that not only can we survive, but we can also thrive remotely and do not need a central physical space to work, learn, and live. Online teaching creates constraints and allows us to breed creativity to rethink and reimagine in-class exercises to effectively flip the classroom in an online environment. Let us take the best of what online course materials we developed this past year and bring these back into the classroom. To that end, I'm providing a blend of both online and in-class course materials to allow students flexibility and create a more vibrant learning atmosphere.

2. Student-centred design
   As a practitioner of design thinking, we never lose sight of the primary end user when considering human-centred design and user experience design. Taking these concepts and applying them in academia, we as educators are putting students first and this should form the gravitational focus for course delivery. I was fortunate to have Chris Hoang (a former student starting in Fall 2019, teaching/research assistant in 2020 to present, EdTech Examined audio producer/sound engineer, and now colleague) to strategize how best to continually improve our courses to enhance the student's learning experience. This year provided an opportunity to experiment with new assignments, course material, deliverables, rubrics, etc. and we've further refined these going into the Fall semester. In April 2020, some academic development colleagues suggested having high frequency/low stake assignments as a best practice for online course delivery. After trial and iteration, this Fall we've streamlined assignments

to avoid overloading students by simplifying their deliverables.

3. Tech-instinctive
   The pandemic has proven to be a transformative inflection point and technology needs to intertwine with an educator's pedagogy. The best way to predict the future, is to help create it and that's exactly what being open to incorporating technology in the classroom does. Technology is a tool like any other—and don't use tools for the sake of having tools. I've seen first-hand students struggling with the learning curve when being presented with multiple technologies, and I now suggest implementing fewer tools in classroom to allow students to focus on mastery of the technology to utilize the full suite of features.

Thank you to both Chris Hoang and also Erik Christiansen for their support and providing their insightful feedback this past year.

ABOUT

**Kris Hans** is an ideas generator capable of turning dreams into reality and truly a social entrepreneur. He continues to undertake diverse roles and responsibilities that bring his skills and experience to serve Calgary's many communities—a testament to the value that he places on civic participation and social enterprise. Currently, Kris is co-founder and strategist at Market Grade, an interdisciplinary consultancy focused on marketing, design, innovation, and strategy. Kris teaches business management, design thinking, economics for business, entrepreneurial thinking (opportunity identification & technology for entrepreneurs), global challenges, strategic planning, and strategic selling at the University of Calgary, Canada. At Mount Royal University he's been teaching business communications since 2016 and he taught entrepreneurship and marketing in the past. Kris also served as the first-ever entrepreneur in residence at W21C in the O'Brien Institute of Public Health, Cumming School of Medicine, University of Calgary. Kris continues to work with students and start-up ventures to help grow their businesses and diversify the Alberta economy.

**Erik Christiansen** is the subject librarian for psychology, counselling, health and physical education and the Music Conservatory at Mount Royal University in Calgary, Canada. Erik has experience working in information technology, and previously he provided instructional design, education technology and research support at the University of Alberta's Faculty of Education. His research interests are centred around open education, integrating information literacy into the academic curriculum and web usability. He is an active member of the scholarship of teaching and learning (SoTL) community. Erik has a long-held interest in computing, interface design and music.

# Tom Burns

Senior Lecturer/Academic Developer, Centre for Professional and Educational Development, London Metropolitan University, United Kingdom

Interviewed November 2020 by *Sandra Abegglen*

SA *Tom, let's start with you introducing yourself and telling us about what you do.*

TB I'm a senior lecturer at the London Metropolitan University. I work within Centre for Professional and Educational Development, which is a professional development team that runs the master and the Post Graduate Certificate of Learning and Teaching in Higher Education (PGCert). On that, I am a module leader for FSL— that's Facilitating Student Learning—and a co-tutor on CED, which is Curriculum Evaluation and Development. My background is one of a non-traditional student. I left school at fifteen, went into the building trade, had a great time and did some community theatre at the same time. Then at twenty-six, College called, and I went back, and I haven't left since.

My background developed into an interest in literature and texts, and deconstructing texts, which then opened up the way for me to get involved in learning development, and then academic development. I find the theory and tools that I've learned within literary criticism and film theory that I taught at the University of Essex, are applicable to academic discourse and academic practices. Within these, I'm thinking of good ways of transmitting information to and engaging non-traditional students in academic discourse, academic practice and how to be themselves within these environments.

Coming from my background in literature, I felt that it helped me to figure out really quick short, sharp mechanisms to enable students to understand exactly what academic study involved and what the essay was, for example, and to have their say exactly as they meant it. That practice was developed, and we created an Essential Study Skills Guide for students. But since then, I have found the whole field of learning development to be much more nuanced. The students have changed—the student never stays the same. But also, what was taken for granted in my day, which was the welcoming and supporting of non-traditional students, became diminished with a widening of participation. So I've actually found that there has to be a much more holistic approach to learning development and study skills when dealing directly with students, and now developing that with staff on FSL and CED.

SA *With COVID, everything had to move quite quickly to the online world. How did you experience that move and what were the challenges when moving online?*

TB Well, I had already been engaged in online learning and approaches, so initially it wasn't a shock. As time wore on and I became further involved in that realization that it was all online, it did become quite a shock. And now, I'm supporting staff with their online course design and teaching. The staff are reporting back to me, giving me feedback, that students had moved seamlessly online, and it was working well. Attendance and engagement levels are even increasing. It seems really positive.

But since then, time has been spent dealing with staff and their particular issues. My work is dealing with support staff, learning developers, academic liaison librarians (who do work directly with students, but who provide a slightly different approach), and directly with subject staff. This is the wonderful thing about my work with these

*"The positive was noticing that it's not about reproducing what you do face-to-face; rather, it is starting from the beginning."*

two bodies coming together in that same space. Subject staff could reveal to the support staff some of the issues that were arriving—and that their students were feeling—and vice versa. In a way, what this means is that we are re-examining practice, and re-examining what we actually mean by engagement online—and also re-examining the different ways that we as staff can support each other.

I always found it "clumsy" that attendance was thought of as a proxy for engagement. Locked down students might—or might not—be attending for a whole range of reasons. These are all things for further research and collaborative conversations with support staff, subject staff and wider support staff for technology and student services. But yes, it has been a shock.

Initially I felt okay with teaching online and thought I understood what it was, but when it actually happened, and you had to walk the walk, I examined my practice and what would've been taken for granted. It's made me reflect on exactly what the mechanisms are and what makes my face-to-face teaching successful and then to consider how to reproduce that online. The positive was noticing that it's not about reproducing what you do face-to-face; rather, it is starting from the beginning. What is social engagement? What does an induction look like? What does an icebreaker look like online? Now that I'm in a virtual world, what capacities are available there that I can harness?

SA *Is there a favourite software, tool, resource or theory you like to draw upon when preparing for your teaching?*

TB I suppose really, the dialogic is the theory. The tool that I found most useful for that is actually **Blackboard Collaborate**, and video chats within **Microsoft Teams**, where you can have joint meetings, and one-to-one meetings and employ the chat box. I know not to bombard people with e-mails, but what I find really useful is to e-mail students or participants, and say, "I'm going to call you." Or, "Can I call you at this time?" I call, then support that with a document, an article to read or a piece of work to give feedback on, so you're making that contact and supporting and scaffolding it. Being face-to-face on video has been really nice. In some ways, it can be more personal than actually being in the classroom. You're both in your own non-neutral spaces, where the classroom or the office is always someone's office. I find that to really be revelatory, actually, a very effective way of communication.

SA *Where do you think we're going with higher education in terms of teaching, especially now that it is mainly online?*

TB I envision that it is going back to what it was before. I know from my own work—and don't tell the bosses this—but I've been able to be so much more productive working from home. I've actually found it can be a lot more meaningful because you're picking and choosing to have those conversations with people. I actually find that they can be a lot more engaging because they can be less intimidating than being face-to-face. I see many positives of being online.

On the other hand, students should experience university. I went to a campus university for my undergraduate degree, and it was just wonderful to be with thousands of people who were all immersed with doing their degrees. The clubs, the societies that were active and that you couldn't avoid being involved with because someone would drag you there. You would come out of your lectures and there would be a quartet playing classical music at the bottom of the stairs. I'd never experienced such a thing and I wouldn't have experienced that if it weren't for being at a campus university.

The drama, the theatre and the politics. Yes, my university produced many politicians and dramaturges. I suppose these are important asides for a non-traditional student like myself. It is not simply traditional performance, assessment and outcomes driven. The universities can offer much more than that. With this move toward education being more outcomes and evaluation driven, rather than process driven, moving online will amplify this. Online just doesn't have the serendipity.

The best resources there for us as staff are our students, and the engagement and feedback they give us. I think that will be our strength as we move forward. In any circumstances, these times highlight the important issues—the importance of human contact and the humane aspects of university. And save your sanity as well. You must remember; stay sane!

## REFLECTION

### Let's Dance

We come to bear witness to the post-apocalypse
one year on
everything changed
and stayed the same.
The best of times.

The worst of times.
You stayed strong and clapped the NHS.
You gave an inch … They took a mile.

Beans to be counted
not counted on.
We remember the tune—but not the chord:
“All in this together!”
Subsumed by the metrics, the metadata.
We are on thin ice again.
Let’s dance again.

Like the songs on the underground in the Blitz,
chestnuts roasting on an open fire,
jumpers for goalposts.
Washed away. Again.
You are all in this together,
beans to be counted
not counted on.

No more heroes anymore.
No free school milk
no homes for heroes
no more heroes
no survivors.

Let’s stick together
Again.
At a distance, online, agile, flexible
Again.

ABOUT

**Tom Burns** is a senior lecturer/academic developer at the Centre for Professional and Educational Development at London Metropolitan University in the United Kingdom. He is developing innovations with a special focus on praxis that ignite student curiosity and develop power and voice. Tom is also a co-author of *Teaching, Learning and Study Skills: A Guide for Tutors,* and *Essential Study Skills: The Complete Guide to Success at University* (4th Edition). He has taken a production of *Bouncers* on a tour of Crete music venues, written and made a feature film *(Eight Days from Yesterday)*, and has produced teaching and learning courses and materials in a range of settings—his *Take Control* video won the IVCA gold award for education.

# Brian McDonough

Course Leader BA Sociology, Solent University, United Kingdom

Interviewed August 2020 by *Mac McGinn*

*MM Brian, can you tell us a little bit about yourself and about what you do?*

BM I'm course lead of sociology at Solent University in the UK. It's a sociology BA course and I lead a number of modules, such as the social inequalities module, sociological imagination, and research in the social world. I'm also an active researcher. I've published two books this year, one called *Universal Basic Income*, which was a co-authored text published by Routledge, and another sociology and research methods text called *Flying Aeroplanes and Other Sociological Tales*, also published by Routledge.

*MM I'd like to understand a little bit more about your research on the differences between online versus face-to-face communication.*

BM Actually, this distinction between online versus face-to-face was a key feature of my doctoral research, and it was based around my interviews with a number of experts in various fields—from schoolteachers to doctors to bankers to aeroplane pilots. There was a key theme that emerged from my qualitative data, and the key theme was that some people just hated talking via a screen and some people absolutely loved it. It was really quite difficult writing my thesis to try and work out what "online"' or, as I call it, "mediating technology" was about. Why do some people absolutely love mediating technology and why do some people absolutely hate it?

At the time I was reading a book called *A History of the Concept of Time: Prologomena* by the philosopher Martin Heidegger, the phenomenologist. And Heidegger actually gave me the answer. It was a short section in Heidegger's book, where he talked about the Weidenhäuser Bridge, which was down the road from Marburg University. Heidegger said, there's two ways of understanding the bridge. You can go down to the bridge, in which the bridge is bodily present, or you can go down to the local shop and you can get a picture postcard of the bridge, and the bridge is represented via a representation—he said that there was a layered structure to picturing things.

Now, obviously, in Heidegger's time, there was no Internet and there was no online distance learning, but there were representations of things. There were picture postcards. You could go on holiday to Paris, and you could send picture postcards of yourself. Okay, they'd take a few weeks to arrive. But some people would say this is the same thing. Seeing the picture of the Eiffel Tower in Paris is the same as me going to Paris. Why do I need to go to the Eiffel Tower?

That same idea was coming through with my research participants. The doctor was saying, look, I don't need to see my patients to know what's wrong with them. I can just do a video call. But then there were other people in the banking sector saying, look, I need to go to the other side of the world to shake hands with someone. That's how important bodily presence is.

This is a really interesting discussion. And that question that you asked I think is a really important question. What is better out of online and face-to-face or bodily presence? I use the term, following Heidegger. I think that these two things are completely different. Heidegger said they were ontologically different, and we might experience things ontically. So, the ontic is what you like and what you don't like. That's one aspect. Some people like it, and some people don't like it. But Heidegger's point was that these things are ontologically different. They're completely different in terms of human existence and in terms of human experience. They're very, very different.

I think that's quite key. Because there's a lot of researchers out there who are saying there's no difference between being face-to-face and being online. And, of course, if you follow that small section in *The History of Concept of Time,* which I did, you can pursue the argument that there is a difference. It's a very clear difference and it's an ontological difference.

*MM* *You mentioned that you're also a teaching and learning champion. Could you explain a little bit more about that and about overcoming different problems and barriers for online learning?*

BM I'm a senior fellow in a higher education academy, and to achieve that I had to demonstrate various forms of teaching. One form was using distance learning, and also using a blended learning approach. Obviously, right now, during COVID, it's not so much blended, it's more online. That's really been a key part of my teaching strategy for some years, engaging students with online materials. But some people prefer a hard copy set of notes. Some people just like you to e-mail it via online. I used to do both. I used to actually produce hard copy reading materials and give them out to all of my students at the beginning of term. And I also used to send them out to them via e-mail, so they had them both ways.

I'm aware that, again ontically, some people just prefer to physically have a book. With the **Kindle** and book technologies where you can buy a book online, people expected to see books disappear overnight, but they haven't. One of the reasons they haven't is because people like to sit on trains and sit on buses and actually physically hold a book. I think that's quite key to understanding what people actually want, and how people perceive the difference between online learning and learning in more physical spaces.

You get some students who physically turn up, but they just don't want to switch on their screens. And then you get the opposite. You get students who are happy to switch on, but they don't want to physically turn up. These are preferences, and beneath that preference there is something very human about being face-to-face with people and having a special kind of relationship with them.

I think that it's superlative, being face-to-face. That, again, ontologically speaking, it's superlative and the online stuff is deficient. Why is it deficient? It's deficient because it lacks bodily presence. So again, I'm talking about deficiency in an ontological sense. It's not deficient in the sense that some people actually prefer online tutorials, while other people prefer face-to-face tutorials. It's understanding those dynamics, I think that is really important to delivering high-quality teaching and learning.

*MM* *What types of opportunities do you think are created through online learning?*

BM I think the switch to online has actually benefited lots of people in lots of different ways. My 25-minute drive, which can sometimes be 45 minutes in bad traffic, was instantly just done away with. Turning up late at my parking lot and finding that there were no spaces available. Turning up, forgetting my office card to get into my office and having to go and speak to Estates to let me in. That's a problem I can forget. A lot of problems that were resolved. I've also got a one-year-old baby boy, Huxley. So, looking after Huxley is obviously really important, and obviously having more space to actually work from home is a huge advantage.

But obviously there's disadvantages too. Mental health is a big issue right across the globe. People have just been locked in the house, 24/7, not doing their usual thing. Sometimes when you just walk to the shops, you meet people along the way, and that can make a huge difference to your mental health. I think it surprised me actually. Because when COVID first happened, I thought, oh, this is great. We all sit home. When I say, "great," I obviously do not mean in terms of the deadly disease, but in terms of affecting how you work, and your teaching and learning. I thought, well, this is all right. Loads of advantages here. But quickly I realized that I wanted to go back to how things were before. People will have different preferences to this, and it will depend on their circumstances, but I think there are lots of opportunities.

I would say before, I was using probably about ten per cent of the IT tools on our online—we call it SOL at Solent University—Solent Online Learning platform. I was probably using about ten per cent of SOL last year, and now I'm probably using about 85 per cent of SOL. I'm using far more online games, online checklists, and online tabs for opening up videos and readings. I'm using a lot more and it made me question why wasn't I using this before? Why wasn't I doing this just six months ago? It has opened up opportunities.

MM *Is there a favourite resource, tool, or software that you have discovered recently that's helping with online learning and teaching your students?*

BM There's one called **VideoScribe**, which is really just very basic. You can download the app and you can write, and basically it plays music. It's a bit like an intro. It can be used as an intro to a module or course. Or it can be an intro to an assessment or a set of ideas. And I think it's really good because it's focused on words. Students will read what it says, but the music also is really engaging, and it also brings some excitement to the course when you see a video that's got music and it's makes it sound exciting. So, VideoScribe is something I've used recently, which I think is really useful. I'm using things a lot more like **YouTube** and some of the most common platforms that maybe I didn't use a great deal before.

We've also got some lecture apps. **Panopto** is one. My university is well adapted to the use of it. So as soon as I upload the video, Panopto recognizes who I am. And it's quite easy to use. Those are just some of the technologies that I've been using—some of them for the first time.

What's really interesting is that I teach a module called Research in the Social World, and my students are doing some research for a real research organization. But the research organizations, because of COVID, are actually doing online interviews. My modules are all set up for teaching how to do online interviews, and I'm also teaching online. So, you've got this really interesting experience from the students' perspective where they're getting real-life work experience

*"... is technology going to keep changing things? Not on its own. Technology doesn't work like that. There need to be other factors, human factors that work too."*

working for an organization, and they're doing that in a pandemic. They're using the software that the organization is using and they're carrying out some research interviews for that organization. Absolutely, it's a learning curve, but not just for me, for the students and the other organizations as well.

MM *What do you think higher education will look like in the future, for example, in ten years or so?*

BM That's a really interesting question because, as someone who has carried out research on technology, some writers and authors have noted that people believe that when you create a new bit of technology that it's going to change the world. And like when we were talking about the Kindle, people said books would be dead, but they aren't.

When the computer was introduced, people were talking about having a paperless office. Everything's going to be online. But the questions you're asking me are on a piece of paper, right? So, this idea of the paperless office just never happened. Some people make predictions now and say in ten years' time, higher education is all going to be online. We have a university in the UK, the Open University, which is very famous for doing online courses. And people say, oh, but we're all going to be like the Open University. Everything's going to be online. But actually, I don't think that's the case.

There needs to be more to make sure it's a shift and social change in society, there need to be other factors. COVID is a big factor. It's played an enormous role in changing what people do, and I do think that, because of the pandemic, higher education has changed. That's not because of the technology. That's largely because there's been this huge social shift, where working from home has become more culturally acceptable. Learning from home has become more culturally acceptable.

I do think in ten years' time things will be different, different to what they were six months ago. But is technology going to keep changing things? Not on its own. Technology doesn't work like that. There need to be other factors, human factors that work too.

## REFLECTION

The discussion about online teaching and learning draws on a number of theoretical concepts from the philosophy of Heidegger. In this interview I, a sociologist at Solent University (United Kingdom), draw on *The History of Concept of Time* (1992). I developed these Heideggerian concepts in my doctoral thesis and I described my use of them in this interview. Heidegger himself draws on his own teaching at Marburg University in Germany. Down the road is a river and the Weidenhäuser Bridge. The bridge can be viewed from the picture postcard, bought from the local souvenir store. Or the bridge can be perceived by placing oneself before the bridge, in which it is bodily present. Heidegger says that the bridge, perceived via the picture postcard, has a layered structure because there are such layers in picture things.

I draw on these ideas in my research on mediating technologies, and in this interview I stated that teaching online has a layered structure to it. When we see students, we see them via a screen, not with their bodily presence. Heidegger says that bodily presence is superlative in an ontological sense. Online teaching is ontologically deficient because it is deficient of bodily presence. It's simply "not the same" to teach students online as it is to teach them face-to-face. Of course, some people prefer the superlative mode of teaching and others prefer the deficient mode. This is an ontological distinction, and we should not confuse this with what we prefer or like, in the purely ontic sense.

The pandemic has brought these ideas to light because it has changed the ways in which teaching and learning are delivered in higher education. There is so much debate over what is better or worse (online or face-to-face) and we can cut through these debates by using Heidegger's philosophy to examine how these distinctions can be better understood. One mistake is that computer designers (ICT experts) are often trying to make online teaching "just like" face-to-face teaching. But drawing on Heidegger, this is impossible. Because these are different modes (ways) of being with our students—they are distinctly, qualitatively, different. The "close" between online learning and face-to-face learning cannot be rescued because it is incorrect to think of these as being on one continuum. They are ontologically different—it is as simple as that.

ABOUT

**Brian McDonough** is the course leader of the sociology BA at Solent University, United Kingdom. He leads a number of modules, including social inequalities, the sociological imagination, and researching the social world. Brian has published work on expertise and the use of technology at work, including an article and book on flying aeroplanes and using autopilot technology, as well as a book on universal basic income. In the UK, Brian is a senior fellow of the Higher Education Academy, having supported his course team in the use of new learning and teaching methods and technologies, and he is also a member of the British Sociological Association.

# Robin Whitteker

Graduate Student, Master of Architecture, School of Architecture, Planning and Landscape, University of Calgary, Canada

Interviewed August 2020 by *Mac McGinn*

MM *Robin, why don't we start with you introducing yourself and telling us a little bit about what you do.*

RW I am a student in the master of architecture program at the University of Calgary. I'm going into my M1 year, or the first of the two-year program, following the foundation year that the school offers. I've been in the industry for a few years working with KFA Architects and Planners, who are also my employer for the summer. They are an Ontario-based firm and I've been working with them purely remotely, which has been an interesting experience.

MM *You have the perspective of a student and also some real-world experience with working remotely in the field, so you have some experience and knowledge on both sides of what we're discussing. As a student, what has been the biggest challenge when we had to switch to emergency remote learning in April of this year?*

RW It was a tough situation and I think the school responded pretty well to it. Overall, I would say that the quality of learning was fairly impressive given the situation, but there were definitely some drawbacks. The most obvious among them is that architecture is a studio-based, in-person, discipline and when we went online the replacement had to be **Zoom**. We definitely lost the element of being able to just lean over and talk to someone and say, hey, what do you think of this? Or, what about this idea? I think it definitely impacted the way that I was working.

The feedback that you can get from professors was also somewhat impacted. Knowledge of using the online platforms was a big learning curve both for professors and students. Simple things like time limits on Zoom calls and screen sharing took a lot of time to figure out. You can't just point to a physical object anymore, so ensuring everyone is talking about the same element on screen can be a challenge. The lack of model making was also another big impact. Everything became a lot more about the digital quality of the work instead of the physical aspects, which I think was definitely a loss.

Participation was another challenge with some of the lecture units. Replacing the ability to stick your hand up and ask questions sort of works online, but it's not as organic. I think I felt this to a certain extent. In class you raise your hand, you can pipe off a random question or say something that pops into your head. When it's remote, there's a certain reluctance. I think we're going to have to either learn to overcome this reluctance or we're going to lose that important element of participation, which, I think, would definitely be negative. Being able to talk about the things that come across your mind is an important part of learning, because it can bring up something that you weren't aware you didn't know, if that makes sense. This is how you get a full, well-rounded education. You're not just learning the facts that are presented in front of you. You're pursuing the things that are interesting to you. I think participation is a big part of that. I would like to see us as students pushing ourselves to overcome the digital barrier there.

MM *Absolutely. Putting some of the onus back onto the students is important in order for us to be more engaged, rather than putting all the responsibility on the professors and educators.*

*"Knowledge of using the online platforms was a big learning curve both for professors and students."*

RW I think that's probably going to be a comfort thing, but engagement and participation in online education should also be a conscious collective effort on our part.

*MM Switching gears, what opportunities did you see were opened up by that switch to emergency remote learning?*

RW At the very beginning, I wasn't really sure how it was going to work but I think we ended up with a fairly comprehensive solution. A greater focus was put on the digital side of things, and this opened up the opportunity for us to get a lot more practice with the digital tools that we use in our program such as the presentation platforms and techniques. Also, based on my experience working during the summer, one thing I would say is that being comfortable in a virtual working environment is going to be a good life skill moving forward, and I think that this was good preparation for it.

*MM Absolutely. One opportunity that I noticed was the ability to pause or go slower on the lessons that were now being recorded and made accessible online. You had a different ability to understand the steps that were happening, but it also comes down to the educator explaining things properly in those recordings. So, I'm not sure if you felt the same, but I thought it was good to work your way through that process.*

RW Definitely. It was a blessing, because the traditional way of solving these technical questions is having to go outside of class time, track down your professor, or track down another student who can show you how to do it. It's tough. Part of it is just adapting to a different way of working. I think the recording of lectures is a great benefit, and it's definitely something that should be continued going forward.

Another benefit is that when students are participating and asking questions in the online classes, a lot of the time it's being written down.

This means we don't have any issues with missing the information that is being contributed by whoever is participating, as compared to us trying to hear the person speaking over what other people are doing in class. It's a small benefit, but it's one of the silver linings.

MM *Great point. So, the next question is, what is your most-used software tool in terms of collaboration, meetings, and things like that?*

RW Last semester it was definitely Zoom. I think that was kind of the natural choice. It's a simple, powerful piece of software that has a lot of the basic elements that you would look for in video chat. In terms of sharing next semester, what I anticipate it would be something more in line with what I've used during the summer at my work, which is kind of a chat-based system where you can have multiple threads. The one I'm currently using is **Slack**, but there are a number of different programs like this. I'm hoping that the school will set up something like this. I think that having some version of a dedicated system of communication is going to be key. It will have to be paired with file sharing abilities for any kind of team or group projects. Group work is a big part of architecture and being able to tackle that is going to be interesting. I don't think video or e-mail is going to be quite up to the task, because a lot of it's going to require the ability to facilitate the micro communications that go on between a team working together on a project. When you're working on the same file, this communication and ability to file share is going to be paramount. Those things have enough challenges, even without the distance.

MM *From a student's perspective, what would be your recommendations for online education as we move forward?*

RW I really hope that universities invest in centralized solutions. I hope they're going to ensure that the educators are proficient in this online software before the semester starts, so that the educators can then, in turn, make sure that the students are proficient, just so we can move past the technical difficulties and get on with the learning. I think that's going to be the first thing.

The second thing is which software they choose. I think there are a lot of really good options out there. I certainly am not qualified to say which one's best; I'd leave that to the experts. But the selection of that software is going to be a pretty important choice, because at the moment, a lot hinges on it.

I would like for there to be an option for some sort of blended learning where we can go and do some things in person, and I would one hundred percent take advantage of that. There is really no alternative to being able to just look over and get somebody's quick feedback. I think that to lose this would be to completely change the spirit of what we're doing. To a certain extent, I felt that last semester as I'm sure you did as well, Mac.

I think that completely digital architecture is not the way that the school should be leaning as a long-term plan. The industry is already leaning toward architecture as being experienced too much through the digital, in terms of there being too much emphasis on the image of the building, rather than the building itself. I think we are making architecture too much of a digital profession.

MM *What do you expect the architecture program and higher education to look like in the next ten years?*

RW I think that you're going to see a lot more of the digital aspects, although in architectural education there is a lot that I would encourage to go in different directions. I think that increasing the amount of digital learning we do is fine for something like history, or even to a certain extent, a course like graphics where you're learning more technical skills. That's absolutely fine. But when it comes to the design and crafting of architecture, I think there's no substitute for an in-person, collaborative effort. That's how it's done in the real world, and that might change over the coming years, but I don't think it's going to be exclusively digital, nor do I think that it should be. Architecture has a digital presence but when it comes down to it, a building is an object in the real world and we need to keep that idea alive, and that starts with education.

MM *Well, I'd just like to say thank you again for participating with us in the TALON project and being an expert voice from the students' perspective.*

RW Thank you, Mac, thanks for having me.

## REFLECTION

It's difficult to say what the future of architectural practice will look like post pandemic, but it is clear that along with other office-based businesses, there will be some element of remote work in practice and remote learning in academia. There is much that can be gained by this transition, more control over where we live and work, a reduced dependence on centralized offices or institutions, a reduction in the time spent commuting—the list goes on. However, it is always important to remember that the work of architecture is not fundamentally digital. For the past two years great strides have been made in remote workflows, but as yet there is no substitute for the synergy made possible by in-person collaboration. This is doubly true for those who are learning the basic practices of architecture. Being isolated from the daily example of how others work prevents aspiring students and young professionals from learning by example. It can not only be isolating but may also lead to stunted growth in terms of soft skills like in-person networking or hard skills which are not widely publicized online. While those negative outcomes are likely, conversely, it may also lead to younger members of the architectural discipline gaining a greater ability to self-teach the majority of their hard skills and will almost certainly improve their ability to engage, share and cooperate through online platforms. This will, of course, come at a cost. More time invested in learning, higher stress levels, and let's keep in mind, remote learning and work can, in some cases, potentially lead to strong feelings of isolation.

Fortunately, we, as a discipline, can help curb these issues. We must look for opportunities to engage in-person with colleges or for fellow students to help navigate the shared hurdles of taking on architecture. In the long term for academia, this will likely mean a return to the studio. In the coming years we will be in the position to take on the lessons we've learned in the past months to leverage the personal flexibility, and the power of some of these new tools to communicate designs, while minimizing the drawbacks of remote work. There is the possibility of shaping a more flexible, healthier architecture industry with its members having a better understanding of how to leverage the digital tools available to us. However, through this one thing must not be forgotten: Architecture is not the tools we use to communicate it. It isn't the Cloud model, or the rendered video walk-through. It is not even the scale drawings. "Good" architecture is the physical building after all that communication is done, and our goal in school and in the profession must be to understand the physical reality of our designs. This is something that is easily forgotten amongst the plethora of new modes of production and, long-term, this must be our ultimate guide as we re-shape the discipline.

ABOUT

**Robin Whitteker** is a graduate student in the master of architecture program in the School of Architecture, Planning and Landscape at the University of Calgary, Canada. In the 2019–2020 academic year when the COVID-19 pandemic began, he was taking the foundation year courses. Before his masters, he worked for four years in Toronto at KFA Architects + Planners, practising residential architecture. Among his many interests are critical design thinking and sustainability.

# Anna-Maria Meister

Professor of Architecture Theory and Science,
Technical University of Darmstadt, Germany

Interviewed August 2020 by *Sandra Abegglen*

SA *Anna-Maria Meister, I'm interested to hear what your role is, what your background is and what you're currently doing.*

AM I am an architect and a historian—I was trained as an architect at the Technical University of Munich (a Polytechnic School) and after working in the field I went to the United States for both a master's degree (from Columbia University) and a PhD. I did my PhD at Princeton in history and theory, and my work centred around topics related to norms and regulations as social projections and ways of shaping society. Since September 2019, I have been a professor of architecture theory and science at the Technical University in Darmstadt, Germany. I go to design reviews, I'm involved in the studio culture, but at my chair I teach mostly through seminars and lectures.

SA *Since COVID, how have you been teaching? Have your classes been moved online?*

AM The German semesters run very late in the year. So, in a way, we had the US as a kind of sample study, which made it possible for me, with all of my friends in the US teaching, to get a lot of intel on what works, what doesn't work, and what I might be more careful with. Our summer semester started in April, so by that time, it was clear that it needed to be online. We were still scrambling to get everybody on board and there was resistance in different parts of the faculty, as there often is. And to be fair, it might be easier for those of us teaching history and theory to teach online than it seems to be for those teaching studio drawing or sculpting, for example. But it was clear in the Summer semester of 2019 that everything was going to be online.

In our department, we put together a so-called digital task force, where a few of us who like to explore different formats, work in different structures and software, and are familiar with remote technologies, came together a few times and workshopped ideas and tried to develop solutions. At that time there was already a robust discourse going on in the US, so I was also reading a lot on **Facebook** from friends and on certain blogs about ideas regarding how to restructure teaching formats, especially in design and architecture. Of course, what happened everywhere else as well as in our department was that some people agreed to, or warmed up to, online teaching, but basically performed their regular teaching and streamed it through **Zoom**, without changing the format, content, or methods. What we tried to show was that it's absolutely possible to teach studio and seminars online, but that if you want to provide a valuable learning experience, it also means rethinking structures and formats, and learning new tools. That's how we approached it and I think we were, I would say, fairly successful, as the evaluations show now. But there have definitely been different paths of exploration and embracing the change.

SA *What was the biggest challenge when you had to move your course online?*

AM Last semester I wasn't teaching my lecture course, but a seminar, which I think made it easier to restructure. Next semester I'll teach my lecture course, Intro to Modern Architecture, so we'll see how that goes. The biggest challenge was to find out how to have quality discussion time with the students. The seminar was large with over twenty-five students, and I had to figure out how to facilitate good discussions around the core texts. To minimize students' online or screen time, I decided not to have a Zoom session every week because while I teach two seminars, they take every class online all day every day. Students have a different quantity of exposure to these online mediums.

To counter that I broke the seminar down into a bi-weekly meeting on Zoom with alternating weeks where I gave them writing assignments. I commented on them, as they would then be compiled into a final "paper" after some edits and changes. I think that worked very well as a format, but I had to learn that the number of classes suddenly shrinks to six, which means that there's a long time between the introduction and when you really get into the content as well as between the discussion sessions. Of course, I knew that rationally, but hadn't really thought about it in terms of pedagogical flow.

The build-up of discussion that you have in a seminar, where the weekly discussions start layering on top of each other, proved a bit difficult in terms of momentum because there were always two weeks in between classes. It was difficult in this way to pick up where we had left off. We used an online whiteboard to collect ideas, and the students could post questions on it, and we collected materials in between the weeks, so there was some engagement. I would say, on a technical or a methodological front, that would be the biggest change. For the first one or two sessions I didn't use breakout rooms. I only had the students discuss with myself and one another in a big group. That was only semi-successful, so starting in the third week, I used breakout rooms for the discussions. I gave each room a question and then had them talk in groups of five. I would check in occasionally, and that really worked. So, I kept that model for every class thereafter.

But in all this there were really two kinds of challenge: One was technical and methodological, and the other was social. I think one challenge that I really tried to address up front in every class was that students should let me know if they were stressed by COVID, if they had any changing circumstances, if anything was not going well, or if they needed help with anything, regardless of whether it had to do with the seminar or not. When I couldn't really meet the students, it was more difficult to know what was happening. When they didn't log on to class, I couldn't tell if they were just tired or if they had issues. Even when they were logged on it was hard to know what was happening, if they were super-stressed. It was challenging to make sure that they knew that we as instructors knew that it was not business as usual. I don't think everybody was as open about whether they were struggling.

I and many of my colleagues tried to encourage the students to tell us if something was wrong. We tried our best to make it clear that we wanted to help in any way we could if they were stressed, if things weren't working for them, if they were experiencing issues with their Internet connection, or if they are living at home or losing childcare for their children. It was also difficult to actually help the students who came to us. I had one student who really had issues and I found it difficult to keep them in the loop and keep them on board remotely. I don't know if the US system is similar, but in the German system, you either take the course or you don't take the course. There's not much wiggle room in terms of exceptions, let's say.

As an instructor we lost the opportunities to see a different range of social interactions, where you can feel whether things are off or

*"In analogue teaching, sometimes people just disappear into the second row. Because there is no second row on Zoom, there was a presence in a different way."*

okay. In person you get a better sense of the social dynamics, whereas online everybody's looking at you and you're looking at everybody. I think it's always our job to make sure that students know that it's not the end of the world if something happens to their seminar question of the week, or something along those lines. I feel it was much more challenging to maintain that online.

SA *With the switch to online teaching, what were some of the things that went well for you? Was there anything that surprised you, or any new outcomes or new opportunities that emerged?*

AM It was nice to work across platforms a little bit more. I thought that the diversity in the ways of engaging the students was helpful and interesting. I discovered that the chat function on Zoom was really helpful in the studio or design reviews and in larger discussions around work. The chat paralleled the online live discussions and allowed students to really develop certain arguments and exchange book references and things like that. We didn't really do that in the seminar because it's a different kind of engagement, and I can't moderate the chat and discuss a text at the same time, but there are still more levels that we could have explored. I saw this method working well, but I don't know if that would have been the case in all formats. I had bachelor students in the seminar and they were very, very engaged. Almost all of them logged on every time and were really present, which doesn't always happen in a seminar of twenty-five or thirty people. In analog teaching, sometimes people just disappear into the second row. Because there is no second row on Zoom, there was a presence in a different way. I thought that it worked well.

SA *In terms of the upcoming course you will be teaching, how are you going about planning for it?*

AM This semester, some of my colleagues tested teaching in a studio setting where they would give their lectures and they would be streamed and recorded, but with professional lighting and a good camera—I will need to ask them how that went. I think that I may try this in combination with an online learning environment where we post readings, questions, and information for the class. Usually the lectures are ninety minutes every week. I'll shorten that to, let's say, fifty to sixty minutes maximum. The lectures will be online so that students can either watch them in the actual time slot for the course, or they can watch it before, depending on their preference. I will then reserve the half-hour that I saved by shortening the lecture for a Q&A

with the students live on Zoom—like a standing invitation every week where they can log on and ask questions after watching the lecture. We'll see how many take up that opportunity.

And of course, they can also ask written questions on the learning environment platform, so it's not the only way to get feedback for them, but it could be one moment to actually talk to each other. Usually in the lecture room you don't do your presentation and then walk out, there's a certain level of communication. So that's my plan for now, to not lose that level of communication entirely.

SA *What would you say has been your most-used software or tool? Are there any resources that you often draw from when preparing your online teaching and learning?*

AM I would say the most-used tool is definitely Zoom. It has totally taken over our lives. I use it for the seminar, for meetings with my students when I give them feedback, meetings with my colleagues, and when I have open office hours for students. Zoom is the interface; it's how we meet and teach. We use **Moodle** as a learning platform from the university, which, from what I gather, a lot of people don't seem to like. It may not be intuitive, but it does have a lot of components, and I find it very useful once you get the hang of it. I post all of my texts and briefs on there every week, so the students get the structure and see what's coming in the following week. We use **Conceptboard** to exchange ideas; the platform is like an online board. For recording our lectures, we use a piece of software called **Camtasia**. That is very useful for recording and editing, not just for lecture courses but also short intro lectures to certain topics. And then good old **PowerPoint** still works its magic.

For resources in terms of teaching methods, I researched online and learned a lot from Facebook groups with my colleagues. It is really a shared community where we are were asking okay, so how do we do this? Any ideas? How can we make this work? How do we teach design online? How do we take care of students' needs online? So that community, I think, is the biggest resource. I have amazing colleagues all over the world, I have to say. They're amazing and brilliant and have so many ideas and paths to follow and things that I've tried, and that has been immensely helpful.

And then there's a lot of information-compiling websites by universities. At our own university we have a study and learning department for didactics and methods. They put together a lot of introductions to different software, lots of examples to work off, and online courses. You could call them or e-mail them and ask them questions if you needed to. They would organize the licensing for, let's say, the new software we needed. They did a really great job in making this possible and organizing it. When we created our guide in the digital taskforce, we drew from all of that. In short, the resources on teaching methods, I would say, came mostly from my networks, other design schools and colleagues. And for the skills in technology we drew a lot of those resources from in-house and then from other universities as well. But that didactic preparation, that really worked well.

SA *Where do you think or where do you expect higher education to go on as we shift away from COVID in the future?*

AM I would say there are two answers. One is what I hope to happen, and the other is what I expect to happen. I expect that there will be a certain online component that remains, because I think a lot of people have now gone over the threshold of not wanting to do anything online and have realized that, for certain formats that are repetitive or that present certain basic skills that you teach in every class every year, the online format really is a big step forward. Whether you use the same PowerPoint every year or whether you make a video explaining it, that there's actually something useful in creating an online component for things that don't depend on your ability to critically frame content acutely or teach certain things live. Using these different layers of learning tools like Conceptboard, collective **Google Maps**, class **Wikis** that everybody works on—I think those are approaches that could be utilized much more in, let's say, conventional learning settings. Because it really creates a sense of a shared project that's accessible in a different way. I think those things should stay and I expect them to at least get a stronger foothold.

At least in Germany, there is a very strong resistance to online studio teaching. Definitely not within the next ten years do I see any shift toward online studio teaching or online teaching as the norm at universities. In Canada and the US there's a market model: you need the tuition fees of the people who attend, and they have to be willing to pay in return for a certain experience. Here, because we are teaching in publicly-funded, federally-funded, and state-funded institutions, there is less market pressure on schools, but a very strong political belief that presence and exchange in-person is a political necessity for higher education and the formation of critical thinking. So at least for the near future, I don't see a shift toward online-only in any way.

Now to what I hope for. I do think one thing that COVID has shown us so far in several areas, not just higher education, is that all of the problems we already had, especially in architecture—a lack of diversity, a lack of accessibility, a lack of social stratification, and the exclusion of certain classes and races and abilities, let's say—that just gets heightened. And I think the technology and the tools have shown us how easy it would be to broaden that frame more than we were willing or able to do before. But while I have seen many examples or more accessible formats, I have not yet seen that actually being the case on a large scale; we still need to do much better in those areas. Because we still have issues of infrastructural access, and the social and political problems of teaching in higher education and who can get that education—these are still very present issues. Even if in Germany we have public education that's free, there are still, of course, discriminating structures and systemic exclusion. So those, I think, are the tasks that need to be addressed. I think there are tools available with remote teaching, but the problem is not the tool or not having the tool, but the actual will to change. That is what I hope we will see.

REFLECTION

Since the interview I have taught a lecture course online and more seminars; we have also developed an event series on **Instagram Live** called Tuesday Night Live where we talk to a diverse group of scholars, architects, and critics in an intimate interview setting. One thing I have become more adamant about is the protection of both students and my team: the pandemic has put enormous pressure on many of us, and the culture in academia is not exactly driven by empathy. Hence, I have really tried to encourage everyone in each format and class and meeting to be open about issues, to encourage flexible solutions, and to help, regardless of whether the problem has to do with the university as such. We have also set up a COVID fund in our department to help financially. Because what I said in the interview has only become further exacerbated: the existing inequalities have become even more cruel, and those who take on caretaking responsibilities, who have medical issues or financial ones have taken on more and more of the burden during the crisis. So while much of the debate around teaching focuses on financial or academic topics, the real task is more than ever to further equal access and equal opportunity. From whichever position you can, that is everyone's responsibility, starting with the small things; because that is, as the crisis has shown, still lacking in academic culture on all levels. I have been lucky to have been part of supportive networks and fantastic events, and have seen and heard many formats, where colleagues have taken on this responsibility and really worked toward a more diverse and just life in academia, and they have done outstanding work (for example Esther Chois' initiative, Office Hours, or the many professional societies who have opened their conferences to a broader audience). But it needs structural change from above as well. The deeper issues of inequality cannot be solved by grassroots initiatives; they require dedication, funding, and policy changes.

ABOUT

**Anna-Maria Meister** is a professor for architecture theory and science at the Technical University of Darmstadt, Germany, and works at the intersection of architecture's histories and the histories of science and technology. Her work focuses on the production and dissemination of norms and normed objects as social desires in German modern architecture. Anna-Maria received a joint PhD degree in the history and theory of architecture and the Council of the Humanities from Princeton University, and holds degrees in architecture from Columbia University, New York, and the Technical University of Munich, Germany. She was a fellow at the Max Planck Institute for History of Science, Berlin, and a postdoctoral fellow at the Technische Universität Munich. Her writing has been published in *Harvard Design Magazine, Volume, Uncube, Baumeister, Arch+* and as a book chapter in *Architecture and the Paradox of Dissidence* (Routledge, 2013) and *Dust and Data* (2019). She is co-curator and co-editor of the international collaborative project Radical Pedagogies; the eponymous book was published by MIT Press in 2022.

# Darby-Marie Henshaw

Graduate Student, Master of Planning, School of Architecture, Planning and Landscape, University of Calgary, Canada.



Interviewed August 2020 by *Martina MacFarlane*

MM *Darby-Marie, please tell us about what you do.*

DH I am a student at the University of Calgary within the master of planning program at the SAPL (School of Architecture, Planning and Landscape). In the Fall I will be entering my second year of the program. This summer has been a bit different for me as the pandemic has impacted professional work opportunities. However, I've been doing some research with SafeGrowth in the Marlborough community in Calgary and have created a variety of Crime Prevention Through Environmental Design (CPTED) strategies for the community to implement.

MM *What was the biggest challenge when moving to remote learning in the Winter semester?*

DH I would say that the biggest struggle was creating a routine. In general, during the wintertime, people have a hard time setting boundaries and defining their routine because everyone is burned out and the winter conditions are inescapable. This added an additional barrier for me. I often felt as if it was okay to sleep in a bit longer and it was okay to watch my favourite show a bit more, just because I was at home. It was convenient; everything was at my fingertips and there wasn't any sense of accountability. I longed for the structure that comes with physically being at school.

MM *You go in, you put in your hours, you go home, and you can separate your personal life from your work life. It's hard to do that as a student doing online classes, because we are passionate about our work all the time. Those rigid boundaries are hard to establish when working at home.*

DH For sure, and by losing that rigidness in your schedule, it's easy to fall into a pattern that does not prioritize balance. Because ultimately, having balance is an important contributor to being a better student.

MM *On the flip side of that, what would you say are the unique opportunities created by digital education?*

DH I felt like I could connect with people whenever and wherever and that has been great. I could have a meeting with a group of people from one class, and then have a meeting with another colleague a moment later. The accessibility was unmatched because of the connectivity opportunities presented with online learning. I believe that as we get more acquainted with the available tools and resources out there, the online platform will continue to provide exceptional connectivity.

MM *What would be your most-used software tool?*

DH I would say for me, it was primarily **Zoom** because it is the tool that our classes are delivered on. I've used **WhatsApp** a lot too for personal use and to stay in touch with out-of-province family. I find that Zoom has been a great resource for school as it is extremely user friendly.

MM *What would be your recommendations for online education from a student perspective?*

*"I think that online education can help education become more affordable and convenient for potential students. Maybe it will even encourage more people to apply themselves and dream big. The goal is to have a diverse community within higher education. That's how knowledge advances."*

DH I would say that there must be a thorough breakdown of expectations. I believe that if expectations are not outlined at the get-go, communication becomes confusing, and the direction can be misleading. This ultimately creates a lot of wasted time trying to communicate with people individually rather than as a collective, which is common in the classroom setting. I felt like there was a lot of confusion within my classes for this reason. What are the expected expectations to begin with? And then, what do we do now because it's all online learning? Because a lot of our work is done in partners or groups, we need to know what's expected of others and how we are going to circumvent the barrier of not being able to be with each other. If the professors and students create that threshold of understanding on what's expected from each other then it can be smoother sailing.

MM *What do you expect that higher education might look like in the short-term future?*

DH I do think that this is a great opportunity to take the chance to understand the possibilities of online learning. People move long distances to pursue education. It's a defining stage when someone goes away to school—it changes family and friendship dynamics and it's quite a risk and changes your lifestyle substantially. I think that online education can help education become more affordable and convenient for potential students. Maybe it will even encourage more people to apply themselves and dream big. The goal is to have a diverse community within higher education. That's how knowledge advances. But I also see that, on the other hand, physical presence is very important within education. In-person communication is a tool and a skill that is learned through observation and practice. So, I see pros and cons, but I do think online learning provides more opportunities.

MM *For you personally, do you find that you're liking online learning?*

DH I'm indifferent. I understand its role and that it's a tool that must be used right now in order to get my degree, and I love what I'm doing. However, I'm a very social person and I think everyone in my class would know that. I love checking in on people and making sure everyone is doing well, or offering my help when needed. It's important for me to connect with my peers. I truly feel like part of my experience has been taken away from me in that sense. I can learn online, but I'd prefer not to learn in isolation.

We create such a good sense of community within education, because it's something that brings people together—sometimes it's unlikely that those people would have connected otherwise. Without physically seeing the community, it's really difficult to feel a connection and know that you have support. We can use online platforms as tools to connect in different ways and with different people around the world, but I believe it's a little bit of an ungenuine connection. I think it's great to actually be together. We need that community.

I feel extremely blessed to still be able to go to school right now, even though it's all online. We are learning just by going through this change. This is a great opportunity to practice resilience and work through an issue that isn't ideal, get through it as a community. As someone going into an extremely social field such as planning, it really helps to understand the kinds of barriers that could occur and how to assess these issues and work harder to make it more accessible for future endeavours. This is just another learning moment. I think we can put a positive spin on this and gain some great insight into the opportunities for learning.

## REFLECTION

I have always been eager to learn and to excel. What I didn't realize until now is that excelling within education is not synonymous with the confines of a classroom. The pandemic has brought a multitude of challenges to light, but it has also illuminated our resilience as a collective. Not only did we adapt our educational model in blind faith, but we became actively aware of the existing gaps within the age-old system. Through this process, we have become more invested in being proactive about fine-tuning our approach to learning, whether it be in-person or online.

My personal experience with this transition has been vast. I was a master's student at the height of the pandemic, and I continue to be impacted by it in professional practice, utilizing online services such as Zoom and **Microsoft Teams** instead of holding in-person meetings. I remember being significantly impacted by this change at first. As someone who values in person interaction, it was a change I didn't know how to manage—both personally and professionally. It was uncertain and uncontrollable. However, I've managed to adapt my own learning style and work ethic. I continue to time manage appropriately, ensuring enough balance between screen time and real-time experience. What I mean by real-time experience is incorporating elements of true human interaction—whether it be a walk or a coffee outside with a friend, ensuring that you provide yourself with an outlet is the most vital component to success with online learning.

I also believe that setting manageable expectations is critical. This experience has helped people uncover their feelings and identify their needs. Of course, higher education comes with higher expectations, but by acknowledging both your personal and professional expectations, a critical path can be identified that can prepare you to establish a more suitable approach to learning and living.

While these tools can help identify personal ways to succeed within higher education settings in a virtual format, I do understand that some learning is best done in person, regardless of the tactics applied. I entered my design-based program without any prior knowledge about the design world. I had a minimal understanding about computer software and hadn't hand-drawn much more than a quick sketch. The brief time I had in person was vital for my understanding of these concepts. I learned from my peers through observation, which is something that is extremely hard to recreate within an online format. However, it's not impossible, and I see incredible potential to recreate these seemingly not replicable in-person experiences.

I believe the future of higher education will rely on this experience substantially. As someone who has undergone the majority of a program and successfully completed a professional program during this transitional time to online learning, I see the value and the potential in this platform. I believe that we can leverage our resources to provide more opportunities for people to pursue higher education through enhanced accessibility. Through the sharing of experiences, thoughts, and processes, we can use these online learning tools and initiatives to create meaningful connections in academia that will transcend into professional practice.

ABOUT

**Darby-Marie Henshaw** is a recent alumnus of the master of planning program at the University of Calgary School of Architecture, Planning and Landscape Architecture. Prior to this degree, she completed a BA in criminology at Simon Fraser University, with a focus on environmental criminology and crime prevention. Darby-Marie was born and raised in the Vancouver area of BC, where she enjoys some of her outdoor passions such as hiking, biking, and kayaking along the West Coast shores.

# Charlie Smith

Studio Design Tutor/Lecturer in Architecture, School of Art and Design, Liverpool John Moores University, United Kingdom



Interviewed August 2020 by *Sandra Abegglen*

SA *Thanks for agreeing to participate in our expert Voice series for the TALON project. Please tell us a little bit about the work you do, what you've been involved in recently and what your specialties are.*

CS Thank you, Sandra. It's a pleasure to be a part of the series. I teach undergraduate and postgraduate architecture programs in the School of Art and Design at Liverpool John Moores University (JMU). I also teach the postgraduate MA course on urban design. I am reader of creative pedagogies in the school, and most of my research focuses on teaching and learning in creative programs. In particular, I am looking at assessment and feedback, and how all of these different issues affect the student experience. I also do a bit of research into library design, library architecture and learning space design. I've been at JMU for about fifteen years, and before that I worked in professional practice for architects in Manchester in the north of England. Primarily, I was designing school buildings there. So, I've gone from designing for education to researching for education.

SA *Sounds very interesting and, these days, very relevant. How have you experienced the move to remote teaching and learning?*

CS I think, like a lot of institutions in the UK, we had quite a rapid transition from face-to-face teaching to online teaching. For us it all happened over the space of a weekend. At the end of one week, we were teaching face-to-face, and then from the start of the following week, we were teaching exclusively online.

In architecture, like a lot of art and design programs, the design studio is the focal point of teaching and learning. Studio culture is very much at the heart of the student learning experience. In that sense, we're very much aligned with a socio-constructivist approach to learning, where in the studio, through tutorials and design reviews, learning is very much co-constructed between students and students, and students and teachers. It is all driven by the dialogue that takes place, because we teach primarily through one-to-one tutorials. Over the course of one of our studio days, I might have twelve one-to-one conversations with students, each of which lasts half-an-hour, about their ongoing design projects. So, a lot of our teaching is formative feedback on their evolving design projects. That dialogue, as Susan Orr and Alison Shreeve described it (in *Art and Design Pedagogy in Higher Education*), is the glue that holds the art and design learning environment together. For us, when we made the transition to online learning, one of the biggest challenges was how to maintain that dialogue-driven teaching approach.

This kind of technology is great—we're on different continents and we can sit and have this conversation, and dialogue without one of us taking two long-haul flights with all of the cost and the time and the carbon emissions that would accrue. But I think that whenever you're having a dialogue in this kind of format, there are nuances and aspects of the conversation which just aren't quite the same as they would be if we were talking face-to-face. So, I think, for us, we had to be quite mindful in that move from teaching face-to-face in the studio to teaching online, about how we try to maintain and work with that dialogue-driven learning approach, which is so fundamental to the studio education.

SA *How did the students react to that move? Did they miss seeing you and having that direct contact?*

CS I think the students understood quite clearly why this had happened, and they were generally very willing to engage and very supportive of what was happening. It was about the middle of March that we went from face-to-face teaching to online and we still had several months of the academic year to go, so a colleague of mine very quickly did an appraisal of the different online learning environments that we could use. We settled on **Zoom** quite quickly because it's very intuitive and easy to use and both students and tutors could screen share very easily. Once we had made that decision, we used it continuously because once we'd set a process up, we were quite keen to try and maintain that same process throughout the rest of the semester.

We quickly made the transfer and we managed to maintain the tutorial process pretty effectively in terms of recreating the one-to-one conversation that studio teaching is synonymous with. We'd use our **virtual learning environment (VLE)**, which for us is **Canvas**, and the students would upload their drawings the day before and then, as a tutor, I'd download all of their drawings in the morning. Just in the same way as in the studio I'd have a series of maybe twelve half-hour conversations, I would now have twelve half-hour Zoom calls with the students. I would bring up their work on the screen and they'd talk to me in the usual way, tell me about the ideas that they were having and the direction they were taking their project work in. The great thing was that I could then annotate their drawings and we could draw over it and discuss it, in just the same way as we would in studio. At the end of that process, I would re-upload that work back to the virtual learning environment. So, then they had a record of that conversation, in just the same way that, in studio, we might be drawing over their drawings and then they could take them away with them at the end of the session as a record of that conversation and that formative input into their work. We tried to mirror as closely as possible what would happen in the studio. Design learning is very much an experiential process. It's all about testing ideas.

One limit that we had was that we quite often work with physical models. Students will make scale models of their work and when you're in studio, you can pick those up, turn them around and look into them. That was a more difficult aspect to replicate. Students might still make cardboard models and upload their photographs, but it perhaps wasn't quite the same as it would be in the traditional in-studio environment.

SA *What would you say were the opportunities to newly emerge through that? Did you experience any particularly positive developments?*

CS I think the move to online learning was something of a catalyst for the adoption of technologies that were already there, but perhaps we weren't really adopting them yet in a big way. The process was perhaps quite reactive in that we were responding to the situation by moving to online teaching, but there are opportunities to be more proactive going forward, and to use the best of those techniques.

For instance, we have **Panopto** as a way of recording lectures. When we went into lockdown, any lectures that were still to go ahead in the timetable, were done through the online Panopto platform

*"I think the move to online learning was something of a catalyst for the adoption of technologies that were already there, but perhaps we weren't really adopting them yet in a big way. The process was perhaps quite reactive in that we were responding to the situation by moving to online teaching, but there are opportunities to be more proactive going forward, and to use the best of those techniques."*

CHARLIE SMITH

and the students could then view those lectures online as and when they wanted to. I think things like that are a big opportunity. That technology has been around our university for a little while, but we haven't embraced it until now. I think the move to online teaching has shown us that there are those opportunities, such as, perhaps, to use Panopto more widely.

There's a technique that you might be aware of called "flipped lectures," where students undertake a piece of work in advance of a lecture. You might ask them to read a chapter of a book or ask them to watch an online recording of a lecture; then you use the teaching session or the timetable slot for more of a discursive and interactive session with the students. Rather than just the old "sage on the stage" of an hour-long lecture, there is much more of a conversation. You come back to that dialogue idea, where it's more of a co-construction of learning. Going forward, one of the opportunities that's come out of this is that, like a number of institutions, we're now taking an "active blended learning" approach. Our large group teaching will now be an online discission rather than it just being a transmission model of learning, while we'll still have face-to-face contact teaching and tutorials in the studio. So, I think we will emerge into a blended learning environment that combines both online and face-to-face teaching. With the online tutorials, some tutors actually recorded their sessions so the students were able to play them back. Unlike in-studio, it doesn't just become something that happens at a moment in time, where students come in for a tutorial and then discuss the work and go away. And there's no real record of that conversation, other than any marked-up drawings that we have made. I think the opportunity for students to be able to play back recorded content is excellent as they can remind themselves of what was being talked about at the time and go and relive that piece of learning. So, I think there are opportunities there to use technologies that were already perhaps in existence, but we weren't using as effectively, or we weren't using to try and support students in their learning.

*SA* *How is the in-person element of the blended learning environment going to operate at JMU?*

CS For contact teaching within a socially distant environment, I think the studio model lends itself quite well to that because, within the design studio, we have quite a lot of space. So, we can have a small group of maybe six students per tutor coming in for a half-day session, morning and then afternoon. And we can maintain social distancing within the studio environment and still have that face-to-face contact teaching. I think the way that they present their drawings is likely to be different. We're looking at a strategy of students uploading their drawings to the virtual learning environment the day before, and then the tutor will download the drawings and then we'll project them using screens in the studio that allow us to draw over and review them. So rather than physical drawings, it's more likely to be digital drawings on a screen rather than the traditional drawings on a desk or pinning their drawings to the wall, as has been the case in previous years.

*SA* *What would you say is one of your favourite resources to use, especially when in designing your online course elements?*

CS One thing we have been looking at more is some of the lectures by high-profile architects that are out there, which quite often are available through formats like **YouTube**. We've been creating a resource of online lectures, not only just by ourselves, but also by signature architects or urban designers or artists, talking about their own work. I think that the opportunity to embed links through Canvas to those wider collection of online materials is great, because then the students are not only reading about the material, they're also able to watch it. Within art and design and architecture, it's very much about visual representation. It's about seeing the drawings, the models, the buildings, and the artworks. It's good to use resources, like online lectures through YouTube, in order for students to widen their understanding of the context of architecture and art and design.

*SA Where do you think the direction of higher education is headed?*

CS That's a really interesting question. I think the design studio is a central element of the student learning experience in architecture, art, and design disciplines. I think it's so central to that dialogue-driven, socio-constructivist approach to learning. I hope and I think that the design studio should remain very much a focal point of teaching.

Certainly, there are opportunities within the active blended learning approach for adopting perhaps more digital technologies through flipped lectures or through using the timetabled teaching sessions for lectures to do different things; to have more discursive teaching sessions, rather than, as I say, the traditional transmission-based approach to lecturing. Students with a flipped lecture can watch material beforehand and then come to the session, whether it's back in the actual campus itself or whether it's taking place in an online forum, to have a much more, as I say, conversational approach about what that material was.

I think in assessment and feedback, obviously, our students have been submitting all of their work online. And I think the actual physical reality of those drawings and those physical models is really important. A physical model communicates certain things that a CAD (Computer-aided Design) model can't really do. So, I think, hopefully, we will find a way back to that traditional format of presentation in the studio.

I think certainly technologies like virtual reality would allow a student and a tutor to walk through buildings at their developmental design stage, perhaps in a way that we don't at the moment. So as students build ever-more-refined CAD models of their buildings, there's an opportunity to create a virtual reality walk-through, in which a student and a design tutor are actually able to see what the design would look like from within and without, as the student's going through the design process. So, I think there are technologies out there, things like virtual reality, that may well lend themselves to a more rapid adoption within an online environment. But I think the physical reality of materials and physical models is still really important. I wouldn't want to see that lost in the next ten years. I think a design studio is so important as a dialogue-driven learning space that I think that should remain. It's been there for decades, if not centuries. So, I think it should still stay as a core element of the art and design and architecture curriculum.

SA *In that regard, do you also think then that the design disciplines, or creative disciplines generally, struggle more than others because there are certain elements that are more difficult to translate?*

CS Yes, it has certainly been a challenge. For example, where students would normally have access to workshops and facilities within the building to make their models, they haven't been able to access these as campuses closed down completely, so students weren't able to access those digital model-making materials or the workshops in the same way that they would have been able to. So, I think, going forward, there is a focus on the way in which those workshops can now begin to function under the new social distancing over the next few months, so the students still have access to those facilities. And I think that'll be really important because it is very much, as I say, an experiential process and a key part of that is being able to fabricate models and test ideas out. I know that students are very resourceful, and a lot were making their own models at home using whatever materials and resources they had. But I think once we get back into campus teaching, even on a more socially distanced, limited basis, those workshop facilities should be there for those students to able to access. So, I'm hopeful and confident that this will still be the way.

REFLECTION

Due to the ongoing lockdowns in the UK since my interview, teaching that would have taken place in the studio has continued to be conducted online. During this time, I've become much more cognizant of the different nature of the conversations that used to occur in the studio—the different forms of dialogue. There is a rich mixture, including one-to-one tutorials, informal peer discussions between students, workshop sessions and design reviews (also known as crits or juries). However, I've come to realize that when these different conversations all take place online, in the same virtual space, they become much less distinct from each other.

The design review is a good example of this. In the studio, these are formal presentations of students' work, and are used for formative feedback. They happen every three or four weeks, interspaced between the weekly one-to-one tutorials. As opposed to being conducted around a table, however, students pin their work up, and present it to a panel comprising a tutor, a guest critic who often works in professional practice, and a small group of their peers from their tutorial group. After describing their work to the panel, the student is asked questions that probe their ideas and provided with verbal feedback. These reviews constitute important milestones in the development of the student's project, and they are a key event within studio culture with their own distinctive praxis. However, design reviews conducted online become very similar to the format of another tutorial.

A consequence of this, I've come to realize that they lose their gravity within the pedagogic structure of design learning. I have discussed this with our students, and they have confirmed my perceptions, describing online reviews as more informal than their physical counterparts in the studio, and the dialogic interaction being more of a conversation with the reviewers. Because of this, however, online design reviews lack the symbolic weight of a physical review, which is a significant source of motivation for them to advance their work.

Furthermore, the JMU students also suggested that online reviews may have hindered the development of essential skills, experience, and confidence in presenting physically and before an audience. I've become acutely aware there may be subsequent impacts arising from this, as we return to teaching and learning in the physical studio after such a prolonged hiatus. Public speaking is a demanding affair. On return to the studio, our final-year undergraduates will have not presented their work in the traditional design review format, before a physical audience of their peers and critics, for eighteen months. Some, if not many, are likely to find reviews in the studio even more daunting, and they will need thoughtful support in the transition back to the physical studio culture and the teaching and learning methods that go with it. I believe that this will, however, provide us with an opportunity to reflect on, and take stock of those practices. The design review itself is not without criticism, and the return to the studio could be a timely moment to address those critiques of the crit.

## ABOUT

**Charlie Smith** teaches on the undergraduate and postgraduate architecture programs in the School of Art and Design at Liverpool John Moores University, in the United Kingdom. Primarily he works as a studio design tutor, but he also lectures across these programs. As a reader in creative pedagogies, his research lies primarily in the field of learning and teaching in creative disciplines, and in particular in assessment and feedback, and how these impact on the student experience. His edited book, *Progressive Studio Pedagogy: Examples from Architecture and Allied Design Fields*, was published by Routledge in December 2020.

# Jane MacFarlane

Voice Coach/Sessional Instructor, Drama Division, School of Creative and Performing Arts, University of Calgary, Canada



Interviewed August 2020 by *Martina MacFarlane*

*MM* *Jane, can you please introduce yourself?*

JM I am a sessional instructor in the drama division of the School of Creative and Performing Arts at the University of Calgary. This is my third year teaching and, before that, I was a guest instructor with the drama division. I teach acting and voice for actors—meaning speaking voice, not singing voice. I am also the resident voice coach for Theatre Calgary, the voice and dialect consultant for Vertigo Theatre, and the voice and text coach for The Shakespeare Company. Before that, I spent fourteen years at Mount Royal University as Program Coordinator for the Performance Program. Prior to that I was teaching in the United States. Most of my work is live and in person, which of course, is tricky right now. Because there is no work in the theatre this coming year, I won't be doing any of those other titles that I have, but I will certainly have my classroom studio work. This is with a small cohort, usually about twenty people maximum in a class who are all up on their feet working and present together. This is a really new world for us in theatre education as we try to figure out how to navigate the transition to remote teaching.

*MM* *It certainly is. Jane, am I correct in saying that before COVID, you had not done any online teaching?*

JM That's correct—I am brand new to it.

*MM* *Given that what you do is so physically based in that in-person experience, what has been the biggest challenge for you when moving to remote teaching?*

JM It's making sure the work is still strong, if that makes any sense. Especially when you're teaching acting, it's about the relationship between the two people and, when it's through online delivery, you have to be much more focused and more integrated in a way, because it's not the same as acting on film; strangely enough, it's not like that at all. So that's a real challenge because it's so easy to be distracted. One of the things we always talk about for performers is that they need to be grounded and they need to be present. Anybody who has to give a presentation, they have to be really present and energetic and alive and it's very easy for that to disappear in this medium. **Zoom** has been great because we can still contact each other, but it's really easy to sit back and disconnect in a way that is counter to how my work goes. That was a huge switch in the spring when everything just suddenly shut down at the end of the semester.

We were supposed to do scene work between two people, and we tried but it just didn't quite work. Figuring out how to do the group work was really, really challenging. We tried to have everybody except for the two people doing the scene turn off their cameras and microphones, and then that way have the two students talking to each other through the camera. So that's one way. One of the other instructors who teaches directing did a collaboration with me so that her students, who were supposed to be directing scenes for live theatre, coached my students on their monologues. Instead of directing scenes, which just couldn't happen because nobody could be in a room together, it was an opportunity for the directing students to really learn how to work with an actor. It was beneficial for them to have that opportunity to work quite intimately through this medium.

March 27 is World Theatre Day and we wanted to do something with the School of Creative and Performing Arts in the drama division. I said, why don't I do a warm-up? So, I did just that, and 300 people from around the globe attended. By the end of June, it had had 1,200 views, so I thought, okay, maybe there's something here. I started doing a weekly vocal warm-up through Zoom and people just set their time wherever they were to drop in and take the class, and I did it for free. I just let people come if they could and if they wanted to give me a donation they could do so as well. It worked really well, and everybody who attended had some voice training—not necessarily with me, but they understood the process and they knew what they were doing.

To begin the work is another challenge though, because voice is so physically based. It really requires me to be very clear in my communication. Doing classes like these online takes a little bit longer than being in a space together, where I am able to physically demonstrate. You're helping the student understand what's happening in their own body because you're right there with them. Online, it's a little harder to see what the students are doing physically. I can hear it and I can give the note, but the adjustments and the notes are a little bit harder for the students to pick up on. It's tricky, for sure.

One of the great things I've found with online voice coaching is that I've started working with another organization in Calgary, Skipping Stone, which supports transgender people in their transition. I've been teaching voice for mainly trans women, understanding how to work their voice. It is a safe space for them regardless, as they are in their own place. They can experiment, turn their mic off and just follow along with me. Those have actually been really successful.

All my voice classes are actually in-person this Fall until the numbers spike, and then I'll have to figure out how to do it again. With online teaching, I think the most important elements are the communication, being really specific about what I'm asking, and being really specific about what the expectations are and what the outcomes might be. I don't like to deal in absolutes when it comes to outcomes but if I send you in the general direction, then the student has to be really responsible for where they think they are in the work and be able to articulate it themselves. The communication on both sides has to be really clear.

*MM* *What other opportunities have you seen to be created by digital education?*

JM Well, I think it is the freedom of it, right? This summer I taught a large lecture course that was asynchronous, so people could do it from all over the place. I had one student in Brazil and one student in China. Poor them though, because there were three Zoom meetings that were synchronous in the class, so they had to set their alarms. But there is a freedom in there. Again, as the instructor, you have to be really clear on your parameters—really clear on what the boundaries are around the assignments and deadlines. You have to communicate these over and over and over again. So, to give you an idea, I would record lectures, I would put messages in the news items on **D2L** and also send e-mails. I was making sure I was repeating the message at least three times. D2L offers that opportunity where I have all these different modes of communicating with the students because it's really important, but I have to make sure I say it two or three times, as I would face-to-face.

*MM What is your most-used software or tool for online teaching?*

JM D2L, for sure. I have become the D2L queen. We are not very good about it in the School of Creative and Performing Arts; nobody uses it but me, I think. But now, we all have to get better at it, and I like D2L because it makes sure that there's a contract between me and the student. All the information is available to them 24/7; they can get the information that they need about assignments and due dates because it's all posted. I resist a little bit the idea that I need to be available to students 24/7 because when I was at university, I could not contact my profs on the weekend. So as for those kinds of expectations—forget it! You can wait and I can wait too. D2L has been really great and now I understand all the things that are available that help support the success of the student but also help me to make sure that the course runs really, really smoothly. So that's great. And then, of course, the other thing is Zoom ... I wish I'd bought shares in Zoom.

*MM I'm sure we all do! Are you using a lot of the features in D2L?*

JM I use the **Time Release**. I tried to use **YuJa** to begin with, and I found it to be a really limited platform and really, really frustrating. Because I live with two filmmakers, I don't find that the editing software in YuJa is very useful. For filming and sharing my lectures, I found it much easier just to have a closed **YouTube** channel of my own and then I could drop the lectures into the content. Even though there are great tutorials and guides for YuJa that are accessible through the Taylor Institute, and they made it look easy, I just found it a really useless tool, actually. I think that whatever you've got on your computer, if you know how to do **iMovie** if you're a **Mac** user or if you're a **PC** user, I think those built-in tools actually might be stronger than YuJa.

*MM What is your favourite resource for teaching online?*

JM YouTube, because for my course that I was teaching on creativity, I found so many things that I could use to fill out my lectures and make them more fun and interesting. I only have one thing blocked because I talked about how Robert Johnson, who was an African American musician, created the blues, and rock and roll. There is a myth about him, that he stands at the crossroads of rock and roll where he met the devil and sold his soul for his prodigious talents. The Rolling Stones credit him and this story as the inspiration for "Sympathy for the Devil" but I couldn't use the YouTube track for the song! Everything else though, I could use to keep people watching. I was able to get access to and I was still using the library and putting up readings and things like that. The library and the copyright office were really supportive in helping me put up material to read. Then I'd go out finding complementary resources in the **TED Talks** and YouTube from the actual authors, so it was great to include that material in the lectures.

*MM I feel like things in the next few months are very unclear at the moment, but what do you expect that higher education might look like, say, ten years into the future?*

JM I know the answer is supposed to be more remote learning, but I think it will be less. I think one of the things that we are actually discovering is that what happens in the classroom is actually incredibly important. It doesn't matter if you're five in kindergarten or thirty-five in grad school, the contact between the instructor and student is crucial. The human connection and the ability to work together is lost on this platform. The human experience is all part of the learning process. We learn better when we are together.

I hope that in the future of higher education there will be smaller classes. I don't think that will happen in the immediate future because education is changing so rapidly, particularly in this country, but I do think that down the line, in ten to twenty years, large lectures in person probably won't happen; maybe large lectures asynchronously, but I think the further we go in our education, right through your undergraduate and definitely in your graduate degrees, that remote learning isn't actually as effective.

One thing that we've learned is that we are creative individuals and when we have to pivot, we do it very quickly and effectively. One of the things that I hear a lot from my students is the stress of doing it this way. So that's another reason why I think that we'll do less of it. I think it will be combined more than it will be one or the other.

I know that the expectation about doing more higher education online is common if you're speaking to Albertans, and that's because we're expecting government cuts. Remote education is a way for universities in the near future to try and generate revenue and perhaps that creativity will never be in-person again. I think we're all lamenting the loss. If you look at people who have kids who should be in school and suddenly they're doing home schooling, they're realizing what those true aspects of being in that building with the teacher and their peers are all about and the strength of it. We learn better when we're together.

*"The human experience is all part of the learning process. We learn better when we are together."*

## REFLECTION

The pandemic education year 2020/21 proved to be a challenge in ways that I don't think we anticipated after the quick pivot to online learning in the spring of 2020. Zoom provided opportunities for courses to continue but the intangible parts of one's educational experience cannot be replicated via remote learning. It was particularly hard for students to stay engaged, to be present within the structure of the class and focused, and to feel successful in the work. I also think learning expectations and outcomes were compromised because the stress and challenge of remote learning were so great. While I was grateful to be able to continue teaching in any capacity, everything became a kind of survey course, because the hands-on nature of being in-person was lost. Students who are not as engaged, easily slipped through the cracks. Technology and Internet challenges exposed accessibility issues and the economic fragility of students who did not have great equipment or Wi-Fi. Having to tell students to turn on their camera, get out of their bed and be present at times was a difficult request because they were working in the only space they had and were dealing with huge mental health issues. The isolation made it very difficult for a majority of students to be able to do their best work. Being in person provides focus, energy and support in a way that online cannot. I think we learned that there are possibilities in terms of straight up, large lecture courses being delivered online, but the full educational experience is one that happens in a relationship with other people.

## ABOUT

**Jane MacFarlane** is a sessional instructor in the drama division in the School of Creative and Performing Arts at the University of Calgary. She has taught at such institutions as York University, Harvard University, Southern Methodist University, Mount Royal University, and the University of Alberta. Jane is also a director, actor, and voice coach. She is the voice and dialect consultant for Vertigo Theatre, a voice and text coach for The Shakespeare Company, and the resident voice coach for Theatre Calgary, where she has coached over sixty-five shows since 2000. Along with teaching Acting and Voice for the Actor, Jane teaches Voice and Presence for a variety of sectors through her own business, Voice Activated, and is currently coaching voice training for Skipping Stone, a "nationally recognized agency that connects trans and gender diverse youth, adults and families with the comprehensive and low barrier access to the support they need and deserve." She spent the spring and summer of 2020 pivoting her teaching practice to both remote synchronous teaching and fully online asynchronous learning.

# Sandra Sinfield

Senior Lecturer/Academic Developer, Centre for Professional and Educational Development, London Metropolitan University, United Kingdom and author of the #Take5 blog



Interviewed December 2020 by *Sandra Abegglen*

*SA* *Sandra, please introduce yourself.*

SS I work in an academic development unit where I work with staff to develop their learning, teaching and assessment practice. The practice of academic development that I do is both theoretical and practical in terms of what can be done both in the classroom and online.

*SA* *Sandra, I know that you have years of experience in what you do, and you have also published widely on the subject.*

SS Yes. Years ago, we produced a book called *Essential Study Skills: The Complete Guide to Success at University*. This was very much aimed at helping students make the most of their time at university. We put a lot of emphasis on creative ways in which students could think about studying and organizing their lives around their studies. We've also developed a staff textbook on that, and we found recently that many different staff across our country are using our textbook to develop their staff practice. So that's quite interesting, and nice to know.

*SA* *With COVID springing up and changing the educational landscape and delivery of courses, what was the biggest challenge for you and how did you experience that move from the classroom to remote teaching?*

SS It was very frustrating because, quite often, courses like ours for staff are very theoretical and didactic, but we'd thrown all that up in the air. We have a very creative, embodied, hands-on workshop approach and we want the staff to experience the strategies we are teaching, as if they were real students again. When we suddenly had to switch to online teaching, everything became a huge challenge to overcome. Translating that important experience into a virtual classroom was tough.

*SA* *What would you then say was an opportunity when having to move to remote teaching?*

SS In trying to find creative solutions, the biggest challenges became the biggest opportunities. This, I think we did manage. At our university, we have the **virtual learning environment (VLE)** where we can meet to teach and gather staff into discussion groups very easily, but we do more than that in the physical classroom. We had to find ways of enabling people to write, produce ideas and brainstorm together; to make, play and create together. Although this was a challenge, the solutions were very creative. We feel that we've only gone part of the way there, so if we're still online next year, we'll have more time to develop a really creative online course.

*SA* *What would you say is the most-used online teaching tool for you?*

SS Our university invested in **Blackboard** as their virtual learning environment, and it is Blackboard that we have to use. That is where we can store resources, but it's also where we teach. We have a **Collaborate** room, which works a bit like **Zoom** so that we have the audio plus visual contact. We can use **PowerPoint** in there if we want to and the breakout rooms, but within that there are some really useful tools that we've used a lot. Actually, we use them even when we do face-to-

*"In trying to find creative solutions, the biggest challenges became the biggest opportunities."*

face teaching. We have online discussion boards where everyone on the course can engage with each other. I find that people won't use a discussion board unless there's a real reason to do it though, so we ask all of our participants to write a learning log to reflect on their experiences. Living within the discussion boards, these take the form of reflective blogs in which they reflect on their learning, and also comment on each other's thoughts. Through the VLE blog function, we get the staff to post their emergent writing and to peer review one another's contributions, offering supportive, critical feedback on the writing that they do. In this way, they engage dialogically as the course continues. Another tool that we found we could use was **Google Docs** so that in our class the staff could produce individual or collaborative, synchronous writing. In the VLE, there's also a **Wiki** tool, which allows for collaborative writing over time; synchronous asynchronous collaboration, where people can edit what other people write. Sometimes we've used that to get the class to produce a glossary of useful terms on the theories and concepts so that they're engaged in making sense of the course together. These tools allowed us to be able to keep up the sense of actively working together.

SA *In terms of pedagogy or approach, is there any resource you come to regularly that you find very inspirational?*

SS I would say that it is Google Docs because I love collaborative writing myself. It's the only way I really feel that I can write, but the resources that I might draw on then would be resources from DS106, which is Digital Storytelling 106. It is a fantastic resource of ideas for digital storytelling, creative and multimodal assignments. They share ideas, and student work. Whole classes can sign up to be part of this thing—this entity or movement. This is what I would recommend to other people.

I think that collaboration is essential. People shouldn't think that they have to solve all of these problems on their own. There's a wealth of experience out there and the people in this area are very generous. They want to share their ideas and their experiences, and they want to work with you.

I also reach out to people on **Twitter**. I think some academics are still very hesitant to use Twitter as a space for sharing ideas. They think it's just about sharing your breakfast. Reach out on Twitter and find the right people to follow. Find those that are inspirational in this area and the whole thing becomes so much more supportive. It feels like a growing experience instead of a solitary one.

SA *Where do you think that we are going with higher education?*

SS Well, I suppose my worst fear is that there will be an elitist division in higher education in the future where the elite and the children of the elite will go to wonderful physical spaces and there they can engage in face-to-face, online, or blended versions of learning and the non-elite will be relegated just to online learning. Now, I do think that online learning can be fabulous. It can be creative, emergent, and inspirational, but I also think there's something very valuable about the physical university. Within the space and the time of the university, there exists that notion that it is your time to be in and to fully inhabit your learning body. I hope that everybody gets to go to face-to-face universities, as well as to inhabit beautiful online spaces.

SA *What would you recommend for tutors, instructors and academics at this time in preparing for the Fall semester?*

SS I think when you're teaching, try and teach without using a PowerPoint. Try and think, what can I get my students to do or make or talk about, even though it's virtual and at a distance? Trust your students. Don't think that you need to be a master of all of the technology yourself. I think you can set creative assignments and challenges so that the students play with the technology and get creative in answering your assignment challenge. They will surprise you. Let yourself be surprised and delighted by your students.

And so, what are my thoughts on the future of higher education after the pandemic, the "pivot" and a collective experience of online teaching, learning and assessment?

Firstly, I cannot believe that sixteen years after the UK government published *Harnessing Technology*,[1] its vision for e-learning, we are still talking about technology enhanced learning (TEL) as if it were separate from teaching/learning. The world is digital and multimodal. We, for example, use collage, painting, poetry, writing, reading, making, doing, animation, video, podcasting and more in our practice.

Some context: in 2009 my colleagues and I published *A Journey Into Silence*, a discourse analysis of the Harnessing Technology document, with a special focus on university teaching and learning.[2] We agreed with David Noble that this policy revealed a dystopian picture of higher education with students as "consumers" rather than actors and agents in their own learning;[3] where the economic model of unit cost takes pedagogy and educational judgment away from the expert tutor/subject specialist and places it firmly in the hands of management; and rather than "education," we have only "a shadow of education, an assemblance of pieces without a whole."

In *Digital Diploma Mills: The Automation of Higher Education*, Noble argued that what we now call TEL is inextricably bound up with the denaturing and de-professionalizing of higher education, both for staff and students. He stressed that whilst the push for TEL is predicated upon cost cutting, rationalization and staff reduction, "education" relies on the quality of interpersonal relationships, and good education requires a labour intensive, personal relationship between students and quality academics.[4]

*Harnessing Technology* marked a fundamental shift away from the practitioner as an innovator and toward a systemic and politically driven model of TEL delivering the "training" that facilitated the development of "IT skills for business" (where any assertion of the self is subversive) and where

---

1 Available online at https://dera.ioe.ac.uk/1423/. This version was amended in 2015 and bears little or no relation to the document published in 2005 that we critiqued in our article "A Journey into Silence" (See n.2).

2 S. Sinfield, D. Holley, and T. Burns, "A journey into silence: students, stakeholders and the impact of a strategic governmental policy document in the UK," *Social Responsibility Journal*, Vol. 5, no. 4 (2009), 566–74. https://doi.org/10.1108/17471110910995401

3 David F. Noble, "Technology and the Commodification of Higher Education," *Monthly Review*, vol. 53, no. 10 (2002), 4. https://monthlyreview.org/2002/03/01/technology-and-the-commodification-of-higher-education/

4 David F. Noble, *In Digital Diploma Mills: The Automation of Higher Education* (Monthly Review Press, 2003).

"hard to reach" students would be plugged into remedial packages to be "fixed," and would be grateful to experience "anywhere, anytime" education online. More disappointing now is how pertinent our critique remains.

Post-pandemic, TEL policies remain driven by financial, managerialist and technocratic concepts rather than pedagogical ones. Many staff who have been creatively teaching online for eighteen months are being called to new ways of working: clear their desks and pick up their "surveyed" equipment; and stand ready to work in silence in bookable "work zones."

We know that students need "owned" space, dialogue with their peers, playful practice and respect for the experience they bring to the educational encounter in order to facilitate significant learning. Yet, despite the expertise that academics have gained over the intense pandemic months, they will have to work to yet another management-generated version of TEL over which they have had no say and have no control.

The future of higher education? Many academic staff will be on-site, office-less and more isolated than ever. They will have no say over their pedagogy or how they integrate the digital in their practice. Harnessing technology or harnessed to it? *Plus ca change. Plus ca meme chose.*

ABOUT

**Sandra Sinfield** is a senior lecturer/academic developer in the Centre for Professional and Educational Development at London Metropolitan University, United Kingdom. She is a co-founder of the Association for Learning Development in Higher Education (ALDinHE), and co-author of *Teaching, Learning and Study Skills: A Guide for Tutors*, and *Essential Study Skills: The Complete Guide to Success at University* (4th Edition). Sandra has worked as a laboratory technician, a freelance copywriter, and an executive editor (*Medicine Digest*, circulation 80,000 doctors). With Tom Burns, she has developed theatre and film in unusual places—their *Take Control* video won the IVCA gold award for education. Sandra is interested in creativity and play as emancipatory practice in higher education.

# Christal Ramanauskas

Assistant Clinical Lecturer, Department of Occupational Therapy, Faculty of Rehabilitation Medicine, University of Alberta, Canada



Interviewed September 2020 by *Martina MacFarlane*

*MM Welcome Christal. Can you say who you are?*

CR I am an assistant clinical lecturer in the Department of Occupational Therapy at the Faculty of Rehabilitation Medicine at the University of Alberta. I teach a varicty of different courses, but my main emphasis is on mental health and clinical field work. We have a satellite campus in Calgary, and we have distance learning as part of those classes, but online teaching is brand new to me.

*MM Through this transition, what is the biggest challenge that you've experienced in moving to remote teaching?*

CR I would say the biggest challenge that seems to be ongoing is student engagement. One of the things that I have found really challenging and, frankly, exhausting at some points, is trying to facilitate the same type of quality interactions that would typically be had in the face-to-face classroom. The experience of having to transition to teaching online has really demonstrated how much learning is facilitated through students and instructors sharing the same physical space. It takes a lot of energy to create something that's similar in terms of engagement experiences. With COVID, we've lost the hallway chats, the questions in between breaks, students dropping by in office hours just to say hi, and just all of those interactions that automatically occur when we're all sharing the same space together.

*MM Have you come across any ways to creatively deal with the challenge of student engagement?*

CR Previously in the Winter term, I was holding virtual office hours by keeping the **Zoom** call open, and that was successful to some extent. Another thing I do is if there's correspondence happening over e-mail, I ask to hop on a Zoom or **Google Meet** call so that we're still trying to have some semblance of a personal connection. When it comes to doing a synchronous lecture and I'm rolling through a shared screen, it's really hard to have that sense of engagement. I'm relying on the chat box "blowing up" or for people to be "chiming in." I do try to encourage students to put themselves out there and just holler at me, because if not I'll just keep ripping through the slides. That tends to work okay, but again, that ability to gauge where my audience is at is almost impossible unless students are really putting it out there and letting me know whether or not what I'm saying is landing.

One of the cool things with our occupational therapy (OT) cohort is that they've been very proactive in organizing a professional development month, where faculty and other external lecturers are coming in and doing talks and workshops on a variety of topics. The goal is to bring in more practice and opportunity for clinical skills development. In the spring, clinical fieldwork placements had to be cancelled, so this is a way to bridge the learning that otherwise would have been happening in clinical fieldwork. The professional development month is receiving good engagement from students and faculty alike and in terms of engagement issues, this has been a big way to help.

There is also another significant element that is impacting clinical skills, instruction, and practice, which is that there's so much communication that happens through real-life interactions that's implicit and non-verbal and that is what really makes your learning experience. For example, when I'm practising interviewing skills or mindfulness exercises with OT (Occupational Therapy) students, it's a whole body-mind experience that a student is engaging in and learning from. Doing this online reduces and strips a lot of that communication, and it simply doesn't get transferred. You don't see my whole body and vice versa, and you're not getting the full read on someone.

*MM* *What are some of the opportunities that are created by digital education?*

CR Oh man, that's where things get really exciting. So, there's the whole phenomenon where the non-verbal communication is reduced, but it also creates opportunities. For example, I taught a module that incorporated an interviewing tool that the students had to learn and facilitate themselves, and one of the things I noticed is that because it took some of the emotional charge away from the role play with me as their interviewer, students consistently did a better performance than I had previously observed when we did this exercise in person. It actually helps grade the activity a bit, and it frees up some of that cognitive load that comes with learning something new and putting something into practice. I would say that this is especially great for students who have concerns around performance anxiety. This might be a nice way of helping people work up to doing these interactions in person. Another example that's been really interesting for occupational therapists in particular is that this time online has shown us how much of our practice is actually language-based, and the extent to which we as occupational therapists can help our patients through an effective and productive therapeutic conversation.

I also really like that I'm able to do asynchronous lecturing, because it enables me to have more control over my content. I'm able to hit on my key points and give the comprehensive overview of the topics that I'm teaching, and the product is more of what I wanted it to be. I get to do more with visual and design elements in my slides and video footage and I can go back and edit too. I'm better able to incorporate elements such as pop culture references and jokes, turns of phrase—little things that make your lectures more engaging and fun to listen to. I've received consistently positive feedback from students that my lectures were enjoyable to watch and learn, and in those we're talking about four or five hours of lecture content. So, when it comes to some pretty dry content, there are great opportunities in simply learning how to jazz it up and make it entertaining. I think it's really important to exercise or develop your design skills, and I see this as an opportunity to enhance student learning. In a live lecture, you're more or less beholden to your audience for a particular amount of time where you're hoping that you have your speaking points down—and that's fine; that stuff is really important. But for me, knowing that there's so much more that can be said about a topic than what is said in lecture, I get to be more comprehensive through online teaching, and I think that has been really good. Basically, I get to cram in more information.

There's also another opportunity, and I think this applies across the board for all students regardless of what they're learning. I believe that digital education is going to help students learn to be more adept digital content creators so that we learn how to use communication

> *"I believe that digital education is going to help students learn to be more adept digital content creators so that we learn how to use communication technology, assistive technology, software, social media, and all those things more effectively."*

technology, assistive technology, software, social media, and all those things more effectively. We're recognizing that learning how to design more elegant interfaces can actually improve the connection and accessibility for people, and that this in and of itself is health promoting. It really challenges and pushes students who are eventually going to be health providers to engage in things like app development, which has tremendous potential for health promotion. I know that we have some OT students who are working on app development projects, and they have exciting potential to make clinical practice more efficient and effective.

And then, my goodness, in terms of the opportunities for the field of occupational therapy, one of the big things with digital education is that it's really helping us to realize the possibilities of telerehabilitation, which is an exciting enterprise for OTs. Usually, telerehabilitation is more of a subspecialty that happens outside of the classroom, or it might be a module of additional learning, but it's something that we're starting to integrate as being more of a core component of our curriculum, just by virtue of everything going online. Basically, what this is enabling us to do is to refine our clinical interviewing skills, which has been a strong and ongoing interest for me, in particular as a practitioner and educator. It's been really cool to see how students are developing their relational skills over the online platforms we use, and how one of the fieldwork sites that I supervised has successfully transitioned to a telerehabilitation service provision. So, a number of students are learning how to do telerehabilitation, and that's one opportunity that I think is pretty neat.

*MM* *It is indeed very exciting to think about all of the opportunities that may come from an increased knowledge and awareness of online platforms in healthcare, especially those opportunities for accessibility. Could you tell us a little more about telerehabilitation?*

CR Telerehabilitation is an occupational therapy service provision that takes place over an online video conferencing platform such as Zoom, or a dedicated piece of telerehabilitation software. It can involve a variety of occupational therapy evaluations, interventions, or follow-ups. It can be used to facilitate an intake session or an initial interview to identify client priorities; it can be used for things such as cognitive or psychosocial screening; and it can be used to do physical assessments just by observing the patient carry out the instructions to help with their range of motion, strength and balance.

One great thing about telerehabilitation is that you get to see the patient or the client in their own home, and that makes it more accessible. For people who have mobility concerns, difficulty accessing a service, or complications arising out of lockdown or physical distancing, all of these things make it more difficult for patients to access health care services. Opportunities in terms of accessibility for these types of things are fantastic. I know that one of the hospitals in Edmonton that offers a cancer education group that's run by occupational therapists has been able to continue it by doing it through Zoom. Rather than having to cancel this education group, they've been able to successfully continue it in an online platform.

*MM* *Absolutely. These are extremely valuable takeaways from the switch to emergency remote education. What is your favourite resource for teaching online?*

CR My colleagues! Typically, we'll debrief a class and have a conversation about what went well, what could be improved, how was the balance of synchronous versus asynchronous content delivery, and things like that. I've also been actively consulting with students about their learning experiences over the past five months to get a sense of what it's like to be on the receiving end of online learning, and what's working for them. I would say more than anything, my favourite resource is talking to students and hearing about the level of success in their learning facilitated through different software. The feedback on the type of delivery is really useful, I would say, more than anything else.

*MM* *What do you expect higher education to look like in ten years' time?*

CR I expect that higher education is going to keep moving more and more to online delivery. Given the changes to higher education that we're currently seeing in the province of Alberta, I don't think that online education is going away. I think that what we are experiencing right now in the switch to emergency remote education is going to change the way in which education and higher learning is going to function. I see it putting more pressure and expectation on teaching programs and departments to offer some edge or value, or something that really conveys to potential students why it is that they should come and study at that particular institution. With online delivery, it means you can have people from all over the world come in and start to access your program, and if it frees people up from having to be in a particular geographical location, then those potential students are going to be looking at different criteria to base their educational choices on. I also think that with things moving more and more toward digital learning, there is an opportunity to free up class time and to make prep work more engaging because really, how many students actually do the required reading? When I think of OT skills and OT learning, I see there being more skills practice, more opportunities to have those higher-level discussions and to engage in scholarly practice. Making and crafting the learning experience to be more of an enriching experience will have more of an emphasis in the future.

Overall, information delivery will be more engaging and information dense; at least, I think it should be. Well-designed content is more engaging, and we know that people like to learn when things are fun and interesting. If we can make our learning more fun and interesting, we're going to come out knowing more, as well as with an increased reasoning capacity. And that's going to free us up, so that we have more time as educators and students to have interesting conversations and good dialogue and to start to do more innovative things.

MM *Are there any final points you'd like to add to the conversation before we wrap up?*

CR I have seen really positive outcomes in student performance. In my experience with teaching a module on mindfulness and clinical interviewing where most of the content is largely asynchronous lecture material, and also where the students are in their first year of their education without any prior field work experience, the quality of performance that I have witnessed has been very impressive. I could see that there were learning outcomes that I hadn't encountered before.

Lastly, one of the things that we could all do with is better software. I think, especially for telerehabilitation, there are platforms being used that are not as elegant as they could be in the user interface. Engaging and usable software is especially important when working with patient populations that aren't computer savvy because online platforms can be confusing, and that detracts from the experience you're giving those people. So, if there's anybody out there who's working on a platform that's as smooth as a **Mac OS** type of interface, I'm really excited to see that come through. It feels like a lot of learning is detracted by clunky, cumbersome, buggy interfaces, and it doesn't have to be that way. Remote platforms are here to stay, and they're obviously a work in progress, but I'm curious to see how things evolve.

## REFLECTION

Since the interview, and with eight months of digital teaching experience to reflect on, I've come to appreciate how important it is to manage digital learning fatigue. Fatigue has a significant impact on student performance and wellness. One of the realities of digital learning is that we are always limited by fatigue, and the best way to address fatigue is to prevent it. On the one hand, I've experienced some of the strongest performances from students via digital learning, with respect to their ability to articulate clinical reasoning and engage in complex theory, which I attribute to the efficiency of learning via engaging in digital content. On the other hand, I've learned that this learning fatigue can quickly spiral into students feeling overwhelmed, and at times becoming demoralized. Prioritizing student wellness is central to optimizing the digital learning environment, and student wellness is best addressed through a time-efficient, less-is-more approach. I've had to consider the most efficient ways of delivering information and clarifying the objectives of my lectures and learning activities. The demands of digital learning have challenged me to be more succinct and clearer in my delivery:

- Speak slowly and clearly: Slower speech makes it easier for students to follow along and engage in the learning material.

- Enthusiasm energizes: It's important to offer positive energy to engage students in material.

- Vary the media sources for self-study/prep: I now use a mix of reading, podcasts, and pre-recorded lectures.

- Less is more: Less content to cover makes the task of teaching and learning less overwhelming for everyone involved.

- Be directive with time use: I tend to specify when I want to lecture without interruption from students, when I will facilitate discussion, and when I will take questions.

- Learning activities go a long way: Anything you can do to incorporate student engagement in the digital classroom helps. Sprinkling in brief discussion questions or experiential exercises helps translate lecture content.

- Offer a generous time cushion for lectures and discussions in synchronous sessions. If I get through the synchronous session with time to spare, I consider that the class has finished done early. These extra time cushions are important for students who are doing 8+ hours of online learning.

- Use flexible due dates: For example, I have an assignment that can be submitted at any time in the term.

- Create engaging content: To encourage engagement in learning, I made "scribble vids" using the **Concepts App** to draw out ideas and recorded clinical interviewing role plays, etc. all of which received positive feedback from students who had to rely on digital content for their learning.

ABOUT

**Christal Ramanauskas** is an assistant clinical lecturer in the Department of Occupational Therapy in the Faculty of Rehabilitation Medicine, at the University of Alberta, in Canada. She teaches a variety of different topics with a primary focus on mental health and clinical field work. Christal is a certified acceptance and commitment therapy matrix facilitator and an administrator of the ACBS (Association for Contextual Behavioural Science) OT Special Interest Group.

# Portraits

By Julian Salinas

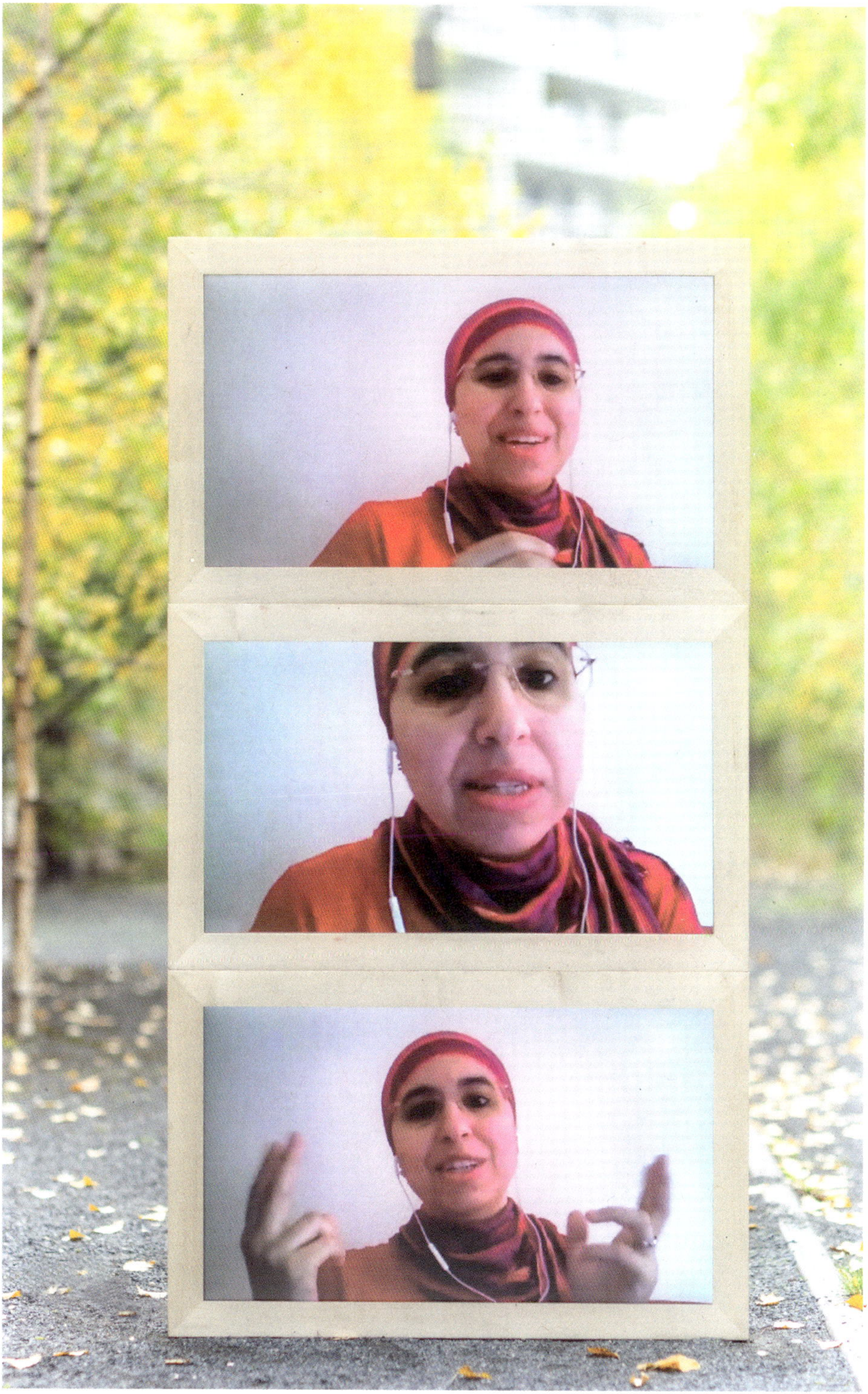

ВЫСТАВОЧНЫЙ ГРУЗ
Росвнешторг
БРУТТО 30 КГ
НЕТТО 18 КГ
ОБЪЕМ 90 60 40
СОВЕТСКАЯ
ВЫСТАВКА
В Г. БАЗЕЛЬ
ЯЩИК №2/6

CALGARY

# Rationale for Portraits

Julian Salinas, Photographer

When I was asked to shoot the photographs for this publication, I saw a challenge. The task of creating portraits from Zoom video recordings appeared to be outside my usual workflow and I had never worked with videos as a starting point for stills. Generally, I work with physical settings and real people, using my camera to capture that space and that relationship. As a professional, I have used digital photography since my university days. Yet, in these pandemic times, where our world turns increasingly digital, it appeared a logical next step for me to engage with "moving" online portrait material.

Because of the challenge involved in trying to create meaningful portrait pictures from existing videos, I initially considered re-photographing the interviewees. This would have allowed me to get to know them and to produce portraits that capture their different, diverse personalities. This is a process I am intrinsically familiar with, having focused on portrait photography for many years. However, this appeared not only impractical because of the difference in time and space but it would also have meant losing or disconnecting from the moment in which the interview was conducted. This led me to explore options for working with the existing video material. It resulted in a process that took as a starting point the practice established over the first few months of the pandemic by the TALON project team in their exchanges with the collaborators.

The video material posed a challenge in that all videos were in a different form and format. For example, some interviews were self-recorded, whereas others were recorded on various online meeting applications by the TALON team; some interviews were conducted with individuals, whereas others were held with pairs; and some interviewees used digital background pictures, whereas others showed their home office spaces. In all this variance, I was looking for a solution that could create a reusable and consistent "image" that accurately represented the people portrayed. I experimented with different ideas—extracting stills, and juxtaposing people and backgrounds.

In the end, after extensive experimentation and discussion with the TALON team, I decided to use three freeze frames from each interview, with each of the three frames showing the interviewee with a changed pose and posture. The idea was to create a "moving" portrait that showed the interviewee in action and that hinted at the original video source. My work then centred around selecting the three frames. Individuals were often showing unfavourable or displaying only minimalistic expressions, and I had to do a systematic search for the right moments. In addition, the selected freeze frames not only had to work in succession, but also on top of each other, meaning there had to be a sensible selection of visuals that could be displayed side by side and as a continuation from top to bottom. This proved to be more challenging than I had initially thought.

I then used digital screens to display the three selected freeze frames inside wooden frames that were purpose-built for this project. The frames were stacked vertically to create a sculptural effect. The idea was that the final picture would become something more than a collection of stills extracted from video recordings: each picture would become an art piece in its own right, with a specific expression.

The wooden frames with the projected freeze frames were photographed arranged in locations at my studio. I set myself the goal of finding a suitable background for each portrait picture. Even though I had never met the interviewees, I used the selection of the frames, the composition, and the physical setting to create this interpretation.

The final portraits reflect the complex tension of the digital and the physical—moving pictures that were translated into stills projected onto physical frames, which were then re-photographed for print publication. The portraits also mirror the translational, transformational process of the book project itself, where online education was explored through virtual interviews, which then got translated into chapters in a physical book, thus capturing a moment in time.

## ABOUT

**Julian Salinas** was born 1967 in Düsseldorf, Germany. He has lived and worked in Basel and Zürich (Switzerland) as an artist and freelance photographer. Since 2013, he has been a lecturer for architectural photography at the FHNW Institute for Architecture. He is also a member of the Haus Oslo Ateliers co-operative in Dreispitz, Basel.

Julian attended the Kunstgewerbeschule Basel, and since 1995 he's worked independently on photos and videos for exhibitions and publications, as well as on commercial assignments for large companies. He has shown his work in solo and group exhibitions in a number of well-known galleries and has received numerous awards for projects in the field of art and architecture. His work is part of important collections such those as at F. Hoffmann-La Roche AG. His fifth monograph, *Where is Martha?*, was published in 2018 by Christoph Merian Verlag.

# Series Two

September - December 2020

# Maha Bali

Associate Professor of Practice, Center for Learning and Teaching, American University in Cairo, Egypt and Co-Founder/Co-Director of Virtually Connecting and Equity Unbound

*Self-recorded interview* September 2020

Q *Maha, can you please tell me about yourself?*

MB I am an associate professor of practice at the Center for Learning and Teaching at the American University in Cairo in Egypt. The majority of my work is faculty development. I help other professors improve the way they teach and integrate technology in the way they teach. I give consultations and workshops, I help them assess students, but I also help students give feedback through course and instructor evaluations. Part of my work involves helping people use digital education, and part of it is just education in general. In addition to this main part of my job, I also teach a course on digital literacy and intercultural learning for undergraduates. In the past I've taught teachers as well, and I've taught part of a creativity course, with a section on educational game design.

I'm also the co-founder of two grassroots open initiatives. One of them is Virtually Connecting. Virtually Connecting is a grassroots movement that challenges academic gatekeeping at conferences by creating hybrid conversations between people who are on-site at conferences, and virtual folks who cannot make it to conferences. That often excludes a large chunk of people who are in the global south, who are women, who care for young children, adjuncts, people with disabilities, and graduate students. So, Virtually Connecting allows them to be part of a conference even though they're not there, and to speak to people in these "hallway conversations." It's not about the presentation so much as having access to the hallway, the informal conversations, and the networking. Virtually Connecting has grown a lot over the last five years and it has become a way for marginal academics—especially in the field of education and educational technology—to have a voice at the conferences that they can never attend in person. Virtually Connecting was founded by me, alongside Rebecca Hogue, and now we have five co-directors, including Autumn Caines, Christian Friedrich, and Helen DeWaard.

The other grassroots organization that I co-founded is Equity Unbound. I'm the co-facilitator along with Mia Zamora and Catherine Cronin. Mia Zamora is in the US, and Catherine Cronin is in Ireland, and now we have an Iranian from Japan, Parisa Mehran, and we have folks from Canada like Bonnie Stewart, and a whole host of other people jumping in and out of it as we go along. So Equity Unbond is an equity-focused, open, connected, and intercultural learning curriculum. It started out as a way to supplement my existing course on digital literacy and intercultural learning. It was born from the need to address intercultural learning and digital literacy by starting from an equity and social justice perspective, and also as a way to integrate connected learning into that kind of curriculum. It has grown into other branches, and it now has within it a continuity of care and goals that came up during the COVID era, and an inclusive academia project, which is influenced by the Black Lives Matter movement in an attempt to make a difference to how academia addresses race and injustice in the academy itself.

I write and speak frequently about social justice, critical pedagogy, and open and online education. I recently co-edited the volume *Open at the Margins: Critical Perspectives on Open Education*. I co-edited this with Catherine Cronin from Ireland, Laura Czerniewicz from South Africa, Robin DeRosa from the US, and Rajiv Jhangiani from Canada, and what we've done is collected perspectives about open education that come from people at the margins. They provided perspectives that had not been spoken about by the dominant white majority of people who were writing about open education beforehand. We collected them because they were offering a very different way of looking at open education, and we put them all in one volume. These were things that were maybe published in blog posts or in speeches, but not in academic journals, where people could find them more easily. We thought that putting them together would make it a lot more intense; you'd be able to see all of the marginal views in one space, rather than them being lost in a sea of dominant whiteness.

*Q* *What will your teaching look like in 2020 and 2021?*

MB I would say that the most important thing about my teaching right now is that it's focused on the care and well-being of my students, more than anything else. Because of the situation we're in with the COVID pandemic, a lot of people—my students, my child, myself, my colleagues—are going through different kinds of trauma. Whether it's a health crisis, a mental health crisis, or an economic crisis, to me this involves a shift of priorities and in what we need to be doing and how we spend our time when we're together. I have a lot more empathy and I'm doing a lot more listening than I would normally. My teaching has to be dynamic. I have to respond to the situations happening in the world, and to the way that people are reacting.

*Q* *From your experiences and perspectives, what are the opportunities that are created by digital education?*

MB There are a lot of opportunities that are created by digital education, but it's really tricky because these opportunities are not evenly distributed. For someone who has access to digital education and access to the infrastructure and who has the digital literacy to be able to use digital education, then the biggest opportunity is in terms of how it can flex time in different ways. I think that doing things like asynchronous and semi-synchronous learning helps give people a lot of agency over how they're going to spend their time in the digital space, where they can do things at different times, and come back to it again. There is space, there's a flexing of space and there is time together. When we're all together in the same room, there's a limit to someone speaking, and someone else cannot be speaking at the same time. Digitally, we can all be speaking at the same time in text, and we are all still able to contribute. There is a space for every single person to participate in that way, and not be interrupted by anyone else. Semi-synchronous spaces are beautiful. Through spaces like **Twitter**, **Slack**, and **WhatsApp**, you have people all talking at the same time and, because the texts are small, it feels like we're all together chatting and if someone misses the moment, they can come back later and still find it. It allows you to have that immediate conversation if you need it, but it also doesn't exclude people who weren't there in that moment, and I think there's a lot of beauty in that.

It's also really important to think about the social justice angles, because a lot of the time we have an automatic tendency to think about digital education as accessible to everyone. There is more than just the economic angle of having access to devices and infrastructure. There's also the aspect of digital literacy, and how well you know how to use what you have. There are the cultural and political angles, bringing up questions such, as whose perspectives are you exposed to, when you use/ look in places like **Google** or **Wikipedia**. A lot of the time, this is a white Western male perspective. Even having access to a tool like **Zoom** doesn't mean that you're someone who's comfortable being in a synchronous conversation with your camera on. And so, just having access to the Internet does not mean that this is social justice. It is also about who sets the norms of a digital environment, and what does that say. As we design our digital environments, it is really important to keep in mind the people who create these educational technologies, and which interests they represent.

The other opportunity is glocality, working together and openness. There is a lot that we can learn from each other. For instance, when I do professional development for professors at my institution, I can do it locally, but I can also have a global angle on it, where other institutions who are doing similar things can join us and we can all learn from each other. Most of the time, there's no reason to just keep it local. You need to have the local part, but there's so much value in the global part. This summer, I'm participating in something called DigPINS. I facilitated the American University in Cairo version of it, but there were versions in four other US institutions. This has been going on in the US for quite some time at different institutions. It started out at one university, and then it spread to several universities in the US. For people who are interested in learning more about digital identity, digital pedagogy, digital networks, and digital scholarship, these are things that you can discuss across the world. It might have different nuances in different local spaces, but there's so much value in talking about it with other professors. Sometimes a professor of mathematics in the US, Germany, Egypt and Japan has more in common than they do with a colleague in the same institution who is teaching in different disciplines because they're teaching the same thing. There's a lot of value in that.

Then, there's also a lot of value in openness. Even if you're going to create something local, there's a value in posting it online. For example, when we created our guide for going online during COVID, a lot of universities kept it open, and we left ours on our website as well. Anybody could benefit from that. You can adapt it. There's no harm, and there's also a lot of benefit in doing that, right? First of all, you are making it easier even for your own local folks to benefit from it, but you're also helping other people. We are influenced by other people too and having that information easily accessible without having to go through a password or a paywall is a really useful thing, and I think a lot of things in education can be done that way. We can save people time so that they can focus on their connections and relationships with each other, and we can make content available so that people can focus on communication, and connection, and community building. That's what I think.

Q *What are some of the challenges that you've experienced with remote teaching?*

MB I did my master's in e-learning at the University of Sheffield and finished it in 2006 and, because of that experience, I don't think I had any particular challenges that I faced in my own teaching. Before the closures, when COVID happened, I had tried out Zoom with my students; I had Slack, we had blogs, we had all kinds of things going. I think the main challenge has been the trauma from the pandemic itself. When I learned from Mays Imad, and from Karen Costa about this concept of trauma in the form of teaching, it gave me terminology for expressing this anxiety, and the difficulty of this whole situation helped me describe what was happening to my child, what was happening to my students, what was happening to me, what was happening to faculty that I was supporting. It was difficult.

The cognitive load and how that affected people's ability to manage their time became something that was a really big deal to keep in mind. So, what I did last semester, which to me was not a challenge, was that I shifted my focus in my life sessions to listening to the students and helping them express what was bothering them about what was going on, and trying to take what I'd learned from them back to my institution, and my faculty development worked to pass it on in the way that I advise faculty on how to deal with the pandemic. I'm trying to make sure that everything is equitable for students who are coming from different perspectives, and who have different abilities, different circumstances and so on. That is a really important aspect of my pedagogy, and my practice as a whole.

I think that what I did struggle with in my role in faculty and professional development is that I was used to doing online professional development, but mostly in smaller groups. Usually I'd have between five and fifteen people, but now when we have more than twenty, it gets really unmanageable. We usually try to split them up into smaller groups, and I wasn't really sure how to handle this with the workshops that I was doing online, until I attended a workshop on liberating structures. This was a full day workshop with professionals who know how to do liberating structures properly. This transformed my thinking and my practice because I was in a six- or seven-hour workshop and I felt engaged the whole time, and I felt it was really useful.

Every single activity that we tried had an impact, and I think every single one that we've tried, I've tried again since then. Since then, I've both transformed the way I teach, and transformed the way I do these professional development workshops. I went back to my colleagues at the Center for Learning and Teaching and demonstrated some of the grading structures to them. The grading structures are ways of structuring conversation and dialogue to make them more equitable so that everyone's voice is heard and to make them more effective, so that you can reach good outputs and outcomes in a very short amount of time. They're very energizing, and I really enjoyed doing them. There were so many of them. It was a good reminder. I already knew about the grading structures, but I wasn't confident, and I wasn't aware of the entire spectrum. I knew it existed, but I had not tried them myself with someone, so that I could feel the confidence to actually try them myself as a facilitator.

I think what was missing in this pandemic was the socio-emotional aspect. People didn't have outlets for socio-emotional learning. You needed to establish a sense of intimacy in people when they were together, instead of putting them in groups of thirty where they are a sea of faces. Putting them in breakout rooms where there could be in groups of four or five, where they could see each other, and look at each other's faces and sort of feel like they're alone in a room, this makes a huge difference with online learning. I think the grading structures help structure that conversation, so that when you leave them alone in a room of five, they're not lost for words.

Here is a moment I'd like to forget about, a very specific moment, but it has helped me better structure Q&A sessions and workshops. This one is about a participant who came to one of our workshops. It was a workshop of around seventy people, so a pretty large attendance. She kept interrupting me to ask questions and to make points that were very specific to a particular context. It turned out that she had just had surgery and was taking medication that were making her a bit uninhibited. I felt really sorry for her because there were a lot of other participants, and they were really frustrated with her. I couldn't find a way to politely ask her to stop talking. After that we decided to do something different. For all our questions and Q&As, we decided to use something like a **Slido**, or a poll that does upvoting for questions, so it doesn't become like the first person who unmutes their mic is the person who gets to ask the question. Instead, everyone types their questions, people upvote, and then the most pertinent questions that the majority of people have are the ones that we answer first. I decided that this was maybe the most equitable way of doing Q&A in the first place, so it came out well.

*Q* *What is your most-used tool or software?*

MB I'd say Slack and Twitter. Both of them are semi-synchronous spaces and they are places where you can have informal conversations. They're neither a formal workspace like e-mail nor a learning management system, and they're not like your home spaces. So they're somewhere in between; I think for both colleagues and for students they're a place where you can share jokes and GIFs and just talk about random things sometimes. This is really helpful for building community, and really important right now when people can't as easily meet in cafes and things like that. I use Slack in my classes and with my teammates to connect virtually. With Virtually Connecting, people tend to think of it as a synchronous thing because they see the videos of us having conversations in a conference. But actually, there's a lot of asynchronous planning happening in Slack, and in **Google Docs** and things like that.

The other main tool that I use is Twitter, which I use mainly for interaction, and obviously my blog, which is the space for public scholarship. The blog is broadcasting in a sense, whereas Twitter is for soliciting responses to a greater degree. A Twitter private message is more valuable to me than a Twitter public space. We have a Twitter DM with maybe twenty people, and this is the continuity with care dimension of Equity Unbound. It's a group of people who got together to have a conversation about care during the closure, and then we just kept this Twitter direct message conversation going. We talk to each other about our frustrations and what's happening at our institutions; we learn from each other and we share our celebrations. It's been really important for my well-being. Without that group, I would not have been able to survive this pandemic. They helped me prepare for my keynote at the Online Learning Consortium conference this year, because I was struggling with a few things and I wanted to test out some ideas, and a few of them actually helped by taking a look at my slides. I don't always do that but for that particular conference I felt like it was a really important presentation and I wanted to get it right. So it really helped, because there were a diverse group of them from different countries and different spaces in academia. It was really helpful to have caring friends to give me that critical feedback in that session.

My favourite resources for teaching online, or remotely, are ones that I recently helped create. These are the community building online resources that I created in a collaboration between Equity Unbound and Virtually Connecting, with OneHE. OneHE is a network of global educators that hope to improve teaching. I'm on their advisory board, and I'm a co-facilitator of Equity Unbound. OneHE is a series of community building activities, and we tried as much as possible to keep intentionally equitable hospitality in mind. Intentionally equitable hospitality is a notion that we developed in Virtually Connecting, which is about how you ensure that the spaces that you create are hospitable to different kinds of people, because it's not necessarily equitable. In order to be hospitable, you must consider that what you do may not work for different people. You need to be very intentional about this, and very careful about how to make sure that everyone participates on their own terms in the way that makes them comfortable, and that makes them feel at home in the spaces you create. I think the most important thing we need to know right now is how to create community online. Some people think there's a stereotype of online learning in that it does not create community. It's the idea that we can't do it, so it's okay, we'll just do lectures. But that's not at all what online learning is. Online learning is supposed to have a social dimension, we all know that. I wanted to help people think about straightforward ways of making it happen and recognize that this is a social justice issue, and that sometimes you need to make room for marginalized people, which may mean silencing dominant voices. We try to do activities here to make adaptations.

There are all different kinds of activities. There are introductory activities, such as what would you do in the first day of class synchronously and asynchronously. You can do it visually, like the surrealist free drawings that Autumn Caines suggested, or there's the human scavenger hunt that Susan Blum's suggested. There are all kinds of things. Some of these come with a video of us demonstrating the activity, and some of them are just text based, telling you how to do it. There are also sets of liberating structures. One that I really like is Conversation Cafe, because it structures a conversation in rounds to make sure that everyone has a time to speak, and nobody dominates the conversation. There's a lot more that you can take a look at. There is a list of people who have been helping us develop even more to come. These are just some of them. There are things to do as ongoing engagement—one example is the Daily Creates. These are from the Digital Storytelling DS-106 course. They're just daily creative things that people can do—five, ten, thirty minutes—and share. It's fun, and it also gives people an opportunity to express themselves and develop their digital literacy at the same time.

Q *What do you expect higher education to look like in ten years' time?*

MB I really don't like answering that kind of question. I don't like speculating about the future. I always try to make my future. Just before

*"Higher education should support the development of the human being to help students become critical citizens, and to work within a community of learners so to be independent and autonomous learners."*

MAHA BALI

COVID hit I was part of a project at my institution that I was collating, where I was asking people to futurize their course; imagine their course in ten or twenty years. We started doing workshops and I was also futurizing my own course. I got a couple of my students to help me out with this and in one of the sessions, they came up with what they thought were the essential elements of my course, which turned out to be care for students' well-being and building community, rather than any content. They said the content would change. We can find our own content. We can be together in the same room or not. They didn't know COVID was going to happen, but they basically developed a high flex model for class, emphasizing the teacher's role in building community and caring for students' well-being, rather than giving content, because they thought the content they could find on their own and they could figure out what they were interested in. And so, I think those students were wiser than a lot of other people.

What they said is what higher education should be like. I know that not all higher education can be like that, but I do think it should be more human focused. Higher education should support the development of the human being to help students become critical citizens, and to work within a community of learners so as to be independent and autonomous learners. I think it will be like this over time. Content will be even easier to reach. I think it's important to note that a lot of the content that is openly available right now is very highly dominated by the Western, and Northwestern world, and that needs to open up more so that knowledge is broader and minority and marginal knowledge is heard as well. I think that the role of teachers will be more about promoting critical and creative thinking, offering wisdom, social and emotional encouragement, and helping people develop the judgment regarding how to find content and then how to think about how they choose what they use in their life. They can be role models for how to behave in the world as well. Learning is not just an act of cognition, you know. There's a lot more going on there. Of course, it's not that teachers will stop having the expertise to give content. Open content should be created by teachers as well, especially university professors who are experts in particular things.

Everyone can create the content that they're expert in, and then use the content from other people who are expert in the other stuff and then focus their class on interactions with students and helping them individually and as a group together, and giving students agency. When there are a lot of open resources, students can have a choice of what to focus on more deeply if they're interested in it. So the teacher becomes the curator and the facilitator; still the teacher creates some of the content, just not every single thing that they use in their course.

When we use a textbook, we don't write the textbook. Someone else has written it. But if it's open, then you don't have to choose one textbook. You can take bits and pieces of stuff that different people have written. I don't use a textbook in my teaching anyway, so that's no different than what I already do, but there's also a lot of stuff that I would like to use with my students that isn't open. And so, the more that we have that, the easier it will be to do that kind of thing. So, for me, I hope students will have more agency and teachers will be able to focus on the socio-emotional development and critical thinking of students, rather than having to worry about passing on content.

## REFLECTION

In my video filmed in Fall 2020, I talked about the importance of care and well-being. I also talked about the importance of building community. These were already central to my teaching pre-pandemic, but during the pandemic they became more important.

Here are some tiny tales of some of the ways I infused this into my class, referring to particular resources in the OneHE/Equity Unbound community building resources:

1. My students felt validated when they learned about trauma-informed pedagogy, when they learned how the stress and anxiety of the pandemic was affecting their ability to think, learn and manage their time. The video with Mays Imad became a central element of my teaching, letting students know that I understand what they are going through, and making them feel heard.[1]

2. I learned about gratitude journaling from colleagues in my department and we created this resource together that showcases different ways of using it.[2] I used gratitude journaling with my then nine-year-old daughter, and it has helped her well-being so much: she managed to find a few things to be grateful about even in the period when I had COVID and her grandmother was hospitalized with COVID.

3. I learned, even more than usual, how important it is to listen to students. To invite them to annotate the syllabus (https://onehe.org/eu-activity/annotate-the-syllabus/), not so we know they have read it, but to create a conversation around what interests them, what confuses them, what they might like to change. I surveyed students pre-semester to help me plan the course, and co-authored blog posts with them on things like how they feel about cameras on Zoom.[3]

Caring for teachers is also important. Because I speak a lot about how teachers should care for students, some teachers, understandably burned out, and asked “what about us?”. So I blogged about it, and I think there are three main areas where teachers can receive care.[4]

---

1 Available at https://onehe.org/resources/trauma-informed-pedagogy/.
2 Available at https://onehe.org/eu-activity/gratitude-journal/.
3 The survey is available at (https://onehe.org/eu-activity/survey-students-early-in-the-semester-pre-course-survey/); the blog posts are available at (https://blog.mahabali.me/educational-technology-2/students-talk-to-me-about-webcams/)
4 The blogs are available at (https://blog.mahabali.me/pedagogy/critical-pedagogy/pedagogy-of-care-caring-for-teachers/).

1. From each other, in the community. This has been a lifeline for me and others, both from communities within one's own institution and outside of it where you can vent more freely sometimes.

2. From students, occasionally. The relationship with students will always be imbalanced: as teachers, we have power and responsibility, but this does not mean that students cannot reciprocate in small ways sometimes and it makes all the difference. My students were gentle and kind to me when I had COVID. One day I lost my voice and the students stepped in to say aloud what I had written in the chat.

3. The third way for teachers to receive care is from their institutions, and I don't mean well-being workshops! I mean modifying working conditions that exploit some teachers over others, and make some people do affective labour that is unrewarded while others do none of that and get rewards for other things like research. These structures need to change.

So these are my top tips … or the ones on my mind today as I head to campus to teach in-person with masks for the first time!

ABOUT

**Maha Bali** is associate professor of practice at the Center for Learning and Teaching at the American University in Cairo, Egypt. She has a PhD in education from the University of Sheffield, in the United Kingdom. She is co-founder of virtuallyconnecting.org (a grassroots movement that challenges academic gatekeeping at conferences) and co-facilitator of Equity Unbound (an equity-focused, open, connected intercultural learning curriculum, which has also branched into the academic community activities, Continuity with Care and Inclusive Academia). She writes and speaks frequently about social justice, critical pedagogy, and open and online education.

# Ruth Healey

Associate Professor in Pedagogy in Higher Education,
University of Chester, United Kingdom

Interviewed September 2020 by Martina MacFarlane

*MM* *Dr. Healey, could you please tell us what you do?*

RH I am a lecturer in geography at the University of Chester in the UK. I think I've been invited to do this primarily because of my interest in students as partners and the research work I do in that area. I'm delighted to be here and to talk a little bit more about the current situation, and how we're approaching teaching in my context.

*MM* *What does your teaching look like in this term, in the 2020/21 semesters?*

RH My institution adopted what they've called the "Chester Blend," which is effectively a form of blended learning so that we have some asynchronous online materials, the work that students do in their own time, and then synchronous work as well. Now, some of the synchronous work is via **Microsoft Teams** and some of it is face-to-face. We had plans in terms of timetabling and then in the UK the social distancing parameters moved from being two metres apart to one metre plus. So we were able to get a few more people into a room and that slightly changed how many classes we were doing with face-to-face sessions. But it's all quite flexible at the moment, because we're just in a situation where the cases are rising (September 2020) and we're uncertain whether we might be going into another national lockdown. I'm not entirely sure what that will mean for higher education. Everything is just a constant marathon of flexibility.

*MM* *From your experience in the past winter term, what opportunities do you think are created by digital education?*

RH In some ways, I'm quite excited about the opportunities. For one, my own learning. I was in a fortunate position that when everything happened toward the end of March 2020, the majority of my teaching was already done. I was able to attend a lot of webinars and seminars to learn more about what was going on and what we could do in terms of the online side of things.

I also like the flipped classroom idea. With the Chester Blend version that we are now doing, there's a possibility that we might be taking these models forward. There are opportunities within the flipped classroom model that can make learning and teaching more flexible for both students and staff. From my perspective, with the opportunity to use that face-to-face time in whatever form, we get to spend much more time discussing, actively learning, and developing ideas.

I know that the flipped classroom is quite an old model. It's been around for a long time, but it's not been a common practice in a lot of institutions. This is an opportunity to experiment with these ideas and try things out in quite a low-risk environment because everybody's understanding is that this is new to everybody. I'm hoping that it will build capacity and confidence for both students and staff. Then hopefully when we return to face-to-face teaching there will be more emphasis on learning from one another, both in terms of staff and students, and students and students.

I appreciate that there are a lot of challenges still within the flipped classroom model, not least of which is being able to ensure that the online content up is interesting and engaging, but also in terms of motivation, which is one of the things I've been talking with my students about. Undertaking asynchronous work, getting your head around that and in a timely manner that is relevant to the timing of the class is challenging. Support for this can come from tutors, in terms of the design of the asynchronous material but also by emphasizing why that's so important and demonstrating how it then connects with what we do when we are together in the same room. Hopefully, we're all learning together.

MM *Could you tell us about your interest in student-staff partnerships?*

RH In my mind, student-staff partnerships are about working together and working collaboratively on what we do. It's generally been my practice to work in terms of active learning, which I think is a form of student-staff partnership. Sometimes it's the constraints and expectations of university structures that make it difficult to undertake. We're quite fortunate at my institution that we don't have fifty-minute lecture slots. We have two-hour sessions with our students, which enable a lot more opportunity for those activities and interactions. Unfortunately, some colleagues will just lecture for two hours, and I'm sure they have activities in there as well, but it's more content driven, whereas I view those face-to-face opportunities as ways of working *with* students and making it more research-based by enabling students to identify and develop skills that they then think they can take forward. It's not about just knowing stuff, which, if you have a memory like me, will go out of your head very quickly. It's about developing the skills to be able to undertake research and understand issues that you can then go on and use in the future.

MM *Wonderful. What are some of the challenges that you've experienced when moving to teaching online?*

RH Well, not all people have the devices or the Internet connections to be able to use these kind of mediums and interact online. There are also the issues surrounding how ... I think that it's great to have people with their videos on, but some people are in environments where they don't want to show where they are. They're working in their own bedrooms, spare bedrooms, they've got family situations, and so on. That means that there are certain people who, because of their circumstances, may not want to contribute to discussions in this kind of medium. They don't want their videos on, which immediately disenfranchises them slightly. I think there are other ways in which you can engage people in these mediums. For example, the chat function can in some ways be more interactive than some of the lectures I've been to. Some people don't want to put their hands up but are a bit more comfortable with texting in the chat area. And of course, there are always technological challenges across the various platforms. The main interface we use is **Moodle**. That is always a little bit slow in the first week of courses and requires a bit of refreshing. Then there is Microsoft Teams, which usually seems to be working okay, but then there are occasional glitches with things such as uploading **PowerPoint** presentations and so on. It's the little technical things, which if you're comfortable and have had a chance to play with stuff you know your way around and you can figure out alternatives. But it knocks people's confidence if they can't figure it out. If you're a student, particularly if you're new to

*"To some extent, these are skills that you're going to need in the workplace, so these challenges are also opportunities to build those and develop those skillsets."*

the university, you're not having the chance to necessarily ask other people because you might not know your peers yet. I think that's really hard. If you're a bit more established, I think sometimes people are forgetting that you may never have used these interfaces before.

Some of these are the challenges that I've seen, but of course, there are different challenges for different people depending on their particular online experiences beforehand. We're always trying to cater for the common situation, not necessarily the extremes of this because we can't cover everything in one go. I suppose that's exactly the same in face-to-face teaching—it's going to work for some and not for others. I think it can be more intimidating online for students to try and connect and ask the questions that they need help with. It's a different form of interaction, and a different level of confidence is needed. To some extent, these are skills that you're going to need in the workplace, so these challenges are also opportunities to develop those skillsets. With the change to remote learning though, this all becomes a little more complex.

MM *So, as you move forward and try and deal with some of those issues, what is your most-used software or tool?*

RH The most-used tool is Microsoft Teams. What I've found nice, is that I've started using it to message my students. My sense is that there's a greater comfort with that format as opposed to e-mail, which feels more formal. Our institution went down the Microsoft route rather than using **Blackboard** and other similar programs. I think the updates that have happened with Teams over the last few months, things like breakout rooms, are absolutely fantastic. **Blackboard Collaborate** has this great function where you can write on a white slide so everyone can scribble away. I quite like that, but unfortunately that's not there yet in Teams.

They do now have another tool, **Padlet**, which I'm using to facilitate a sort of whiteboard space, which I'm sure many people knew about already, but I've only started using it within the last couple of weeks. It was recommended to me months ago, but I never got around to testing it out, and now it's like, oh, this is actually really cool. I can work with this. I can see this working on a whole range of things. That's probably my newest exciting piece of software and we'll see how that goes. A Padlet where people can write at the same time together is more inclusive than a physical whiteboard on one wall in a face-to-face classroom where maybe two people can write at the same time. Everybody has equal access to it, and then there's a chance that somebody who perhaps wouldn't have volunteered to contribute to the whiteboard will be willing to write online, particularly if you set it as anonymous ... although there are issues if something's anonymous, and someone wants to be cheeky. However, there are ways around that in terms of the settings, so it's okay. You just need to maintain a certain amount of confidence that it's going to work out no matter what happens.

MM *Moving to a broader picture, what do you expect higher education might look like in the next ten years?*

RH Such a big question. What do I expect, or what do I hope? These are slightly different. I think that there is really great potential for partnership working on the back of the changes due to the pandemic. One of the things that I noticed very early on in the pandemic was how much my students were caring about my welfare in terms of the context we were in. We were very much connected, because we were all experiencing the responses to COVID at the same time. I think it was very much a levelling experience. I would hope that we maintain this opportunity to recognize and break down those barriers to enhance the ways in which we can work with students and that students recognize their expertise as students in developing and enhancing higher education. Then we might be able to work on creating these knowledge and learning-based communities by having opportunities to interact with each other in different ways that aren't necessarily so focused on the kind of "sage on the stage" model that predominates in lectures. In a way, the students were literally being brought into my home at the same time as I was being brought into theirs. It helps us recognize the power relations that are inherent in a lot of higher education structures—that we're genuinely all in it together.

REFLECTION

Since recording the above in September 2020 and writing this in July 2021, in the UK we have been through two more lockdowns and are experiencing an ongoing intensive vaccination program. We are now expecting to open up fully on 19 July 2021, with no more legal public health requirements, e.g., wearing masks and socially distancing. This appears to be a high-risk strategy with rapidly rising cases of the Delta variant. This uncertain context, on the back of a year of perpetual change, reminds me of the importance of being flexible to adapting my teaching to ensure the best pedagogy in whatever format is possible at any given time.

Whilst we were able to undertake the Chester Blend up until Christmas, for the rest of my teaching in this academic year we were entirely online (lockdown 3, which prevented most HE students from attending classes in the UK ran from the end of December 2020 until the middle of May 2021). This included running a virtual field course in February 2021. Instead of spending four days in Snowdonia National Park, we worked with the Carneddau Landscape Partnership—a scheme to help people discover and care for this culturally important area—to enable our students to focus on projects investigating the impact of climate change, sustainability, tourism, and questions of access, especially around disadvantaged groups in the area, but at a distance. I missed several aspects of face-to-face teaching, particularly the informal social contact, but I have also been astounded by the way in which many of my students have embraced such a difficult situation to make excellent academic progress and achieve their potential.

In addition to the anxieties due to the pandemic, more recently students and staff (including myself) have had to face further uncertainties as financial losses on the back of lower student numbers, both domestic and international, have led several institutions across the sector to propose redundancies. This presents a bleak picture for the future of higher education. But there have also been successful Union campaigns that have been successful at either reducing or cancelling the redundancies. Students and staff have come together to demonstrate the value of individuals and/or departments and have succeeded in their goal to recognize how universities are the people that work and study in them.

When we fully emerge from the pandemic and it is possible to re-start traditional modes of delivery, I hope that we will remember what is important. It is the people, and the connections that we make with one another, between students and staff, between students and students, and staff and staff, which are the basis for academic learning communities. There is no one fixed way of teaching that works for everyone, and we should remember that the new methods have worked very well for a significant proportion of the HE sector, whilst recognizing that for others they have significantly limited the experience. The term "HyFlex" has begun to be used to refer to the simultaneous face-to-face and online delivery, enabling students and staff to teach and learn in a more personalized way. Whilst many would like to return to campus, as a sector we can no longer refuse to offer flexibility to students and staff who for a variety of reasons may not be able or willing to join them. Fundamentally, HE institutions can no longer offer a one-size fits all model. These are strange times, but by working in partnership with students and staff we can identify how best to adapt in our individual contexts to develop adaptable and inclusive learning communities.

ABOUT

**Ruth Healey** is an associate professor in pedagogy in higher education at the University of Chester in the United Kingdom, where she has been since 2009. In 2016, she also joined Healey HE Consultants. She has actively researched learning and teaching issues since 2004. Her pedagogic research interests include teaching for social transformations, debates, ethics, and students as partners. Ruth has written over thirty pedagogic papers, chapters, and reviews, with her work being cited over 450 times. Ruth's article about the "power of debate" was shortlisted for the *Journal of Geography in Higher Education* Award for Promoting Excellence in Teaching and Learning 2012–13. She became a senior fellow of the Higher Education Academy in 2014; in 2017 she was awarded a National Teaching Fellowship (NTF); and in 2019 she was awarded one of nine inaugural fellowships of the International Society for the Scholarship of Teaching and Learning (ISSOTL).

She is on the editorial board of the *Journal of Geography in Higher Education* (2009–) and is one of the inaugural editors of the *International Journal for Students as Partners* (2016–). She is chair of the Geography and Education Research Group (formally the Higher Education Research Group) of the Royal Geographical Society.

# Rujuta Nayak

Graduate Student, Master of Architecture, School of Architecture, Planning and Landscape, University of Calgary, Canada



Interviewed October 2020 by *Mac McGinn*

*MM Rujuta, let's start off with you telling us a little bit about yourself.*

RN I'm living in Mumbai, India, right now because of the pandemic. I got admitted into the master of architecture program at the University of Calgary in 2018. I'm so glad that the school came up with plans quickly so that we could join online and still continue studying. I'm doing my M1 this year and, although it's online, so far it's been great. I struggle with the time difference sometimes, but I'm just glad that I am able to do what I love to do.

*MM How has your learning changed in 2020 compared to other years?*

RN I was born and raised in India and my education has not been particularly technical, in that I've always gone to school by attending in-class. It's a completely different atmosphere that I'm going through right now, but everyone is quite supportive. We're all new to this and I don't think anyone is well-versed. We are all holding each other's hands and getting along and doing what we can. It's interesting and just a very new experience.

*MM Absolutely. So in that light, what are some opportunities that you think have been created by the switch to online education?*

RN One of the most positive aspects of digital education for me as an international student is that I can be with my family. They mean the world to me. It's such a relief that I can spend time with them and do my courses at the same time. In the foundation year, it was a completely different story because I was living in Calgary, by myself. It was my first time living alone. Coping with taking my master's and being without my family was a difficult situation. Having the ability to be with my family this year is only possible because of online education.

*MM People always say that it's pure isolation when you're doing classes remotely, but many students like you also get to spend more time with their family. There's definitely a twist there. What challenges are you seeing from remote learning, especially as an international student?*

RN I would like to touch on two primary challenges that I'm facing. One is that I'm not getting the chance to be in person with classmates like you. That is a challenge because we don't get to connect informally, though we do connect formally over **Zoom** calls where we have all our meetings and discussions. We even break out into informal conversations sometimes, but I think if I were there, it would have been even closer and more intimate in that sense. We could have even gone for coffee or maybe just hung around at each other's place or something like that. So I think that is one of the primary challenges that I'm facing.

The second challenge is the time difference. Because I am in India, it is around eleven and a half, twelve hours ahead of Calgary. When it is morning out there, it's night here and when it's night here, it's morning out there. That's a challenge in itself but you get used to it eventually. Getting used to it is the only solution to the second problem. I started practising a month in advance by getting myself used to the Calgary schedule. But honestly, I can't even get into the Calgary schedule because I'm living a life here. I still need to do things like buy groceries

*"One of the most positive aspects of digital education for me as an international student is that I can be with my family. They mean the world to me. It's so relieving that I can spend time with them and do my courses at the same time."*

and go to the makerspaces for my projects. In that sense, I feel like I'm not living in the Indian time zone, and I'm not living in the Calgarian time zone either. I'm living in maybe the UK time zone. It's somewhere in between, but it's fine. I'm getting used to it.

*MM* *With these different challenges that you're presented with, what types of tools are helping you with remote learning?*

RN The primary tool is Zoom. Anything like Zoom or **Skype** is really helpful for connecting with people. I even tried **WhatsApp** to call my groupmate in Mexico. My peers and I use **OneDrive** and **Google Docs** for sharing documents. We also obviously use **Gmail** or our e-mail programs. There are tons of tools we use because everything is digital. We use anything and everything that's available.

*MM* *Other than tools, do you have any favourite types of resources that you use for remote learning?*

RN Of course, I use **D2L** a lot because most of our content is posted there and it's where we get first-hand information regarding our assignments and course content. Then that leads to a lot of research. Being in architecture, we frequently use ArchDaily, Dezeen or other websites like that which are architecturally relevant. I also use the UCalgary library portal. It's quite helpful to go to the library website and download books, and handling the information is easy because we can copy-paste everything we need into documents. Although I do miss going to the library and picking up books in person. I prefer having books in my hand over reading them digitally.

*MM What do you expect higher education to look like going forward?*

RN Honestly, I'm happy that I'm experiencing this atmosphere right now. Had this pandemic not happened, we probably wouldn't have moved or had this shift so suddenly. In general, if you ask me about developed countries like Canada or the US, it might be possible for us to keep using these online platforms for our benefit. For example, students can connect on Zoom and work on their projects independently, while also working together. Doing this enables you to get each other's feedback and have those more informal conversations, similar to what happens when we're in the studio. We have the flexibility to do this, but we don't yet have the acceptance of doing it online. I don't think we've got fully comfortable with having a group of people online working on their own in a purely informal setting. Moving forward, having the option to work online together like this would be nice.

If you consider developing countries, or countries which still do not have a lot of facilities like here in India, there has been no contingency plan set up for students, so the students have not yet moved forward into the next year. I'm glad I'm going to a Canadian university, but not everybody gets to have a foreign education. I don't see the online transformation happening here in India anytime soon. I feel it's going to take a lot of effort and financing to get set up with online learning; we're just not prepared. For the future of higher education in countries like Canada, the US and the UK, there might be a combination of both in-person and online learning. You can have in-person learning but at the same time have the informal setting where we can all be online together at the same time. I think a combination of both would be quite helpful.

*MM Thank you, Rujuta. It's interesting to have you share your international perspective and to know that certain countries do not have the ability to create these contingency plans.*

RN Yes, for example, if you go just two or three hours outside of Mumbai, there's still the challenge of not having adequate Wi-Fi and Internet connection. This costs a lot and students are on their own; there's no financial support from the government or additional help from the community. I think a lot of students out there studying in these small villages, outside the city. They are suffering. There's a wide socio-economic gap, where there are people who are really rich and people who are really poor. They don't even have laptops for studying. At schools here, having a laptop is not mandatory because you still read from printed textbooks and write your notes by hand. It's a different world. I really feel sad for these students because they've had to put their studies on hold for an entire year and the government has still not come up with a contingency plan. It's sad because there's very little anybody can do about it. Because of the high population of India, the other challenges the government is facing are huge. But this is something that's happening to a lot of students. There are students who have been accepted at universities in places like the UK, Canada or the US, but they haven't been able to do their final exams yet and they're still here. Had I been studying at a school in India at any academic level, despite having financial stability, I would have been left out too because there's no plan B. For me, honestly, I just got lucky.

REFLECTION

The COVID-19 pandemic has certainly impacted on each one of us in many ways. My journey in the last year has been no different, as I have personally learned and experienced the transition from in-class learning to seeking education in the online world while in my master of architecture program.

On the master's program, which is one the most integral stages for academics, the shift from in-class to online came with its own set of challenges, including learning through different mediums with little scope to have a deeper understanding of the software, a lack of practical learning, and the inability to interact with the cohort informally. However, learning online has taken the Internet by storm as most millennial students, including me, are dependent in terms of the use of various online platforms to seek education. This has eventually compelled many of us to seek collaborations and group learning which help in resolving many of the challenges. For instance, I recall the Spring semester being one of the shortest semesters, with immense schoolwork on hand that had to be generated in a short period of time, with the groups assigned. It seemed difficult in the beginning. However, brainstorming over long Zoom sessions helped us in resolving most of the challenges collectively and enabled us to sail through the intense semester successfully. I believe that as time passes, each one of us will get a stronger hold of the situation and we can respond positively to the circumstances presented.

I recollect, early on in Fall 2020, when the shift to online teaching was made, I was nervous to begin learning online as I was living away in my home country, India. Factors such as the difference in time zones and lack of physical presence of the faculty and cohort made me think twice about continuing the program. However, the situation then was getting worse in India. Realizing the fact that many students in India were not availing quality education due to the circumstances, I found myself to be fortunate for being associated with the Department of Architecture, SAPL (School of Architecture, Planning and Landscape), and the University of Calgary, as they were swiftly upgrading and providing the transformation that was desired by many. I quickly, without any hesitation, enrolled in the courses and since then I have been glad about the decision that I made.

To touch upon the current educational situation in my homeland, I feel the shift to online education has led to a steep rise for many EdTech companies, including Byju's, a Bengaluru-based start-up, capturing substantial world markets. However, on the one hand, we have the EdTech giants scaling new heights and on the other hand, we have the situation of inaccessibility and unavailability of devices and infrastructure problems on the grassroots level in rural

India, making it impossible for students to seek education. Given the flexibility of balancing my professional and personal life and being able to stay in my home country while availing myself of a master's from a premier University in Canada, the shift to online education has impacted me in a positive sense. But making an equitable position for all is very challenging considering the socio-economic disparity and infrastructural unavailability for many countries. Though I feel the online mode of studying should persist due to the benefits it has offered, although the lack of physically learning has certainly impacted my education in ways I am yet to discover. However, I am truly grateful for this experience even though I did not plan for it!

ABOUT

**Rujuta Nayak** is a returning graduate student in the master of architecture program at the School of Architecture, Planning, and Landscape, University of Calgary, Canada. In the 2018–2019 academic year, she was admitted to the program and took the foundation year level courses. Before pursuing architecture, she graduated with a master of commerce from the University of Mumbai, India. She also has an apprenticeship certificate from the J.J. School of Applied Art, a premier school for art and architectural education in India. She is passionate about travel, the environment, and the socio-cultural impacts of society.

# Dimitri Giannoulis

Graduate Student, Master of Planning, School of Architecture, Planning and Landscape, University of Calgary, Canada and President, School of Architecture, Planning and Landscape Student Association, University of Calgary, Canada

Interviewed October 2020 by *Martina MacFarlane*

*MM* *Tell us just a little bit about your background and what you do at SAPL (School of Architecture, Planning and Landscape).*

DG I am originally from Calgary and I have a background in geography from the University of Victoria. I'm now in the second year of the urban planning program at the University of Calgary and I'm also the current president of the SAPL Student Association.

*MM* *You've stepped into your Student Association President position during all of this, and I imagine that you've seen a lot of changes. How have things changed in general, and how has your learning changed for the 2020 year?*

DG When I first became president in May, I sort of figured that everything would be back to normal by August. But by July, it was clear that the Fall would be virtual, and so there was a lot of work to try to prepare for that. For me individually as a student, I was in a weird position to transition online because I was doing most of my work from the school computers because I found it was better for the software than using my laptop. I think I was at school more than your average student, so it's been a real change not going into the school as much this year.

*MM* *You experienced a big change completely shifting where you do all of your work. Have you been using the lab computers remotely at all?*

DG No, I haven't. The pandemic year sort of forced me to accept that I had to use this heavy software on my **Mac** laptop, and I found out it wasn't even that bad. It gave me confidence, whereas before, I had the impression that it just wouldn't work. I haven't had to use **AutoCAD** or any **GIS** on my laptop; these would be the only barriers. In particular the GIS is a bit more difficult, but I haven't really had to use the server because this term the assignments are focused more on **Adobe Creative Cloud**.

*MM* *What do you think are some of the opportunities created by this shift to digital education?*

DG One of the opportunities is affordability for those who would normally have to move to attend school. However, the degree of economic opportunity will play out differently for everybody, depending on the situation. In terms of the actual learning, I think it's just a different format. If we think about just going from one format to another, how well it works for you sort of depends on your personality. The switch to digital education does affect each person differently depending on how you learn.

*MM* *How has the switch to online learning been for you personally?*

DG I don't like it, but it's been fine. I'm fortunate because I've been living with my partner instead of alone and we have friends in town that we can still hang out one-on-one with, so that makes it easier to not have in-person socialization through school. Also, I'm lucky to have the benefit of knowing all my peers in my cohort already from last year when we were at school together in person.

*MM I would imagine it's a whole different challenge for students in their first year who have only met their classmates over Zoom.*

DG I completely agree. The SAPL Students' Association put out a survey to students asking how their experience has been, and after reading through the submissions I know that many first years are having a hard time. They don't have those social connections established and it can be awkward to meet people over **Zoom**.

*MM Are there other challenges that you're seeing with remote learning?*

DG I definitely wonder if students are now learning less. Sometimes it can be hard to pay attention. For the school, it's no easy task to change the format of class schedules, but some of those longer class times that would work previously in person are simply just too long in this online format. Although within that challenge, there is also the opportunity to be able to just turn off your camera, get up and do a quick stretch or whatever you need to do to get comfortable. I am definitely a fidgety person at the best of times, so it's been nice for this reason. These are things you can't really do in class. Another challenge is that it's now so easy to pop open a new tab and get distracted. It's not that I'm scrolling through **Facebook** and tuning out what's happening on Zoom, but there is that sense of distraction that's always present when you're alone at home. In a sense, it's harder to focus and really get into it.

*MM Absolutely. There are all these external sources that you can quickly dive into, and before you know it your brain is somewhere else. So, speaking of all the things you can get into online, what is your most-used tool for remote learning?*

DG By far, it's been Zoom in the format of single-group lectures and questions. I would say we spend about half of the time on Zoom with presentation material up, and half the time we're just chatting. I've also used **Miro** in one of my courses. It's a cool tool but there are definitely limitations with it too. Between the instructor and all the students there are so many files being put on Miro and this can really slow things down. But overall, Miro and Zoom are the tools I use the most.

*MM Do you have a favourite resource that you look to for tips or inspiration?*

DG Not in particular. I'm not actively seeking out resources, but I'll use some that I happen to come across. For example, having used Miro I know that there are some Miro games. The SAPL Students' Association might use these for one of our upcoming online social nights.

*MM Dimitri, we've come to the last question, and it's a big one. What do you think or hope that higher education might look like in the next ten years?*

DG I've thought about this before, and my understanding for universities is that because they have their in-person infrastructure already in place there are all these new pressures on the business side of things. I think that the university wants to get back in-person. I can't imagine them choosing to say okay, we're selling our buildings, or leaving them vacant.

*"I imagine then that things will go mostly back to normal. I think that it's going to feel like a big shift. I'm not saying that this is a vacation, but I imagine that when the school says, okay, we are going back to in-person classes, it'll sort of be like summer vacation is over. We've all developed our little habits of working at home and I think it's likely that students will feel a sense of oh wow, how would I ever go back to school? But then on the first day, we'll say okay, I guess I better get up and go."*

DIMITRI GIANNOULIS

The transition back will be tough too. I think that if universities take on the hybrid model of both in-person and online education it will be really challenging. It could be that we have, say, ninety percent of students back in class and the rest are still remote learning. I don't really see that being very viable, or even desirable. Overall, though, assuming that we develop a vaccine or something like that, at some point the pandemic will end. I imagine then that things will go mostly back to normal. I think that it's going to feel like a big shift. I'm not saying that this is a vacation, but I imagine that when the school says, okay, we are going back to in-person classes, it'll sort of be like summer vacation is over. We've all developed our little habits of working at home and I think it's likely that students will feel a sense of oh, wow, how would I ever go back to school? But then on the first day, we'll say okay, I guess I better get up and go. Hopefully before we know it, we'll be adjusted right back to our in-class habits again.

I think that when we do get back, those who are in-person aren't going to want to have that digital component. I think it's a consensus amongst students that once classes are back at school, they just want to do things the way they were before. That's been my experience in terms of my involvement with the SAPL Student Association. For us, the virtual realm has been tricky. Students already have so much screen time and we have to decide if planning social activities online and stretching the amount of screen time even further is something we can do.

*MM* *Are you finding that people are responsive to those sorts of digital sessions?*

DG The responsiveness has been less than in the past when these events happened in person. There are students in their first year who may not know any of their peers, and those who are in different time zones. These are monumental challenges for student involvement. Going forward there will be the question of how to advocate for these opportunities if they're in person, because hosting them offline will make them exclusive to only those who are able to attend in person. It's a bit of a Catch-22.

*MM* *Thank you for sharing your experiences with us, Dimitri. Is there anything else that you'd like to add?*

DG I've heard from students that it's been difficult to learn all the new software for our programs online. Nobody is near you to help you troubleshoot and it's harder for the instructors to gauge where everybody is at. Difficulties with teaching and learning software over Zoom was a significant finding to come out of the survey we sent. This is definitely something we need to keep in mind as we progress through the changes to online education.

## REFLECTION

I'm writing this reflection on 3 July 2021, an interesting moment to reflect on my interview nine months ago. In Alberta, we have just entered Stage 3 of our re-opening, removing nearly all restrictions. In my interview, I only hoped that a vaccine would be developed, but now I have had both doses. However, at the time of this reflection, COVID-19 continues: people are still dying from the disease in Alberta, and globally, it seems like wealthier nations have been able to force themselves to the front of the line for vaccinations. But in many ways, in Calgary, life seems almost normal for the first time.

I have graduated and a new president is leading the SAPL Student Association. I am working full-time now, and I have been transitioning from working at home to working in the office. I still use Zoom and Miro regularly, and I appreciate having virtual tools as an option when needed. I am finding working from home different than online schooling, particularly when it comes to feeling restless or unable to concentrate. I find concentrating easier while working remotely because it's more involved than just listening to content, and because I know I'm on the clock, that gives me a sense of obligation that prevents me from getting distracted. Another contrast is that remote schooling has the added difficulty of being all the time: you have no shift or end time, which I found was taxing.

At this point, universities and workplaces seem to be offering in-person and digital options for their employees/ students. For some people's personalities or life circumstances, digital methods are simply preferred and may offer personal benefits. However, I wonder what the effect would be of dividing workplaces and courses into those two groups, whereby the two never meet. I worry that it would negatively impact collaboration.

I wish that I had been able to return to in-person learning before graduating, and I am excited for those who will be able to. I hope that the students who began their studies digitally will be able to meet in person and feel a stronger sense of connectedness to their peers. For me, the physical spaces of a school are part of the experience and those physical spaces for education are important for making the education experience memorable, tangible, and meaningful; you get nostalgic about school walking by your former school because it's a space filled with memories for you. Five years from now, I doubt it will be the same form of nostalgia when I remember working from my laptop in my apartment; that spatial disconnect is significant, and I am excited for the opportunity to reconnect with spaces as much as with people. Even if the pandemic is not over, the end finally feels in sight.

ABOUT

**Dimitri Giannoulis** is a proud SAPL alumnus, having completed his master of planning degree at the University of Calgary, Canada in 2021. During his final year, Dimitri was the president of the SAPL Student Association. His most recent professional endeavours have involved bike share operations, main street activation, and he is now a planning and development officer with Foothills County.

# Mary-Ellen Tyler

Professor and Associate Dean, Landscape and Planning, School of Architecture, Planning and Landscape, University of Calgary, Canada



Interviewed December 2020 by *Mac McGinn*

MM *Mary-Ellen, let's start off by you introducing yourself and telling us a little bit about what you do.*

MT I have a varied background, but I came to Calgary in 1988 as the dean of the Faculty of Environmental Design. I am now a full professor and, for the last three years, I've been acting as the interim associate dean for the master of planning and landscape architecture programs at the University of Calgary. I teach in both landscape architecture and planning. I generally do studios, regional planning, design studio, professional practice studio, and climate change adaptation courses.

MM *How has your teaching changed since the start of the COVID pandemic?*

MT I started off being very concerned. We had to switch online in literally less than thirty-eight hours. It was pretty dramatic, but we did it. The courses were over halfway through the term at this point, and so we had already built up a lot of background, some trust, some communication, and our projects. Nothing was starting from scratch. This year, everything is starting from scratch remotely. When you're at square one, it takes longer to build a rapport with the students and between students around what's happening in the class, the intention, and the communication, because there's a whole conceptual and cognitive development that comes when you're thinking abstractly about problem solving.

It's a very different kind of learning engagement and it's taken a little bit longer than in person for the students to adapt. In my check-ins with them every couple of weeks, it seemed to me that it didn't start off great. Now it seems to be growing nicely. We're almost six weeks into it, and I think most students are getting comfortable as they start to go through the assignments, having had opportunity to talk to each other outside of class in multiple ways, both through their workspaces as well as online. Now we are having discussions on **Zoom** that I think I would have fully anticipated having in person. So I think we're seeing some good signs.

I have seen real difficulties with my Landscape Ecology courses. It's not possible to really give students the conceptual framework they need to undertake some of the work if they are never able to understand the regional landscape, and there's only so much you can do for someone who's never been in it before. If people are familiar with it, then, yes, representations like **Google Earth** give them enough to be able to make that leap. But if they're from a different country and they've never been here, it's really difficult to try to communicate or visually explain the dynamic processes at the landscape level. I'm certainly going to have to re-evaluate it all at the end of one entire term remotely, to see if anything changes. I believe that learning should be hugely experiential at the professional graduate level. This is really restricting the experiential opportunity for some students who just aren't from here. I've worked on a number of major consulting projects, twenty years ago, that were in China and trying to figure that site out before I actually went there was really difficult, so I can certainly appreciate the experience that those folks are having trying to make head or tail of a place you've never been.

MM *What opportunities do you think are created through this remote or digital education that we're in now?*

MT Well, clearly, I think it's the fact that it opens up this portal, essentially, for international or distance communication both in terms of connecting with expert resources, as well as for having students being able to dial in. A few weeks ago now we had a course in which a number of international speakers met with us on Zoom to talk about new ideas for downtown Calgary and what we might be able to implement from their perspectives, from where they are in the world, that might have some traction in terms of being customized to Calgary. We would never have been able to do that before. That really enriches not just student learning, but also thinking. Being exposed to new ideas, new concepts, different cultural perspectives, that really makes a difference.

*MM What types of challenges do you find, in terms of pedagogy, have been created through this?*

MT Like they say in real estate: location, location, location. When it comes to this, I say: time, time, time. The time constraint was huge in trying to think through alternative ways of presenting and trying to understand it from a student perspective. It's not simply figuring out how do I now present, but also where are the students coming from in terms of what their perspectives are, and what are the steps that have to happen in order to make it accessible to them. So the preparation this summer took a huge amount of time.

Once the term started, another challenge was the response time. Because of remote learning, students need more individual tutorial time with you. And then there's the class time in addition to the scheduling of all of the individual meeting times, to supplement that. A one-on-one component is really needed, particularly in both of my courses, as they work through a series of exercises. For me, I really need to maintain a very high level of engagement with each student in terms of their individual perspectives around the exercises, as well as the collective view of things in classes. Then there is the time for feedback.

They're changing the format of the assignments, so that you're able to give them feedback on what you need from them. Marking, evaluation and review always take time, but it isn't so much the comments. What takes extra time now is putting the comments into the work in a format that they can understand. Again, everything is spatial in landscape architecture, so it's like, okay, here's what you did; here's another view of it. You're showing them a different image or a different drawing. I think it's helpful. But again, it's a huge amount of time for an instructor. At the moment, as the associate dean, my primary job is not as an instructor, so it's really added on to the workload for me in terms of trying to carry other duties. And I'm sure it's increased the workload of the instructors without administrative duties, but who are still trying to do research and publication.

*MM That must be quite the challenge to you to balance those two different workloads together with being associate dean.*

MT That's right, and I don't think we're the only victims. I think that the students are feeling a huge overload too. I gather from those who I've talked to that this seems to be a large source of the stress that they are dealing with right now. They feel absolutely overwhelmed by all of this time commitment. It's especially so when they're used to doing school alongside some part time work. So I think the workload comes on both sides. That's something we're all going to have to figure out and manage more effectively, even if we move back into the classrooms. We may have to start thinking about maintaining the hybrid models to alleviate some of this. Our sense of time is going to have to be adjusted.

MM *In light of discussing the new challenges of time in remote teaching and learning, are there certain resources or software tools that you would use to help you manage time or teaching more effectively?*

MT One thing I've learned is that the old-fashioned stuff isn't bad. At the beginning, everyone, including me, thought that we could handle the regional landscape courses using 360-degree cameras and the new, sexy technologies that are available along with those tools. In reality, the video footage would go too fast, and although as the instructor I understood what we were looking at, that didn't mean the students could understand, especially at that pace. After wasting some time doing this camera work, I realized that I had students who weren't familiar with this landscape and many who really didn't have any background, so then I went outside and simply started taking photographs. In a very old-fashioned way, I put them into my **PowerPoints.** I put graphics on top of them and I laid them all out in the format that I wanted: the arrow goes here; the trees are going to grow there; in ten years this is going to look like this. I can implement graphics and animate them so that what I'm showing the students can be slowed down. They can run it all through if they want to. It was important for me to put this content in a format that students could access at their own speed. So I found that just going back to plain old photographs and PowerPoints with graphic annotation was a better method that enabled the students to access it as fast or as quickly as they needed. I was actually imprinting the information on top of the image, rather than assuming that everybody could see what I saw. This is the gist of what field work is. As an instructor, a lot of it is teaching people to see. When you are learning this type of content, it all sounds crazy until you're out in the field and someone is actually explaining it to you.

As for other technologies, I haven't leaped into anything really new yet, and it's just because I haven't had to. But, certainly, I've heard from others that they're trying some new things and I think that's great. It's as though the technology gives us an artist's palette. You're going to have more than one colour and use it as you think best.

MM *What do you expect higher education to look like in ten years' time?*

MT Ten years is a big leap, and I think we will see some significant changes. One change we're already experiencing is that students are needing to work more and more as time goes on, and as the cost of education is increasing. Given the pandemic and the impact it's going to have on the economy, it's hard to tell whether that's going to be any different in the next ten years, but I don't see that changing. I do see education becoming more customized so that students will be picking more specific modular types of packages of education or knowledge, which they will then combine in ways that suit them for whatever changing ideas that they have. Students are going to be very entrepreneurial in terms of creating an education that they want that can be individ-

*"I see higher education having a lot more choice, a lot more variability and being a lot more lifestyle driven. It's going to be more like a buffet. How are you going to put it all together?"*

ualized or customized to their interest. I think there'll be a lot more choices. I think people also want that four-year degree timeline to change so that you have more flexibility to work and have time for education, and technology will absolutely help with that.

I think that one of the most significant changes going forward will be a hybridization of education. We may actually move to what I call more of a "conference style" delivery of courses, where students do their work and then come together for three, maybe six weeks of the term. They'll give their presentations, get to know each other personally and then go back to wherever they are. I think there's going to be a huge role not just for instructional design in the sense of content delivery, but also design in the sense of restructuring these courses. Perhaps we will see something along the lines of learning modules or learning pods, so that people are getting their technical skills, then applying those skills, and then moving on to put them into practice. I see higher education having a lot more choice, a lot more variability and being a lot more lifestyle-driven. It's going to be more like a buffet. How are you going to put it all together? I can't envision the exact product, but I think it is going to be hybridized in terms of in-person and online. I think it is going to be highly customized and a bit deconstructed and it's going to be a lot more entrepreneurial on the part of the learner.

It's quite exciting. I come from an era where we didn't have job expectations. I mean, we really did believe in the Seventies that we'd make it happen. We'd just do it. I came from a generation that didn't feel the job pressures that people seem to be feeling now. The assumption was, well, we'll just go out there and make our own jobs. I think they call it naivety—call it genius, call it whatever you want, it is coming back. I think people are realizing that they're going to make it. Whatever happens, they're going to make it happen and I think that's exciting for everyone. We have to support them and offer the opportunity to do that.

## REFLECTION

What I teach is not text based. Unlike some academic disciplines, particularly in the social sciences, where text-based reading and writing are primary, regional planning, landscape architecture, and environmental design require spatial literacy. Spatial literacy is primarily visual and has a physical landscape or geographic context involving spatial pattern, form, and dimension. As such, abstract thinking involves abstractions based on physical analogs, which have a variety of spatial scales and dimensions. Everything students need to think about will eventually have to find a physical form and spatial location on the ground. Information in a spatial context has meaning based on where it is, as much as what is in the spatial context. Visual information is different from text and "reading" an image is not a text-based process.

In addition to spatial literacy, my courses also focus on design literacy. Specifically, regional planning, landscape architecture, and environmental design are "normative" because they deal with what "should be" in some future timeframe rather than analyzing what currently exists. This is a distinctly different perspective. Design thinking is a highly interactive and iterative process in which new information and learning occur through constant engagement with and reframing of the phenomenon or problem domain of interest. In this process, drawing and diagramming, rather than text, are used to represent both the conceptual and physical understanding of dynamic functional and structural relationships in time and space.

Digital and visual software are well suited to this type of visual information representation and provide synoptic overviews, as well as cross-scalar perspectives, spatial pattern recognition and pattern generation. These digital tools also enable the manipulation of thematic spatial information in multiple ways to meet multiple objectives. As such, students can use these tools to visually explore, illustrate, draw, construct diagrams, generate, and simulate information and processes over time and space.

In reflecting on the COVID-driven remote teaching and learning experience of last year in the context of what I teach, it has started to become clear that learning in the context of professional design education at the graduate level in planning and landscape architecture is very different from the old "three Rs" of education. There is no reading, writing, or arithmetic. I don't think I had really appreciated just how different what I am teaching is in a professional education context until I had to think about how to deliver it remotely at short notice and without the benefit of the design studio format, which has been the traditional pedagogical approach.

By deconstructing the courses down to what learners need to grasp, I was initially able to use a minimal technology approach to teaching the basics. While this seems to have worked in the short term to solve the immediate problem in a time effective manner, it didn't explore the potential for digital technologies and software to enhance teaching and learning. Specifically, visual technologies can dramatically enhance teaching and learning opportunities in regional planning, landscape architecture, and environmental design and inform a rethinking of the traditional studio pedagogy.

A return to an on-campus studio delivery format may be possible this year or next. This may be appealing in some ways as a return to "normal." However, this would be massively short-sighted in my opinion. I believe that in retrospect what I have learned from remote teaching will enable me to redesign a traditional professional "signature" pedagogy to realize the potential of visual technologies for fostering visual information and design literacy skills in future regional planning and landscape architecture practitioners.

This is not at all what I was originally thinking at the time of my TALON interview over a year ago. I am now thinking that pedagogical innovation is possible by rethinking the role for visual technologies in creating spatial design literacy.

ABOUT

**Dr. Mary-Ellen Tyler** was dean of the Faculty of Environmental Design at the University of Calgary from 1 September 1998 until 30 June 2003. She holds interdisciplinary graduate degrees at the master's and PhD levels in environmental science and natural resource management. Dr. Tyler has worked in both the private and public sectors as an environmental planner and ecologist and spent ten years with the federal government in British Columbia working with Indian and Northern Affairs on resource development, impacts assessment, local government development and intergovernmental resource management issues related to comprehensive land claims negotiations. During her academic career, she has held tenured academic appointments at both the University of Waterloo and the University of Manitoba, and has taught in the areas of urban and regional planning, landscape architecture and environmental design. Prior to moving to Calgary in 1998, Dr. Tyler was associate dean of architecture at the University of Manitoba and acted as head of the Department of Environmental Design and Interior Design. She is currently a professor and associate dean of Landscape and Planning at the University of Calgary. Her current areas of research, scholarship and professional practice are urban ecology, sustainable urban design, urban watershed management, ecological restoration, and urban environmental management.

# Guy Gardner

Instructor of Building Science, Architectural Robotics and Computational Design, School of Architecture, Planning and Landscape, University of Calgary, Canada and Director of Fabrication, Laboratory for Integrative Design, Calgary, Canada



Interviewed November 2020 by *Martina MacFarlane*

MM *Thank you so much for joining us today. Tell us a little bit about your background and what you do at SAPL.*

GG I am a graduate of the architecture program at the University of Calgary, and of the master of environmental design (MEDes) program. After finishing my architecture degree, I worked for a few years and then came back to the University of Calgary to engage in research through my MEDes degree. I spent a few years working under the supervision of Jason Johnson, one of our profs in the architecture program, looking at creative uses of digital fabrication tools, such as 3D printers and industrial robots. At the end of that research, I completed my MEDes thesis, and then was hired by the School of Architecture to work as the Robotics and City Building Design Lab (CBDL) Facilities Specialist. We have a couple of industrial robots, both on our main campus at the university, and then also in our satellite campus here at the CBDL. I am responsible for these tools, and I help out as a technician, supervising students and researchers who are working with that equipment. I also work out of the satellite campus here, and help students with 3D printing and provide support for any of the research that happens around digital fabrication.

MM *Wonderful. Through SAPL you have lots of experience with digital technology and tools, but with the pandemic this year, things look different in a lot of ways. How has your facilitation and teaching changed?*

GG When the pandemic started, I was in the middle of working on one of our block week workshops. We had just set up our exhibition and wrapped up the student work, and then the next day, the university was shut down. So, at that time I was halfway through teaching that course. I also teach the Introduction to Building Science for architects, and I was halfway through that course too. So, we switched over to an online delivery method and finished up that course on **Zoom**. Having to do that in the middle of the semester was a big adjustment. I think it was actually good for me, because I didn't really have a choice about being able to adapt, and it got me really familiar with the process immediately.

Directly after that, we put together another course called Computational Design, which we could offer in the spring because we wanted to provide some continuity for students. We offered that course completely online, and it was great. We found that the students were really receptive to the content, and it gave us a chance to explore some other possibilities in terms of course delivery. We did a couple of the classes on **Mozilla Hubs**, which was interesting. It gave us a chance to try out some different things.

Over the summer we figured things out a little bit more. We hired a new faculty member and professor of robotics, Alicia Nahmad Vasquez, and toward the end of the summer I started working with her. We set up a way to deliver that class remotely, and that was the first time that I had to think about how we would give students access to the equipment. I think it's really important for students to be able to have hands-on engagement with these kinds of tools and to really be able to understand how they work. I've always been someone who learns through doing and through making, and I think that this is really important for an architectural and design education in general.

Working through some of those problems with that team has been quite interesting. We've come up with some creative solutions and we're still constantly trying to develop and figure out new ways of working.

MM *Overall, what do you think are some of the opportunities created by digital education?*

GG First off, I think it's important to recognize that the practice of architecture, landscape architecture and urban planning has become a heavily digital practice. It's very important for people who are engaging in that field to be comfortable with working digitally, and be able to collaborate with teams in a distributed way, across different countries and continents. I think that using tools like Zoom and being able to work in teams and not necessarily having to meet in person but finding ways to share and mark up drawings and communicate in those ways, is really important from an educational perspective. We need students to be able to learn those processes. That's what I want to keep in mind. This is just the reality of these professions in some ways.

It's also important for designers to be able to construct models and explore tectonics through producing mock-ups and things like that. Those things are a bit more of a challenge. For example, at our workshop we've had to shift things so students are submitting fabrication files of their designs to our technicians. Rather than the students actually going into the shop and cutting the materials themselves, the technicians are producing those parts and giving them to the students so that they can assemble them on their own, if they are working locally. We are having to find ways for the students to get access to the equipment wherever they might be located, and we are making arrangements or alternative plans for students located outside of Calgary so that they are able to make up for that work in some other way. There are ways for us to give students the ability to control those machines from remote locations. Our IT department has been helpful in providing students with remote access to the computers in the labs and we're also broadcasting videos of the robots working, so that the students have real-time access to see what those machines are doing and how they're responding to the commands that are being sent to them. We've actually created an **Instagram** account for our robots so if people are interested, they can follow along @sapl.robots.

The other thing that's been really nice is that, across all of the different institutions, I'm finding that other professors and technicians are being really collaborative, helpful, and interested in sharing the tricks and approaches that they've found to be working. It's been interesting to tap into that larger network of people, who are all dealing with the same challenges.

MM *It's connecting us in different ways than before, and there is lots of opportunity in that. I'm curious about model making. My understanding of classes in my urban planning program is that the requirements for models have been lightened at this point, so obviously, there are lots more concessions being made in architecture to try and make these things happen. Are you finding that things are getting lost in translation during that process, or is there more creative problem solving as a result? How do you think that's going?*

GG Well, I'm still in the process of really testing that idea out. I'm teaching a class right now called Integrative Acoustics where we're studying the acoustics of learning environments and looking at some spaces here in the building that I'm working in. We're doing some simulations and then working toward producing mock-ups for the class that we're hoping to be able to actually test using acoustics equipment. So up to this point the work has all been digital; it's all been using simulation. One of the challenges that the students have encountered is that, sometimes, their own hardware is not as fast as the computers that they would have in the lab, so we've given them remote access to the lab computers so they can run the simulations on those. As we move into production mode, it is going to be interesting to see how the students are able to overcome some of those challenges. One of the ways that we're making it work is that the students are going to be working in teams, so those who aren't able to come in and directly work with their hands are able to contribute in other ways. Part of the whole reality of working in teams, and part of the profession as well, is that there's a division of responsibilities. People need to understand how they can contribute and participate in their own way. Obviously, the documentation of processes becomes really important, and finding ways to be able to take time lapse photos, share the progress with the team, and those kinds of things can be really cool ways of addressing that. It's all a big experiment right now.

*MM We're all in that together, for sure. In terms of online teaching, what's your most-used software or tool?*

GG Right now, definitely Zoom. I feel like I'm on Zoom all the time. I've also started using **YuJa**. It's been nice to have TALON sharing this set of resources and tools; I've found it quite useful. Initially, I was recording all of my Zoom videos and then going back and trying to edit them down into usable clips that I could share with the students. I found that process to be time consuming and onerous, so finding other ways to speed that up a little bit has been nice.

*MM And then what would be your favourite resource for teaching online? That can be inspiration, where you go for guidance, or anything like that.*

GG One thing I want to mention that I found really useful as a platform is **Discord**. I can both make myself available to students, and more importantly, make them available to each other to try and make up for that missing studio culture that's disappeared, which is so critical to architecture school. Normally in the studio, students are able to sit next to each other, look over each other's shoulders, discuss their projects and talk about what techniques they're using and how to address challenges with the software. Trying to replace that through an online server like Discord, or something like **Microsoft Teams**, I think can be quite important. It's really great to try and facilitate ways for students to be able to communicate with each other in that way, so that they can learn from each other. I think students always learn more from each other than they ever do from their instructors.

In terms of resources that I've been using, there are some really amazing online tutorials that I've been just blown away by. One really good example is a **YouTube** channel called **ParametricCamp**. It was

*"There's so much, just this huge trove of information that's been put out there and made available to people. Now is a really great time to engage in self-directed learning, I think."*

started by Garcia del Castillo who is an instructor at Harvard, and he's been recording his lectures and posting live streams of him coding in different software languages. It's been great to see people like that who are stepping up and facing this challenge by sharing more information and being really generous with their time.

That's just one example, but there have been lots. There have been different conferences that have made their proceedings available online to people for free. Actually, as a person who's interested in computational design, digital fabrication and those subject areas, there's even more information available right now than there was a year ago. There's so much, just this huge trove of information that's been put out there and made available to people. Now is a really great time to engage in self-directed learning, I think.

MM *We don't necessarily know what the future holds, but what do you expect or hope for higher education in the next ten years?*

GG Well, I hope that it continues to provide students with ways to be able to find their own path—their own passions and interests—so that they can connect to networks of like-minded people, come together and collaborate, and open up new areas of research and investigation. I think that in any sort of crisis, there's opportunity. I think that the best possible opportunity that could come out of this is that, maybe before, people were a little bit intimidated to go up and approach somebody in person, like a prof, and ask them questions, but I hope that now they will feel a little bit more comfortable doing that online. It will allow for people to really find their niche in design, or in whatever field they happen to be in, and to find access to the resources and the people who can help them learn and achieve some really cool stuff. The technologies for automation and distributed manufacturing and those sorts of things are only accelerating because of this current situation. While it might feel at times that life is on hold, it's moving forward very rapidly. It's important that we stay on top of it and keep working all the time.

MM *Absolutely. I think it's really interesting that you touched on that comfort level, or layer of safety, that comes with being in your own home, and that people are able to take advantage of all these things that are now readily available. These are great positives for sure. So, Guy, you've answered all the questions I had. Is there anything else you want to add to the conversation?*

GG I just wanted to say thanks to TALON—to you guys—for taking the time and taking on this extra responsibility, in the midst of all this. It is appreciated.

## REFLECTION

Since this interview I've learned that we will be returning to in-person classes this Fall, and I am looking forward to it. Despite our best efforts, I'll be the first to admit that remote instruction isn't the same, at least for the type of content I teach. In the interview, I focused a lot on the opportunities provided by technology, but I think it's also important to acknowledge the difficulties we've all faced over the last eighteen months.

There are so many technical challenges that interrupt the normal flow of information and interaction; delays that set things back; and, an occasional lack of engagement or sense of apathy. I think students, instructors and everyone involved has done their best to try to deliver a positive experience, but at times it has felt … remote.

One thing that this year has reinforced for me is the irreplaceable importance of real, tangible sensations and experiences; spending time with friends and colleagues after a long separation and being able to examine details with all the senses and experiencing presence.

As things ramp back up in the coming year, I hope we take forward the important lessons from this pandemic. I hope we continue to refine and share the tools and skills we've found and built to improve access, remove barriers, and share information. Most of all, I hope we maintain a sense of empathy, compassion and understanding of our connectedness to those both near and far.

ABOUT

**Guy Gardner** is an instructor in building science, architectural robotics and computational design at the University of Calgary School of Architecture, Planning and Landscape, and is the director of fabrication with the Laboratory for Integrative Design. His design research explores the intersections of technology, art and architecture, with a focus of design-build and learning through making. He has extensive experience in digital design and fabrication and has collaborated on a variety of residential, public space design and community art projects in Alberta.

# Lisa K. Forbes & David Thomas

Lisa K. Forbes: Assistant Clinical Professor, Counseling Program, University of Colorado Denver, United States

David Thomas: Executive Director of Online Programs, University of Denver, United States and Assistant Professor Attendant, Department of Architecture, University of Colorado Denver, United States

Lisa and David are founders of the Professors at Play community project, online at professorsatplay.org

Interviewed December 2020 by *Sandra Abegglen*

SA *David and Lisa—would you like to say a few words about yourselves and in particular what you're working on at the moment?*

DT As a guy who's been in the online business for a long time, of course I'm busy trying to cope with the reality of everyone being online now. That's been interesting, but in terms of the play work, there are different threads of it for me. One thread I've worked on for a long time has been how to be more playful at work and in organizations. Lisa and I have been working together on this community called Professors at Play, and it's really intersected in surprising and meaningful ways with the whole shift to online learning.

LF Yeah, so I mean, your intro summarized everything. Play therapy is therapy for kids aged 3–12. I do research with intensive mothering practices, trying to change the narratives around motherhood in our culture. David and I met about two years ago, and ever since then we've been trying to meet frequently and talk about play, fun, and teaching. At first, neither of us knew what that looked like or how to do it.

Over the past two years, we've really been working on implementing that in the classroom. This spring, I did a research study on my own teaching practices of bringing play into my teaching, and then this summer we started Professors at Play. Five months later we have almost 600 members in our community—it's just blown up. I think playfulness can be a nice tool to help us be better at our jobs by not being so rigid.

SA *That's very insightful because I how I found you is through the Professors at Play website. Was it started out of the move to remote teaching and learning?*

LF No, it honestly didn't have anything to do with the remote teaching at the time. David and I would come across people who were really interested in play and learning, so we would set up meetings with them and just chat. After each of those meetings we'd say, we should keep connected. Let's see if we can get more people involved and keep the conversation going. We wanted to start a **Listserv** to have somewhere where we could all keep that conversation happening, and it just so happened that it was during the middle of COVID. I think there are a lot of people that joined Professors at Play because they were naturally playful or they'd already been doing this in the classroom, but I also think the majority of people joined because they were struggling with this abrupt shift to digital teaching and learning.

DT When Lisa and I met, I was very focused on the aesthetics of fun, and how it applied to games. Then I realized that the business community were very interested in being more playful. Even though my professional career was teaching and supporting teachers in this online stuff, when I met with Lisa, she said, so how do you make teaching more playful? I'm like, no, teaching is over here, play is over here. Lisa said, no, that's not going to work. I want to know how to do more playful teaching. I said, well, I don't know how to do that, but I'll go with you, let's find out.

So I think that our adventure together, being fearless about how play can change teaching, really was the same story as Professors at Play. We just did it because we wanted to stay in touch with people, and then COVID created a moment in time where there was a crucible of thinking about your teaching. All of a sudden, teaching came to the forefront. Professors, for the first time in a long time, were wondering: Am I engaging my students? Professors at Play was like this light that conveyed that, well, we don't know how to do it either, but come and join us while we figure it out. That's really the heart of Professors at Play. It's an intervention to say, yeah, this just sucks, let's have some fun while we figure it out—and that's where we are right now. Through creating this project, we've mastered a lot of research and a lot of experience. I don't want to sell it short, but Professors at Play really is just a project of pure joy.

*SA* *For those who aren't familiar, could you tell us a little more about Professors at Play?*

LF It's picked up quite quickly. I imagine a tiny snowball at the top of the hill just rolling down, picking up all this snow. It's this huge, massive thing now compared to five months ago. We started the website that you saw, Sandra, where we have a blog and a resource page. We also started with a LISTSERV, which included around 600 people. David and I thought, well, if we have all these people, we've got to do something. So why don't we hold a virtual Playposium? We held that in November, and we had 361 people register. Right before the Playposium someone said, what's the hashtag for the Playposium for social media? And we were like, we don't have social media. We then set up accounts for **Facebook**, **Instagram**, and **Twitter**. We recorded all of our sessions at the Playposium so then we had to have a **YouTube** channel. It's as though the next step just unfolded without us really planning it. It was just the next right thing to do and we created it.

DT Now there's been some demand for additional speakers, so we're actually starting programming for ongoing workshops and talks. Now we're starting to realize that there are all these affiliate organizations, such as the Strong Museum of Play, and we're finding other associations and play researchers. The goal now is to build a bigger network so that we're additive and not just duplicative of things that are going on. So really, I think when Lisa says it's a snowball, the snowball is not even halfway down the hill. It's still gathering speed.

*SA* *I'm curious to know, how do you bring play and fun into your practice?*

DT Lisa is the tip of the spear of these interventions.

LF It's a complicated answer, I would say, first, there is play as an activity. For instance, you could do a game in class, or you could do a playful activity to teach a concept. Then there is just playfulness. That's a way of presenting yourself, reducing the hierarchy between faculty and students, making it more of a safe learning environment where their stress is reduced, and a whole bunch of other elements that go into that. I think it's multi-layered. Part of play can be things like ice breakers. I call them connection formers because I don't like the term ice breakers. I think it has a negative connotation. I call them connection formers because that's what they do. They connect people and they reduce stress. At the start of almost every class, I'll do some type of fun activity that really has no connection to the content. The whole purpose is just to get people in the learning space forgetting about their stressful day and connecting with each other. In my study, the students said that it reduced their stress, and it was like a form of self-care. They felt like they were centred and they could actually approach the heavy topics better because they had that moment of levity. I think that's one way of being playful, but it has no relation to the content at all. Faculty often miss that stuff because they aren't aware of the value of it, as it's not connected to the learning, and they have learning objectives to hit. I think that's an unfortunate thing because I saw from my study what an impact those things have—even if they're not directly related to the content—on the learning process that comes after that. Then there is play that you can design within your class to teach the content. Maybe it's a playful discussion or a game that you've created to really teach that content for that day.

In our Playposium, we had one faculty member named Roberto Corrada. He's a law professor and he does this entire course play where he has the students read *Jurassic Park*. They have to come up with laws and strategy for protecting ... what is it?

DT Extinct animal parks.

LF Extinct animal parks. It's just genius, and that goes across the span of the entire course. So, there are little things that you can do, and there are larger things you can do. It's a complicated type of answer, but that's how I conceptualize it.

DT One thing Lisa said is that some people naturally embody it, but what sometimes people miss is that the professors themselves need to be playful. I mean, we've all been through the whole thing of establishing your social presence at the beginning of class by showing a picture of your dog, and then it's all business. I think that the professors that we connect with the most have a natural playfulness. They invite the students to engage with them, and that really is play, even though it's not what we think of as play.

As I reflect back to before Lisa and I started working on this, I've always been a playful professor. Some of that's just my nature and who I am. Some of that is my gender and my privilege. It's just easy for me to be like, hey, I can be a little looser than my students because they're younger than I am and I'm an old white guy. What became interesting to me is that there's a baseline. You have to enter the classroom with a playfulness and then the techniques really start to pay off. I think sometimes if you divorce the techniques from the playfulness, it really does feel like forced fun. Like why are we doing this? It's like when you do these jeopardy games and then the rest of class is stressful. The jeopardy game isn't inherently going to unlock playfulness in your class. Your approach is your mindset.

LF Yeah, I think that's a good point. I teach mental health counselling and, to cut a long story short, there's this research called Common Factors. It basically says, well, there are five hundred different counselling theories, and more than that, really. How come it doesn't really matter which one you use? Therapy can be effective no matter what the approach is. So what is it that makes therapy effective? Common Factors research has found that the most influential factor in successful therapy is the strength of the therapeutic relationship. I believe it's the same thing in teaching. If you have a strong relationship with your students, the techniques and the tools are going to be much more effective. I think it speaks to what David was saying in that if you have play without playfulness, there's a disconnect and students don't grasp on to that.

DT This is where I have to set Lisa up and say that I think she has a very elegant observational model of how play unlocks in these levels. I'd love for her to share it because when she structured what she was doing in this model, all of a sudden I realized that play is not just the sugar that helps the medicine go down. Play is fundamental to these human practices.

LF I think what David is talking about is ... before I started my research project, I had this theory of how play was meaningful in the class environment, where if you played and had fun, then people started laughing and connecting and creating that bond and community. When there's a sense of community and connection, people are going to be more comfortable and more likely to be willing to be vulnerable. When we're more willing to be vulnerable, we're more likely to take risks, and when we're more likely to take risks, we're more likely to fail. Failing leads to longer lasting learning. So that was the model I had worked up in my head. It's just my research, and the model that I designed out of my research is more complex. It's hard to explain verbally, but that's the gist of it.

DT Lisa has this theoretical model, which I love because I think it's just so good at describing things. Then she's got the research model—the model that actually came out of the research—the more complex model. What I love about it is that it gets people away from the idea that play is just this little bit of delight that you drop into some otherwise painful process. Instead it says, no, this is a healing practice. This is how people connect in human bonds, and through those bonds of community you're willing to risk and explore and think and engage. Play is actually a very human mode of mode of inquiry and understanding, and it's just motivating on the inside.

I'm like, why didn't someone tell me that a long time ago? The work that Lisa has done to bring that to bear in a psychological language has really enlivened all the work that I've done, which has been more about aesthetics and how it looks, how it works, how to recognize it and how to talk about it. It's been a wonderful symmetry of how our approaches work together.

LF It was a qualitative study, so there were a lot of their experiences of play. So you start with playfulness and play, where I talk about laughter, fun, novelty, and excitement, and how it removes barriers and reduces stress, anxiety, and fear. It puts you in a place to learn and approach the seriousness from a more centred place. At the same time, it creates those relationships in that sense belonging, which I call relational safety, because it creates trust. Then from there it awakens intrinsic motivation, where students said they were more focused on the learning process instead of grades like they normally are. They actually enjoyed coming to class and they enjoyed the challenge. Class felt intriguing and exciting and energetic, and they just felt more motivated to learn. That was huge to hear, because that's always been everything I've tried to get from my students. From there it's like this vulnerable engagement where they're highly engaged in the class and activities. It's hands-on and interactive. I don't lecture at people very often, and so within that, peoplc are doing things, trying things, and taking risks. They're open to feedback. This relates back to the idea of relational safety, because if you have a strong relationship with your students, you can give them just about any feedback and they're more likely to be able to hear it. From there, learning is enhanced. I think when I first started this journey, I thought, okay, I'm going

*"... Play is not just the sugar that helps the medicine go down. Play is fundamental to these human practices."*

David Thomas

to make my class more fun and playful and it's going to create better learning outcomes. I didn't realize all this in the middle of these four steps; I think I wasn't quite sure how those are all connected. So that's the visual that keeps me going. I mean, play is hard to do, and my experience is that people don't take it seriously a lot of the time, and sometimes I'll get flack for it. When I look back at that model, I know it works. I'm going to keep on going because I know that for students, it really matters to them.

SA *What has your experience been with playful practice, now that most of us are teaching and learning remotely?*

LF I think being online has actually opened up more opportunities for play in terms of creatively thinking of playful approaches. Before, when I was teaching in-person, I was confined to the walls of the classroom and the perimeter of the university. We're now teaching digitally, and I have the physical environment of each student's home where they can get up, move, and go and get things. I also have access to the entire web and when we're learning digitally, all of the students are on the Internet. So these ideas have expanded in that way.

In a sense, being online is more challenging because it's harder to make interpersonal connections, and so I think that digitally teaching play is even more important than teaching play in in-person learning. It's more important, but it's also harder because it's more difficult to connect through a computer screen, obviously. I think there are some limitations to the model I showed you in terms of the deep level of connection, because I don't know that I'm getting as deep a sense of belonging in my digital classes than I was in my in-person classes. But my students have classes where there's no play and it's just lectures over **Zoom**, and that's hard for them I think. So it's important, but it is harder digitally.

DT I think that when we moved online, it ripped away the veil of "I'm a good teacher." We were pretty naked on Zoom because I can talk in a classroom and I can feel like I'm doing pretty well and keeping people's attention. On Zoom, I'm basically a radio DJ. I'm talking to the screen. There's no feedback.

I think this put teachers in a state of shock ... that they weren't as engaging as they thought they were. I'll tell you that in a classroom say of thirty students, if I can engage half the class, I'm going to feel like the class is engaged. If I'm online and I'm only engaging half the class, I'm looking at fifteen Zoom cameras turned off. All of a sudden we can see the absence that's always been there. If I can get the class to laugh, everyone benefits. It just raises the mood for everyone. Online, if I've got thirty people laughing independently with their microphones off, everyone's isolated. I agree with Lisa. It's simultaneously easier and harder in different ways.

This is where I wanted to tie in Professors at Play, where we just don't know how to do this online thing. I don't think students know how, and I don't think we know how. We're still inventing, and I think that's why people started flocking to Professors at Play, because at least there were people offering methodologies for engaging students in things like crazy ice breakers, escape rooms, funny quiz shows, and full class simulations. All of a sudden we were like, shoot, if I'm going to be trapped in this little Zoom box, I might as well try some of this stuff out. So, I think it's an exciting time to be doing this, and I don't know that playfulness would have been as present in people's minds if they were just doing the same old class, telling the same old jokes, and doing the same old activities.

LF I don't want to make assumptions, but I think another piece is that it is common for faculty to have perfected their classes that they've taught in-person over decades, sometimes, and maybe they do tweaks here and there but generally they have it down. In moving to online and digital teaching, they had to shift completely what they had been doing for so long. Personally, I found it to be an opportunity to try some things differently, shake it up, and step outside the box a little bit because I was having to redo everything anyway to put it online synchronously and asynchronously. I think it was a huge opportunity to just do something different and expand. Hopefully people are seeing that play is a way to do that.

DT And I want to emphasize again, that we're in this too, it's not like we've figured this out. We've just committed ourselves to playing through this mess. This summer, I taught an architecture course that was normally a hybrid class, but this time it was delivered fully online. I found myself facing some of these same struggles and I was doing a lot of things wrong. Lisa's always in the background saying, you should do more of these wacky things. You should do more of these fun things. I'm like, I'm trying to, but I get international students, and these architecture students are a pretty serious bunch. At the end of the whole thing, I did a lot of fun stuff. And by the way, I should tell you, the class was the architecture of fun. So it's a ringer. Like, my class is going to be fun because of its subject matter. At the end I'm reading through the course feedback, and it's just like, we love the wacky activities, we wish there would have been more of them. I learned my lesson, which was that I wasn't brave enough.

LF Or, just listen to Lisa.

DT Yeah. I should just listen to Lisa.

*SA On that note, are there favourite online tools that you use?*

LF I've found that for the connection-forming type of activities, if you just **Google** free computer games, there's a bunch of ideas. Have you seen **Flappy Birds**? It's a free computer game and it's totally pointless. It's just this little bird and you press the spacebar and there's these breaks in the pipes and you have to get the bird to fly through the pipes. It's really hard to do. Most people can't get past level one or two. In the chat box I'll send the students a link to that website. And I'll say, "Open this up. You have three minutes. Whoever gets the highest score at the end of three minutes wins." It's totally just for relaxation, fun and play. I have them unmute themselves if they are okay with that, and the laughter that comes from that is just so heartwarming.

There's this other one. David found a website and it's ... I can't remember the name of it, but it has to be thousands of questions and you just scroll for minutes. I call it "scrolly questions." I'll send the students into small breakout rooms and give them the link. I'll say, one person, share your screen and be the scroller. The person starts scrolling and then whoever's turn it is, say stop randomly. Whatever question the little cursor lands on, you have to answer the question and then just take turns scrolling and answering questions. It seems goofy, but I go around between breakout rooms, and I hear the students having the most connecting conversations that I've ever heard in a classroom situation. Normally our icebreaker questions are kind of surface level, but these are such random questions that it gets into these facets of the students' lives that would never have come out in a classroom otherwise. What are some other ones we've tried, David?

DT I like breakout rooms with weird objectives. For instance, I would send people to a breakout room and say, don't come back until you've found something that you all agree that you don't like. Instead of saying, hey, talk about your favourite place to go for vacation, they come back and they're like, none of us like tomatoes. Who knew? It humanizes people. You're asking about tools, and I think that's what's interesting is that play transcends the tools.

LF I think that's a good point. Mainly I use Zoom because I think you can get better interactions within that. At least that's what I've found. Within Zoom you can post links in the chat box and then they're off into a different cyberspace world. It's like constantly changing the virtual environment, so that they're not doing one thing for too long. I think that's useful. You can use **Google Docs** within that and **Flipgrid**, and within that you can use **Google Forms**. I create escape rooms through Google Forms. I'll send them to smaller group breakout rooms and give them the link to the escape room, and they have to break through all the locks in order to re-enter the main classroom. If they break the final lock, there's a secret pass code to get back in the main Zoom room.

To me, it's less about using a bunch of different tools and more about creating that connection and being creative within Zoom. There's so much you can do that I had no idea about five, six months ago and it's really just about trying things out, breaking the norm, and breaking the status quo of what teaching is in my mind, and just doing it differently to see what works.

SA *Sounds interesting, I especially like the idea that you need a code to come back to class. Rather than the idea that you have to be here right now in this Zoom class; it's reversing the idea where class becomes a desirable space to be—you need to work hard through this fun activity to come back to class.*

LF It's so funny because the secret code I had for the last one I did was "bananas." So the winning group and all the others come in, and we're all just waiting for the last group to finally come back. When people are connecting to Zoom, their camera comes up and then it says the audio is connecting. So you can see people joining the class again, and then they say, "Bananas!" And they're like, oh, because they realized they were the last ones. It's so fun.

SA *Where do you get your inspiration from for things like this?*

LF I'm on a rampage, so I'm surrounded by a bunch of playbooks that I've ordered by a number of different authors, and I'm just reading as much as I can. The Professors at Play community has been really inspiring, especially our Playposium. By the end of that day, I was so overwhelmed with amazing, playful ideas that I needed to go back through the videos because it was just so much. I get inspiration from just connecting with certain people here and there who have a different angle on play, because play means so many different things. I think my whole life I've always really hated traditions, normalcy, and the status quo. When I get to break the rules a little bit, it feels really invigorating for me. There's this internal sense of inspiration that comes when I just get to bend the normal teaching practices, at least that I've been taught and modelled. I'd say for sure that David has been a huge inspiration for me as well. When I first knew that this was a possibility, I went to one of his workshops on wacky workplaces or play in higher ed, and since then he's really been a guiding light in this for me. It's been nice to have him by my side.

DT Yeah, I mean, my answer is almost identical to Lisa's. I've been an academic researcher of fun for a long time. My colleague from New York University, John Sharp, and I wrote a book about the aesthetics of fun and I've been really heady about this stuff. But then watching Lisa teach these classes and just seeing the students explode with delight, all of a sudden I was just like, this is interesting to me. I love idiosyncratic architecture. I love weird stuff. I was just very removed from it. My joke at all of these talks is that, as my wife would say, how can you be the professor of fun when you're the least fun guy I know? I say, I don't like to have fun. I just like to think about it. But through the Professors at Play work and working with Lisa watching people come alive to play, all of a sudden it was just like, wait, this thing that I know a lot about matters. And so it's been really wonderful. At the heart of it, I agree with Lisa. It's like we have built this energy between us that says, this is okay, this is good, this is awesome. Look at the things that it's done. I think that's what Professors at Play is, because I agree one hundred percent that watching all of the presenters from all over the world, I'm like "This is so great! Why don't more people do this?" We've got to get more people talking to us. Every time I meet someone that's doing something and making it work, I just get more excited to keep trying and keep doing more.

There are lots of books on theory, practice, all the gamification stuff, all of that. There's so much out there but it's not in a curriculum yet so it's hard to find. That's the other component of Professors at Play that we work really hard on, which is to try to point people to things like, hey, here's this random book from game studies. Here's Miguel Sicart writing about the ethics of play. If you read the book, it's so relevant to teaching with play. Here's Stewart Brown. This guy writes about why playfulness is important for creating a happy life. Well, read that book too because it's about teaching it. I think that we're just starting to find all these common threads and trying to put them in a place for people to be able to use them.

LF I think for me, it's really been the community. When I first saw David talk and then he and I started talking, we found random people here or there that were interested in this too. Before this, at times I felt like he and I were the only people who were into it. Sometimes I've felt that when I talk about play in teaching, a lot of faculty are like, that's cute. I started to keep it to myself and not tell people what I was doing in the classroom, and so in meeting David, it was like I was given permission to play. Now, every time I talk to somebody in the community or go to a workshop or the Playposium, it's just gives me more fire. It's like, yes, we're a community. There are people doing this. People have been doing this all along, I just had no idea, and there are pouches of people everywhere. It's inspiring to me that the community is getting bigger and bigger.

DT I'd also go back to student feedback. I mean, when you see students all lit up and they're thanking you for teaching and you're like, WTF? Why haven't I been doing that all along? Then I think that you get inspiration from success, and you get hungry, where you're like, I want to do more of this.

*SA So on that note, where do you think that higher education is going in the next decade, and where do you hope it will be going? These may or may not be the same thing.*

DT Well, here's the thing. I've spent a lot of time thinking about the future of higher ed because in a certain sense, that's what I'm part of all this online stuff. I think the future of higher ed is going to be a lot more technologically mediated, and a lot more networked. I think that the era of the closed classroom and the professor as the expert is coming to a close, and that has been hastened by COVID.

Students are going to become empowered, so I think that the role of the professor is going to have to change. Whether or not you like the word play, I always say that play has these two connotations in English. On the one hand, it's child's play, like goofing around. On the other hand, is like mechanical play, where there's a sort of looseness. Really the word means both things. It means moving things around and seeing how they fit together. I think that professors are being forced into a playful pose because students are like, I can look up a lecture, I don't need to sit here and listen to you lecture to me. I want you to help me play with these ideas and put them together and learn the practice of thinking the way you do. So, because of COVID, I think that the future of higher education is going in that direction. I'm kind of hopeful that that will happen as well.

There's another line of conversation here that could be very, very deep, which is that play upturns hierarchy. Higher ed is built on hierarchy. Who knows the most? What's your institution's ranking? What's your GPA? Play is reflective, and COVID is upturning things, and I think play is a response.

When we talk about decolonizing the curriculum or we start talking about racial justice, I don't think higher ed is ready for these things. I think it wants to be ready for it, but I don't think it is, and so I think that something really weird is going to happen. I don't know what that is, but I am pretty convinced that the idea of the fool who doesn't know the danger and just marches through all the chaos may be the emblem that we need. That's what I'm hopeful for. I'm hopeful that we can play ourselves out of this mess.

LF I think the obvious answer is that it's going to become more digital. I think it's been headed that way and COVID has definitely advanced the stages of that. What I think is going to happen is that in ten years, not much will be different, maybe it'll just be more digital. In terms of the hierarchy or the status quo in terms of what a faculty member is, I think those things are probably going to stay the same. That's just the skepticism in me. I was doing some reading for one of the manuscripts I'm writing up right now, and there are a couple of sources that talk about pedagogy. This hierarchical, listen-to-me, lecture-based approach, it's like five hundred years old. There is research more recently that says, hey, that's not the most effective way to teach. But at the same time, faculty sometimes struggle to adopt a more playful or a more hands-on engaging style, and I think that's because we are so used to teaching in this lecture-based format.

I mean, in all of my years in undergrad and graduate programs, that was how I was taught. Now as a faculty member ... it's easy to just do what those modelled to you. I think it's hard for people to think outside the box. I wrote one of our blog posts that said academia killed my creativity, because I think you're just recruited into this traditional way of thinking and being in this status quo. It's really hard to do something outside of that because your creative mind is shrivelled. Also, I think it's scary to do something new and different because you can get a lot of criticism for that—like doing playful things. People say play is trivial, play is a waste of time. My class is too serious for play. There's a lot of skepticism, so if you do it, it's a risk, and I think it takes a lot of energy to rethink teaching in that way.

The other thing that I have to disagree with David on is that students want this more playful approach. I partly agree, but also when I asked my students at the very start of the semester what their thoughts about play and teaching and learning were, they said, well, I don't know how that's going to work because how are you going to get a bunch of grad students to get up and move around the classroom? One student said, I'm not really looking forward to it because I just want to sit there. The lazy student in me just wants to listen to a lecture and take notes. That same student then said, but I don't learn very well that way and I know that about myself, so I know that playful learning will probably be better. I think that student was just saying, my brain is so conditioned to be lectured at. Sometimes students will push back against that, and

*"In 10 years, I hope that higher education will be really playful, and a space where faculty have more time to be innovative and creative in their approaches. I do not believe it is wise to maintain status quos for over 500 years. Things change, the students change, and the things we are teaching change."*

Lisa K. Forbes

I believe the reason for this is due to the concept of neuroplasticity, where what you do every day creates strong neural pathways in your brain. If you're lectured at for decades, that's the way that you feel the most comfortable learning. So of course, when a faculty member stops lecturing and uses play, you're going to be like, wait, what? This is weird to me. Where is the rubric? What do I write down from my notes? I think it's like a little bit of faculty being recruited into teaching a certain way, and I think it's also pressure from students, as if they just want to take their notes and take a test and leave. Sometimes I think maybe it's just because they're used to it.

In ten years, I hope that higher education will be really playful, and a space where faculty have more time to be innovative and creative in their approaches. I don't believe it is wise to maintain status quos for over five hundred years. Things change, the students change, and the things we're teaching change. I'm hopeful that it'll look different. I just worry that going against the status quo is going to be a little too much ... and hence we won't.

DT One of the things I'd add to that is if you think about the last decade or so, the **iPhone** was released thirteen years ago. I mean, the world is different with smartphones. It's just different. I think that COVID may have been that moment in higher education. It's different now. I just don't think that we realize it yet, like we're living in the future and it's going to take us a while to recognize that. Some parts of the university world are going to die fighting for the old way, but I think it's already changing.

I'll give you a quick example. We have a pretty respected music school. Of all things, what can you not teach online? Music. Well, they found out that their opera singers could train with Metropolitan Opera singers in New York City because the opera singers were not busy doing opera, so they had the time. These music professors are already thinking, well, of course, I want to get back into the studio. I want to work with people in person. But, boy, I've got to hang on to this online stuff. I find that so exciting because I think, wait, the future is already here. One year ago, that was impossible, and now that's just the way things are going to be. So, I'm mostly pretty positive and excited, but I do maintain that play is an important component in all of this.

*SA What words of advice would you give to those thinking about integrating play into their teaching practice?*

LF I'm a mental health counsellor, so I think you can give somebody all the tools and resources in the world, and sometimes that won't help because there is an underlying issue or a barrier that keeps people from being able to access those things or see the usefulness in them. So, my advice would be, take some time to reflect on the narratives of higher education, and the narratives of what being a faculty member means to you. For example, what is the status quo that we are upholding and what part of that can you change? When I did that for myself, I realized that the traditional form of lecture-based hierarchical teaching—where I'm the expert standing telling you all of the facts—was not working for me. It was draining. It was leaving me feeling disillusioned about teaching in higher education. Once I was able to see how that's one narrative of teaching, I knew that I needed to create my own narrative.

What works for me is more in line with who I am as a human, and that is just being more free and playful and not taking myself so seriously, because I have a hard time doing that. My advice is to try deconstructing those dominant narratives that have been taught to us for generations, and choosing for yourself which direction you want to go in.

Then it is a matter of figuring out what that means to you in the classroom. How it looks for me is different than how it looks for David and everyone else. It's like personalizing play. I think of it on a continuum of not trying it at all and going way too far. Where can you take one little, tiny step with play? Maybe it's doing an icebreaker and seeing how that works. Take tiny steps because it can feel daunting and overwhelming. So, that's a long answer but I would just say to everyone, go to therapy and talk about the barriers that keep you from being playful and just don't take yourself too seriously.

DT My answer is similar. One of the things that I've been looking at for a while now with Lisa is what I call "the fun wall," and she just calls it shame. People have that experience where you want to try new things but you're afraid. You finally get you up the courage and do it and you're like, wow, that was really fun. People tend to be that way. They have shame and think that they're going to look stupid or they're going to mess up or they're not going to be any good, and it's doubled down for professors. There's no room for error. It's the idea that I am the master of my domain. For anyone that wants to become more playful in their teaching and unlock some of this, you've got to get over that wall. For some people, just telling them that the wall exists, and they'll plough through it because they're stubborn.

As Lisa says, one thing to start with is to pick something easy. If you've never done anything before, sure, do the dumb jeopardy game. It's like the lowest form of play in the classroom, but that gets you started. I'd say find someone that you know in your discipline, or even not in your discipline, that's going to egg you on to go do things. One of the best parts of the Playposium was watching people that I knew had never done any of these things before get so excited watching someone say, "Well, I teach my whole class like this." You could just see the key unlock. If they can do it, I can do it. A lot of it is simply modelling and exposure, but at the end of the day, I think it's just about going out and doing it. I think it's got doubly hard because in a way, we've got used to Zoom. Here's the length, here's the syllabus, here's the lecture. I think it might also start with doing something to break yourself out of complacency.

I have another friend who has nothing to do with teaching. He's a crazy guy that does all of these wonderful, weird events and stuff. He and I were talking about writing a book called "Prank Yourself," about the idea of doing things that make your life more weird and complicated just to break yourself out of complacency. So I would also say that I think if nothing else, even if you're going to do it in your classroom, start pranking yourself. For instance, every day before you go to class, pick a random word out of the dictionary and you have to figure out how to work that word into your lecture. Just do it for yourself. If you're a little braver, tell the class you're doing it and see if they can figure out what the word is.

LF I think it's just about overcoming your fears. I still get nervous about doing playful things. The first time I really tried to do something different, it was a game where I had questions on these little Post-it Notes and I put them down on the table. This was in person before COVID. I gave each of the students those sticky hands—you know, those things for kids, they're all gooey and elastic and they look like a hand and you can fling them. So I gave each of them a sticky hand and they had to come up to the front of the class, do an intro and say their name and what track they were in. Then they'd slap a card with the sticky hand card and whatever card flung back at them, they'd have to answer. It's the most hilarious game, but the first time I did it, my hands were shaking because I was so nervous. Then I remembered David in the back of my head and thought to myself, he's going to ask me how it went after class ... I have to do it. And so I did! I think each time it's going to feel uncomfortable, but you just need to have that person who's going to be your accountability partner; find the courage within yourself and take some risks.

## REFLECTION

Our understanding of play in learning seems to constantly evolve. It started with the idea that learning shouldn't be a drag and that joy makes learning more meaningful and memorable. As we have continued to engage in this work, we have realized that play in learning *is* about fun and joy and making learning stick but it's also about changing the underlying foundation of academia. If anything, since the interview we have become more convinced of, and increasingly bold, about proclaiming the power of play.

We believe that for many faculty, the pandemic was a big push and an invitation to *play* with their teaching. Overnight, academics were forced to drastically alter their methods of delivery—it was not only a necessary task, it provided encouragement and freedom to play around with what we do. It seemed as though faculty suddenly had more motivation to seek out new ideas for delivery and techniques for student engagement. Perhaps more were open to playing and the idea of play in teaching because the timing was right.

Through our work with Professors at Play and our own pandemic-induced re-focusing of teaching, our vision has focused on a possible "playvolution," which we see as a powerful and playful movement that reimagines higher education by breaking the boundaries and bending the rules. Play is at the centre of the playvolution 1) as a way of being: not taking ourselves so seriously; 2) as an activity: harnessing the power of play in learning; and 3) as a philosophy: playing with the status quo to break and then remake learning to be more flexible, inclusive, and expansive.

So, play can be things you do in the classroom, techniques—but it is also more than that. It is also a frame of mind, a way of being and an approach to teaching. The playvolution is about approaching teaching differently all together. And that's where we intersect with some of the brightest scholars of educational reform—playing with the status quo to "create new."

We are hopeful that the pandemic has inadvertently catapulted us into a more playful and flexible future of higher education. We hope that Professors at Play can be a social support and think tank for faculty to continue to play with their teaching. We will continue to offer blogs, workshops, symposiums, and potentially future publications centring around:

- The Ethics of Play: Transforming culture;
- The Playful Professor: Becoming a playful person in the professoriate;
- The Playful Classroom: Teaching your students to play/through play (techniques);
- The Playvolution: Changing higher education.

As we look ahead, we see more opportunities to bring smiles to faces, share ideas, and change how people think about the work we do in academia. What started out as a research project has quickly turned into a life mission!

ABOUT

**David Thomas**, Ph.D. is the executive director of online programs at the University of Denver and assistant professor attendant in the Department of Architecture at the University of Colorado Denver. His research centres around fun, fun objects (like buildings!) and the meaning of play.

**Lisa K. Forbes**, PhD. is an assistant clinical professor in the Counselling Program at the University of Colorado Denver. Lisa is a licensed professional counsellor and is training to become a registered play therapist. Lisa teaches counselling techniques, counselling children/adolescents, counselling practicum, and internship. Lisa's research centres around play in learning in higher education settings as well as intensive mothering ideology, gender conformity, and mental health.

# David Gauntlett

Canada Research Chair in Creativity, Faculty of Communication and Design, Ryerson University, Canada

Interviewed December 2020 by *Sandra Abegglen*

*SA* *David, thanks for joining us. Can you tell us who you are and what you do?*

DG I am Canada research chair in creativity at Ryerson University in the Faculty of Communication and Design. I moved to Canada about two and half years ago from the UK, where I previously worked in a number of roles and had been a professor for many years.

*SA* *How does your teaching look in 2020 compared to before the switch to emergency remote learning?*

DG When the lockdown began, it was right around my birthday, which is March 15. At that point, I was in the middle of teaching an MA class called Creativity, Identity and Making Things Happen. The course began in January, and it was held in person. There were about twenty students in the class and I got to know them because we'd been having very nice in-class sessions where we were doing collaborative workshop-style activities together. I would bring in different kinds of creative materials so we could build metaphors about our thoughts and reflections on different topics. I would stand at the front of the class with big sheets of paper and coloured pens and I'd physically map out the exercises with the students. Then COVID happened and, all of a sudden, we had to switch to doing the last few of these online. Because we knew each other already it was fine, and we were able to work it out so that we could do similar exercises, just with the class all apart from one another, working remotely.

Wrapping up that class online went okay, but then with all the time between the end of Winter and start of the Fall semester, I had to consider how I'd translate my next class to be taught online. That one is an undergraduate course called Your Creative Self, which I had taught once before. It's built to be very hands-on, workshop style, with everybody in the classroom together. I don't lecture much in that course; rather I turn up to class with different materials each time to lead the students in different reflective exercises. The students and I find a lot of joy in this method and the environment it creates to share our creative experiences with one another. When COVID happened and everything switched to remote teaching, I thought that the transition with this course was going to be really terrible. I thought, how would I be able to recreate this experience online?

To add to the complexity, the course was meant to be capped at sixty students but because of an error in registration, there ended up being ninety students enrolled. Ninety students was already too many for one class in person and I remember thinking that ninety students on **Zoom** was going to be a serious challenge. But what can you do? That was just the situation we were in. I had a lightbulb moment maybe three or four weeks before the start of the course when for some reason I just thought, "Let's embrace this." I came to the realization that the only thing you can do is just try to make the best of it. I thought, I'll just try to maximize this time and pretend that the course was always meant to be taught this way. I developed the mindset of, let's make it great. But of course, that is easier said than done. It's not a very clever thought, really, but making the best of the situation was just how I went about it. I simply put effort into being happy and embracing this thing and ignoring the fact that I actually thought it was kind of awful. There was not much point focusing on how awful it was, because we already knew it was awful.

Of course, I wanted to be sympathetic to the students because I anticipated that they were going to come into class having difficulties. They might have recently been bereaved, they might be feeling very anxious in these times, all of that. So, I wouldn't force them to be cheerful about COVID, but I would just teach them as if the class was meant to be delivered online. It worked out as a good plan, and I am actually quite enjoying it. The students seem to like it too.

One thing, however, is that I'm always very aware of the fact that as the instructor, by definition, I'm at the centre of the experience of ninety students on Zoom. Due to the nature of the large class size and the online delivery, the class may be paying attention, or they may be doing something else on their computer at the same time. They might have actually switched off and I don't really know, because half of them have their cameras on and the other half are just black boxes on my screen. I know you can't really force them to put their cameras on, but obviously I much prefer it when I can see everyone. As the instructor in a classroom we expect to be able to see the students as we're teaching them. The fact that you can't see the students' faces half of the time is definitely weird, because who knows what their experience is.

I just keep the energy level high and if I have people interacting with me and we have some good, interesting conversations, then I get a good feeling that it's going well. The number of students who actually talk to me in any of the three-hour sessions is maybe twenty out of the ninety students, which isn't bad, but I don't like to think about the fact that this number is not the majority. I figure at the very least, I know they're there. And you have to consider that online there are different ways to communicate as well—like how the students participate in the chat more than they like to actually speak up. With the high level of interaction in the chat I know that the students are present and paying attention.

SA *How do you bring in the creative aspects of that course online?*

DG I still get the class to do creative exercises and activities, but the big difference online is that I can't use a variety of physical materials as I did in class. It would be exclusionary because some people would have access to these materials and some people wouldn't. I didn't want to have to send the students to their local Dollarama store, so the exercises tend to be things that the students can do on paper.

The activities typically involve drawing and writing on their paper while I give step-by-step instructions. It's like creating a kind of individual worksheet with their paper and pen while I guide them through the process. It's less varied than it would otherwise be, but it operates similarly. I don't know what I would do if I were having to teach sewing or technical skills like design, but in my case, I can lead the class in a way which is not that different to being in a classroom.

SA *What would you say are the opportunities emerging in this switch to online education?*

DG Before 2020, if someone had told me that I was now going to be doing all of my teaching online, I wouldn't have been able to picture it, and I wouldn't expect it to work. But as it turns out, you can do it. I still think it's better to have people in a classroom, but we've now seen that it's not necessarily essential. There is always the cost and difficulty of getting people all into one place and now we are aware of the potential health risks, but the fact that you can do this kind of online teaching is an eye-opener for me. Before I had thought of online education as quite asynchronous and lacking a connection between the learners and the people working with them. Now, I have seen and experienced the new opportunities and different avenues that allow you to have a certain amount of interaction and some level of closeness in this video environment. It's not the same, but the opportunity is there and that is striking to me.

One opportunity that we created is a thing called Creativity Conversations, where my colleague Rain and I invite students to come online and chat with us about their creative projects. Similar to coaching, it's a chance for them to share what they're working on and also to share some of the questions or anxieties and see if we've got anything that we can suggest. I say to people that we don't necessarily have the answer to all their problems, but they can talk about them, and we might have some interesting suggestions. We could have created this space before, in person, and it would have been a place where people would turn up to appointments, but it had never occurred to me before the switch to online teaching happened. I think that for conversations like these, the fact that people can just log onto Zoom and speak to you is a really great opportunity to come from this.

I've done some other things like free public creativity workshops in collaboration with Artscape Launchpad, which is a resource based in Toronto to support creative communities. With COVID, it's like the idea of your children asking you, "What did you do in the war, Dad?" Except this is the war against COVID, and obviously, I haven't got the ability to develop any super vaccines or anything like that. Like many others, I just do lots of free things that are available online for people. It's not solving the COVID crisis, but it is a useful thing that I can do to make things a little easier.

SA *That is fantastic, David. The fact that you've taken these extra steps to exercise what's within your wheelhouse and make this situation brighter is inspiring to us all. So, what tools, software, or applications have you found to be useful for online teaching?*

DG I like **Google Jamboard**, which is a free whiteboard-type platform where lots of people can go on at once and draw and write together. I can easily post the URL for students and there is no login or anything like that, so it's easy to use and straightforward. That's one good tool. After I started using Jamboard I began to search for other tools where people could work together collaboratively in real time. I asked one of my research assistants to spend a while looking and I started asking people about the different kinds of tools they use. I had thought that I was going to come up with a whole list of different ones, but I never found any others that seemed as good as Jamboard. I think it's important to use tools that are straightforward. If you've got a class of ninety, if most people get it, but there's ten people who need some help, it's going to ruin everything straight away because you need *everyone* to be able to use it immediately. So, it needs to be really easy.

I had considered maybe using **Twitch** where we could watch videos together and make comments alongside, but all of those ideas fell by the wayside because it just seemed too complicated. I landed on using Zoom and Jamboard together, because at the very least, you're always connected by audio in Zoom, but with Jamboard going at the same time people can speak and interact without having to switch the platform they're using, and they can have that element of visual interaction. That seemed to work well. Trying out lots of different tools ended up seeming like more trouble than it was worth, and I figured it probably was going to confuse at least some of the people, which would snowball into decreased class efficiency, and so on.

Having said that, I feel relatively unadventurous in my tools now, but using those two things together is quite good. I've found Jamboard to work well with the guest speakers that often come to class. I give the students some preliminary information about the guest and their topic, and then on Jamboard. We have a moment's silence where students can each generate at least one or two questions that we'll be able to ask our guests. This fills up the board with loads of interesting questions very quickly. Students are then invited to have conversations with the speaker. I've found this to be really good. I haven't ended up using any other technologies so far. I just don't want to make it too complicated because any extra platform you add just makes it harder. I don't want to make it difficult for people.

*SA* *Where do you see things moving with higher education into the future? Do you see us going back to traditional in-person teaching methods, or do you think we will trend toward a more blended approach? Or is something completely different going to emerge out of this?*

DG I really don't know. I don't really feel like we know what's going to happen in the next few months, let alone in the next few years, especially right now, where we're at in this moment. I think that because we've had our eyes opened to the fact that you can do quite a lot of stuff fairly effectively online, it will change people's willingness to deliver some parts of higher education in the digital realm. But also, the pandemic has reinforced many people's keenness on having the face-to-face interaction back. So, I don't think that we will be switching to a totally online education when this is all over, because we like the real-world experience. Also, of course, when universities have students paying a lot of money to get that student experience, you've got to deliver. This really does focus the mind as to what "extra" means when going to university. What does university add to your life and your experience, beyond just getting some information delivered to you through a computer?

I do think that being a student at a university should be a wonderful, all-encompassing experience with lots of different dimensions. For many, it's possible that only a fairly small part of that is receiving the information they're being taught, which as we've seen now, can be delivered via a computer. Then there are all of these extra experiences that students get from attending university, all of which can't really be done right now because of the switch to online learning. I think to justify their cost, universities will need to go back to that. That probably raises more questions for universities about their continuing existence, certainly for some of those that weren't so prestigious or those that weren't doing so well before.

*"There are cheaper, quicker forms of education that don't require you to leave your house, which could be attractive to many. It's going to be a challenge for universities. But also, I quite like that challenge because it means that universities really need to do some critical thinking about their meaning and what they do for people."*

Universities and higher education institutions are going to have to show what they are adding to people's lives, because people are now more aware than ever that they could just go online and take courses. There are cheaper, quicker forms of education that don't require you to leave your house, which could be attractive to many. It's going to be a challenge for universities. But also, I quite like that challenge because it means that universities really need to do some critical thinking about their meaning and what they do for people. We have to consider what kind of experiences and sorts of personal development are offered to the students. Learning is more than just receiving content, which you could get from the Internet. Because we are more aware now that the purpose of a university isn't simply to hand you a parcel of information, we've got an interesting question—what do you need a university for? It is important that we ask these questions. A global pandemic isn't fun, but it is thought provoking.

## REFLECTION

That interview took place in October 2020, and I've been asked to write this reflection in July 2021, nine months later. I don't think I have too much to add, especially since my answers above were relatively fresh ones. As the pandemic drags on, but the promise of a "return to normal" remains confusingly elusive, it's difficult not to feel jaded by anything that involves yet more Zoom calls.

This concern about becoming weary or complacent links to one experience from 2021 that is worth mentioning. In January 2021 I started teaching my MA course, Creativity, Identity and Making Things Happen, feeling more optimistic because I had managed to successfully run the undergraduate course Your Creative Self—discussed in the interview above—quite successfully, and had even been given a Dean's Teaching Award for my efforts.

When running the earlier course, I included special guest speakers, because it made things more varied and it filled up one hour of a three-hour class in a useful way, taking the pressure off me a bit. And in the Zoom environment, of course, it's quite easy for guests to call in from wherever they are without having to travel to a campus. I had planned to have three guests, but I added more along the way, so in the end there were six weeks that included a guest—half of the classes.

Planning my course for the following term, I thought—perhaps without thinking about it too much at all—that as I was now more experienced with Zoom teaching I didn't need the prop of special guests so much, and I didn't plan to include any (although later in the term I was able to get in touch with Zarina Muhammad and Gabrielle de la Puente, who operate as art activists The White Pube, and they were our very engaging guests one week).

But going mostly without guests had an unintended consequence that I hadn't anticipated. Students in Your Creative Self were able to see the primary speakers (i.e., me and the six guests) as a mix in terms of race, gender, and sexuality. Being able to speak to outstanding Black and Asian creators, as well as LGBTQ+ and disabled creators, made the course more diverse and interesting, and offered a range of role models to students who didn't necessarily look like me. My increased confidence with online teaching, as well as perhaps a lower level of enthusiasm for having to organize *another* set of Zoom classes, meant that I ended up with a course that was less successful in terms of diverse representation than the previous one. The pandemic, and the Black Lives Matter movement, have sharpened our recognition of social injustices, and these issues are of course just as pressing even when we are individuals, apart, in little boxes on Zoom. So, my "simpler" solution was not better, and we have to always remember that if running an online class gets too easy it's probably because there's more we should be doing.

ABOUT

**David Gauntlett** is Canada research chair in creativity at the Faculty of Communication and Design, Ryerson University, Toronto, Canada, where he leads the Creativity Everything lab. He is the author of several books, including *Creative Explorations* (2007), *Making Media Studies* (2015), and *Making is Connecting* (2011, second edition 2018). He has made a number of popular online resources, videos, and playthings, and has pioneered creative research and workshop methods. He has worked with a number of the world's leading creative organizations, including the BBC, the British Library, and Tate. For twelve years he has worked with LEGO® and the LEGO® Foundation on innovation in creativity, play and learning.

# Kiu Sum

Doctoral Researcher, University of Westminster,
United Kingdom

Interviewed December 2020 by *Sandra Abegglen*

SA *Kiu, you host The Education Burrito podcast—can you introduce yourself and tell us a little bit more about The Education Burrito?*

KS I've just started my second year of my PhD at the University of Westminster in London, in the UK. My PhD looks to explore doctors' nutrition and their diet and health during their shift work. In a nutshell, that's my day job as a researcher. As Sandra also mentioned, I recently started a brand-new podcast called The Education Burrito, where we try to unwrap student engagement and the pedagogy approaches in higher education, and have a bit of fun at the same time. So, yes, aside from doing my nutrition PhD, I'm very interested in student engagement as a side project.

SA *That's a big leap from nutrition to student engagement. What bridges these two different interests of yours?*

KS If I may, I will take you back to where it all started. During my nutrition undergraduate study, I was approached by the wonderful staff at the university who had started a new partnership scheme called Students as Co-Creators. It was where students partnered up with academics to develop a project that mattered to them in terms of changing the curriculum or changing something in that institution that would enhance their university experience. For my first co-creators project with a few members of staff, we looked at mobile technology and its use in learning and teaching. This was a few years back before technology was a big thing. We aimed to determine whether or not using mobile technologies would be beneficial if we were to embed technology in our curriculum. After that first project, I signed up again the following year and I have done it a few more times since then, working on co-creators projects with other students and staff members on other related learning and teaching topics. Student engagement became part of what I do and became one of my major points of interest, aside from my degree. Nutrition is still the bread and butter of what I do, but while at university, these extracurricular partnership projects extend my knowledge and really define who I am, defining my skill set and experience in understanding the university and higher education systems. Through this initiative, I connected with other students studying degrees like architecture, social sciences, and music. It became a way for me to find out what was happening at the university. It became part of me as well, stimulating my interest as I navigated my journey through higher education.

SA *I know that doing a doctorate can be quite a lonely endeavour and it must be even more so these days during the pandemic, especially now that the UK has gone into a second lockdown. Would you say it's also something that's true to your heart, still being a student yourself and working on quite an extensive piece? Would you say it's still related to that desire to also connect to others and advocate for that?*

KS Yes, it's a very interesting question and it's quite different, I think. As an undergraduate, you are very clued up in terms of everything that's happening in your cohort or other cohorts in the undergraduate world. When I moved and completed my master's at another university, this sense of belonging changed because you don't know where you fit. You are just at the university for that one year for your master's course, and so I found myself trying to fit in and figuring out who was who. Then when I started my PhD, I had a somewhat different feeling because I didn't have a class as such. It's you and your PhD. It was somewhat isolating at the start. I wouldn't say my research is the same as others in the office. Other PhD students in school would generally have a lab to use due to the nature of their project, whereas for me, my research bridges both psychology and life sciences. Thus, the definition of "my lab" is somewhat different. I don't do wet labs. I do the opposite. Everything is done on the computer, and I study people rather than cells and pipetting. No white coat is necessary, though I do miss wearing a white coat because it does make you feel like a scientist!

Although it was isolating at first, I got to know people through the PhD Society we have at our university. I started to connect with other students, and surprisingly, not with scientists. I signed up once again as a PhD student for the Students as Co-Creators Scheme to find that connection and that sense of belonging. Since March, I've been working at home, and it has been a good eight months now. It is strange that connection can sometimes be a bit distant when we are all working remotely. Lockdown was different because you have to do so online and through technology if you want to connect with people. I think as a PhD student during this pandemic, it is a different sense of belonging.

SA *After the lockdown started, you seized this opportunity to launch an initiative, The Education Burrito.*

KS Yes, during the lockdown, I started the Education Burrito podcast. I really wanted to find a way to keep working on my interests in partnerships and student engagement, and I thought, why not actually go and find people and talk about what they do? I know that people love talking about what they do, and I thought, why not capture it in a podcast? So, this is my side project, and it helps to keep my PhD sanity going. Otherwise, I'm just doing my doctoral research day and night. It gets me motivated, connected, and keeps me up to date as to what is happening in the sector. It's something different and something that tests my skills and experience. I'm learning every time I'm doing it. I always love to try new things and get involved if I have the time to.

SA *In discovering your interests and taking action to develop these into your learning or your life in general, what advice do you have for those wanting to do this?*

KS I think being proactive is something that I would encourage people to do. I remember when I was in the final year of my undergraduate degree, I really wasn't sure what I wanted to do. I still don't, to be honest. I had opportunities to have conversations with new graduates and academics who really stimulated my mind in terms of being proactive and learning new things because, at the end of the day, everyone comes out with the same degree. When I think back, being proactive is one thing, but another potential risk is being too proactive. Even though you're very passionate or active in what you want to do, you don't want to commit yourself to too many things because you won't have the energy to carry out these passions. I learned that I needed to focus on things that are beneficial and relevant to me, and of course, prioritizing tasks!

My best recommendation is to be proactive and find out what you want to do after your course. I have somewhat of an idea of what I want to do but getting there is another matter. This question still remains for me because I don't know what will come up after my PhD. I don't know where I will be. It's quite difficult to know the future when you don't know the future. We didn't know that we were going to have a pandemic this time last year. So much has changed, and it is more about capturing the now, I think. I've learned to embrace the moments you have with people and embrace the moments you really enjoy. At the same time, I've learned that you need to find out what you want to do and seek to figure out how to get there. Be proactive and learn to embrace and reflect on everything that you do.

SA *There is a lot of wisdom in that. Now that we are all at home online, what would you say are the good channels to connect, network, and get to know people?*

KS I think finding people is easy, but maintaining a network is the difficult part. I like to talk to people and find out more about what they do and who they're connected to through seminars and events. Get involved in activities and committees. Talk to the people you meet as much as you can and follow up on the things you find interesting. The third thing is more about working up the courage to simply introduce yourself to people. I normally just say as an aspiring student, as an inspiring person in this field, I want to find out more about what you do. Social media is a good way to connect with people, especially the Weekly Wednesday Chat, #LTHEchat. They are a community of people who have got a wealth of experience in higher education, especially in learning and teaching!

SA *What are the online tools that you find most useful?*

KS I use **LinkedIn** after I've been to conferences, so if I'm looking for a collaborator in a project, and that person fits, I will then go and search them up. Now that conferences and webinars are now all online, it's a different situation in connecting with those who attend, but I still think it's important to break down those barriers. I was in a webinar hosted by a university in Australia. Even though I was up at a ridiculous time just to be there, it was very helpful because the speaker invited everyone who wanted to connect with other PhD students to put their e-mail in the chat. I thought I've got nothing to lose. About a week later, when the organizer of that webinar distributed all of the attendees' contacts, a group from that community ended up talking as a separate mini group. We ended up organizing a new group between us about procrastination during our PhDs, and despite our different time zones, we all share the same common goal, and it's been really great to connect with others across the world in this way. I would definitely say that engaging in these conferences or events online is a great way to connect.

SA *You've hinted that you are getting an idea of where you want to go in the future or what you may want to do. Where do you see your initiatives going?*

KS I have been in education nearly all my life now and I would like to stay in academia if possible. I think, from my undergraduate to my master's and now doing my PhD and being part of different initiatives, it has just opened my eyes as to how much I enjoy the student engagement aspects, connecting with staff and students at university. I'm hoping to continue my initiatives as I progress throughout my career, if the opportunities arise. I know the challenges that this brings and the challenges of finding a job, so I can't really say for sure. But that's my aspiration, having met the people who have been helping me in my journey thus far.

## REFLECTION

Without a doubt, the pandemic has changed the way we perceive our learning in higher education. As I reflect on my conversation following this interview with Sandra, remote working has become the norm, with fewer face-to-face opportunities due to uncertainty around the pandemic. The use of technology is becoming more dependable, with more opportunities to reach out to others, whether locally, nationally, and internationally, developing new connections for potential collaborations and nurturing our skills and experience through virtual meetings.

Working from home was something I never imagined doing for eighteen months during my doctorate. I am grateful to have had those in my communities and network who have been supportive during this unprecedented time. As such, working from home during the pandemic feels like a really (really) long, dragged-out weekend when you are not physically in the office. Nevertheless, the doctorate keeps me on my toes! Though I do miss working on campus and the opportunity to be in those random conversations with others, it is undoubtedly a learning curve. Yes, doing a doctorate can be an isolating journey, but learning to adapt to working remotely can be even more isolating if there is no strategy to overcome this challenge.

Being involved in student engagement and pedagogy research activities has undoubtedly enabled me to think more outside the box. It has been fantastic to collaborate with various staff and students, via Students as Co-Creators, across the university to work on projects that are directly and indirectly relevant in our discipline; but simultaneously, topics that influence our university experience. As mentioned in my interview, it is an alternative approach to making those connections and learning more about the higher education sector. Through this journey, an idea to create The Education Burrito was developed—this is a podcast that aims to discuss topics related to student engagement in higher education and an opportunity for those in the sector to share their stories and for listeners to learn more about them. As I write this reflection, the podcast will soon celebrate its first birth-

*"... working from home during the pandemic feels like a really (really) long, dragged-out weekend when you are not physically in the office."*

day—time has truly gone by! The podcast has enabled my learning about the education roles there are in the sector, something I did not know before. For example, this journey has shown that in this educational ecosystem, some roles are not as widely known as others and are often behind initiatives implementing changes and making innovative ideas into a reality. Furthermore, the podcast has provided me with the opportunity to develop skills and experiences that I did not necessarily set out to gain beforehand. The podcast has become a side project where I can learn more about the educational sector and provide a space for the community to share ideas, raising awareness of various topics of interest.

In summary, my perception of reflecting on my learning and teaching practice has evolved since my interview. Though the pandemic has nudged us to think about how we can work effectively and efficiently remotely, it has also shown the importance of collaborations, networks, and a sense of belonging in our community, no matter whether there is a pandemic or not.

ABOUT

**Kiu Sum** is a doctoral research student in life sciences at the University of Westminster, in the United Kingdom. With a BSc (Hons) Human Nutrition and a MRes in Clinical Research, Kiu's research interests are around public health nutrition, nutritional behaviour, mobile health, and cardiometabolic health. While studying for her undergraduate degree at Westminster, Kiu found her passion in student engagement and the opportunities to collaborate with staff members on various research projects. Whenever possible, Kiu is actively involved in learning and teaching projects and advocates for the "student voice." She hosts The Education Burrito Podcast (https://theeducation-burrito.podbean.com/) in her spare time, discussing learning and teaching in higher education.

# Lisa Silver

Associate Professor, Faculty of Law, University of Calgary

Interviewed December 2020 by *Martina MacFarlane*

MM *Can you tell us a little bit about yourself and about what you do?*

LS I am an associate professor in the Faculty of Law at the University of Calgary. I teach first year Criminal Law, and Evidence to second-year students. Both are mandatory courses. I am also course director for the Trial Advocacy course in which all third-year law students participate.

MM *How has your teaching changed so far in 2020?*

LS It has not changed the way that I approach my teaching, but it has changed in terms of my own feelings surrounding the practice. I know we like to use the word pivot. I'm not sure if I like that word so much, but I guess that's the way to describe it. It just happened so fast. On March 13 I was supposed to have a special guest in my Criminal Law class. The night before, she emailed me and she said, what do you think? And I said, I don't know. And then, it came out that classes were cancelled. That was a Friday, and I had to teach the next week.

So, then that feeling creeps in where, as an instructor, the situation is out of your control. As lawyers, we like to have control over our files and our information. Preparation is huge for lawyers. That's an important characteristic of a successful lawyer. So, to not have that control in March was a bit scary. Then as we went along knowing that the Fall semester was going to be online, I developed a feeling of okay, well, I am going to really get down to business and learn as much as I can about how an effective course runs online. I started asking myself, what can I do? What are the best practices? In some ways, best practices were what I ended up just doing by the seat of my pants. In March, I flipped my class. I created narrated **PowerPoint** presentations and then spent the time in class doing a lot of problem solving and reviews of the concepts. At the core, I'm doing the same thing this term, but I got there not by the seat of my pants, but by ensuring best practice.

I did a lot during this period. I went to the workshops and presentations offered by the Teaching Institute, and they also offered a North American teaching conference that was outside of Arizona. I went to some of those too. I did my due diligence. I wanted to see if there was anything cool that I could get out of this as an instructor. I wanted to know—are there new innovations? Am I doing this the right way? Does someone have a better idea?

One of the things that I took to heart was looking at my syllabus in a different way. The syllabus wasn't the home anymore. **D2L** had to be the class and the primary platform for what I was going to do. It wasn't easy to embrace that as your classroom environment and it means that you really must put a lot of time into building its structure. I ended up simplifying a lot of my concepts. As an instructor, you fall in love with your syllabus because you made it. You think every single one of those cases is so important. If a student asked you, which one is more important, you'd say, they're all important. You're going to be examined on all of that because it's all important. These are all new students who don't have prior experience, and I've practised in criminal law for over thirty years. So, you can imagine my view that every case is amazing. But what it made me do was let go of some of the small stuff. What I did instead was make lesson objectives for each of my topics, and that helped me to cut things out. I said to myself,

*"I wanted to see if there was anything cool that I could get out of this as an instructor. I wanted to know—are there new innovations? Am I doing this the right way? Does someone have a better idea?"*

LISA SILVER

what do I really need these students to know and what is reasonable, considering they're in their first year and we're now online? I wrote four, maybe five objectives for each class or topic area, and I stuck to it. If there was a case that was doing something other than what I wanted, I cut it. I ended up trimming the course.

The other issue that I had was that our first-year students all take the same mandatory curriculum, and they get separated into three different classes, with about forty-three students in each class. This year though, during COVID, one of our criminal law professors moved back to Victoria. When he left, that meant that my colleague and I each had sixty-seven students. There's a big difference between forty and sixty-seven. The trimming really helped, because I ended up narrating all my PowerPoint presentations using the information that I had trimmed out of the required reading.

So, I ended up looking at my syllabus and deciding that really what I was teaching were modules. I put topics into four of them for the Fall, and four for the Winter. I've got sub-topics under each module, and then for each module I do three activities. Activity One is the reading. Activity Two is the narrated PowerPoints. I've also turned these into podcasts as an alternative in case the students prefer to just listen and not see. And then activity three is the **Zoom** class. I divide my class into two breakout groups because the Zoom class is for quick review and problem solving. I've decided that I'm going to repeat the quick review and problem solving for both groups. I've really tried hard to build a D2L platform that is user friendly, so that all the students have to do when they get to the Zoom class is go into each module, sub-topic or unit, and they know what to do for each one of them. This way they also know what they need to do before they come to class.

*MM* *It sounds like you've really used the opportunity to streamline your content and distill everything down. You've painted a good picture of what your teaching looks like at the moment, and you've touched on some opportunities and challenges already but maybe you can focus in on these and tell us more.*

LS The opportunity was to rethink a course that I'd taught for six-plus years. I always do some tweaking every time I teach, but you don't often do the big rethink. The opportunity was to ask, what am I really doing? Why am I doing it? And those lesson objectives were helpful for me because they made me understand why I was teaching these particular cases and what I expected from the students. I think it gave me an opportunity to do things better, because I think there's always an opportunity to do things better. It made me open myself up rather than saying, no, I'm perfect. It's a perfect course. There's no way I'd ever change it.

As for the challenges, one thing that we pride ourselves on in the law faculty is community. Community matters to me—I always have an open door. I encourage students to come and see me. Students that graduate stay in touch with me and I have a relationship with the students. It's difficult to create that community online. With the way that the D2L for the course was created, some of the students have said that it shows you really care. I mean, I think that helps, but I feel a little sad that it's just not going to be the same as much I try. I stay back after the class for students to ask questions but also just to hang out. In my Group A, I already have two or three students that like to hang out, and they just want to talk. That's awesome. I love it. But in my Group B I have nobody, which I think is funny. It's hard if you are someone who likes the interaction with the students. Of course, lecturing is not the same online. It just isn't. We're not having the same two-way discussion and there's always a time lag. Students have to use that electronic "raise hand" button. It's amazing how different it is when you're in person, face-to-face. There's a flow that's missing online.

So that's a challenge, and to be honest, I think I'll see other challenges after the midterm. I think after the midterm, which is a low stakes exam by the way, I'll be able to see and judge based on students' past performance whether this new format is really working. I am a little worried about that. If they were upper year students, I wouldn't worry as much because they already have a lot of the knowledge on how a lawyer thinks, and how to analyze. But I figured that the other opportunity is the opportunity itself to just try, just do it, and see what happens.

MM *So, in this great experiment of testing, midterms, and those kinds of things, have you altered your approach to creating those tests at all?*

LS Well, the difficulty with the law program is that the marks are one hundred percent weighted on exams. That's the tradition, and we've tried to move away from that approach, but the difficulty is that this is just how it works. Between the three mandatory courses I'm involved in—Criminal Law, Evidence, and the Trial Advocacy course - by the end of a student's life in law school, I will have taught them. I've tried different things for the different courses.

One year in Evidence, I tried to do more small assignments so that the exam would be weighted less. But the reality is that we must be mindful about what the students are doing in their other courses. If too many courses are doing other kinds of assessments, then the students have too much to do during the term. So, it's not just up to me. I can't just say, I'd like to give the students three book reviews. Reading has to happen in my course, I would say at least 20–25 pages a week. So, times that by five other courses, right? It's a fine balance.

What I've tried to do though is self-assessments. Some of my units under a few of my modules in Evidence are D2L only. They're just activities online and they are backed by more background information to get students comfortable with the concepts we're learning in class. I've also done some self-assessment quizzes. They are not marked or graded. I've been using a similar technique in the Zoom class with some very easy polls. As soon as the students get on to the Zoom class, they have four or five questions that are a very big picture, just to make sure they understand these very basic concepts before we launch into more of the specifics. So, I am trying to rethink non-grading assessments. More informative and less summative. I'm trying to do it that way and I'll see if that's successful.

MM *In your journey through this term so far, what's your most-used software or tool?*

LS Well, obviously, I'm using D2L and Zoom the most. Another one is **Google Jamboard**, which I love. I used it in the first class, and it was really good. I've used **Mentimeter** to do word clouds and I think those are great too. I like using those three things, and in Zoom itself, obviously I use breakout rooms.

MM *Just as a curious side note, had you used any of these platforms or tools before COVID?*

LS I hadn't used Jamboard at all. I used it over the summer with Student Legal Aid, or SLA, our student legal services here at the University of Calgary. These are law students who help people who don't have enough money for a lawyer with their simple criminal offences. When I did a seminar for the SLA on evidence, I did a Jamboard to open it up. The question was, "SLA matters because ... " and I almost cried. It is amazing how people can share in this anonymous way, especially when it's a question that is meaningful for them. Many said such beautiful things about why it's so important to help people in need. I loved it. So, I'm a huge fan of Jamboard and these types of resources for this reason, but I also know there's only so much that you can ask people to reflect on. I think reflection is important, but I think you can have fatigue from that too. But no, I had never used Jamboard before COVID, and I think I used Mentimeter once in class. COVID has given me an opportunity to use some fun stuff, for sure.

MM *Like you say, it's interesting to see how people come out of their shell when they're in their own home, in a comfortable space, and feel safe enough to do that.*

LS Yes, because it's anonymous. And what's nice is that it's anonymous in a positive way. I think this aspect promotes a healthy class environment.

MM *So then, what is your favourite resource for teaching online? We have talked about tools, but is there any place that you look to for inspiration?*

LS I look at the Teaching Institute and I feel that their resources have been really helpful. I've looked at resources done by other universities as well. Even in our own library, there are very useful books, podcasts, and audio books. There are lots of good teaching and learning resources out there, which you can either purchase or get for free, that you can listen to, or that you can read. I've also used our tech coaches. They've gave me help with making the podcast and they helped me learn how to troubleshoot some of the technical issues that came up, which has been great.

MM *It's interesting to think about all the learning that is coming out of this situation, at every level. Even those micro-tech things that everyone is learning about. Following all these developments and changes, things will be fairly uncertain for the next few months. What would you expect or hope that higher education might look like in ten years' time?*

LS I do hope that higher education doesn't go completely online. Obviously, it's an important aspect to have contact with the students, and to have the ability to relationship-build. I think it's important for students' own mental health, to be honest, not just because you learn better face-to-face. I think it's just the way we are; we're tuned to be social people. But I do hope that the technology still stays. There is something to be said about being able to teach an online course.

In law, we just don't do that. It'll be interesting to see if this now becomes part of what we offer on a regular basis. That could open up other possibilities too, possibilities such as more international teaching. We tend to shut down come April or May in terms of teaching and we usually don't teach during the summer, but this year our faculty did because of COVID. Maybe we will start offering more courses over the summer, which may mean that students are finishing their degrees earlier. But if that happens, we're a profession, and we can't do things in a vacuum. However, when we change our educational approach, this needs to be done hand-in-hand with the legal community. We have to bring in more of the firms and the law society. If we're serious, we need to approach this in a more holistic way.

MM *Absolutely. Are you seeing collaboration, and these kinds of reflections with the profession?*

LS Well, one of the courses that I am doing in the winter is my Trial Advocacy course. I have 130 students that I break into twelve small groups, and they perform as part of an experiential learning curriculum. I have members of the legal community, and judges from the Court of the Queen's Bench come in and be the group instructors for each class. Normally they would do it in person, and you can imagine how they perform. There is lots of feedback and reflection. Well, now I have to move this whole process online. That's a real challenge, but I have to say, I have well over forty volunteers from the legal community, and they've been great. After one lawyer expressed the community's obvious concern about conducting trials and advocacy online, I asked her to come in and do a little mini lecture about it. I want to record some of the demonstrations that the lawyers typically do live. I've already had one lawyer say, great, we'll take care of it, we'll do one of these demos, don't worry about it. So, I think that my course is really a litmus test for the way that the profession perceives what we're doing. I think they're seeing that there is value in our students knowing how to do lawyering online. Firms are really looking for people who can use this technology.

MM *Lisa, thank you so much for sharing these experiences with us. Is there anything else that you wanted to add to our conversation?*

LS I'd like to mention the mental health aspect. I think we tend to let that slide, and I think it's important both as teachers and learners and for our students, that we really be cognizant of those issues because it is isolating. And I feel it too. You must compensate for that somehow. And I think that you have to ensure that you use your social skills as much as you can. That's important, I think, as a teacher as well.

MM *Do you think that there are ways to build in little catches within courses? It is such an intangible thing, but we're all experiencing it, right?*

LS Well, I'll give you an example. I made a point in my course outline to put in an EDI statement, which stands for Equity Diversity and Inclusivity. I thought it was especially important for online classes because there is now the ability to hide behind technology. You can forget that you are in a class with a bunch of people and that you need to be respectful and inclusive. As part of it, I said that this online classroom is a safe place. If you don't feel safe, then come speak to me because I want to be sure that you feel safe in my classroom. Just recently I received an e-mail about that, and I've never had those issues before. So, I feel that we must be even more responsive to students' emotional well-being, because I think it's easy to feel isolated in a Zoom classroom, and to feel that things aren't right. You don't get the same cues as you do when we are in person. Online, the cues are different. So, I'm glad I did that. It's important to take measures such as these even if you're not online. I did it specifically because I wondered whether my presence as an instructor makes the students act differently. When my presence isn't in person, does it then allow for people to not feel as safe? In criminal law, we discuss a lot of controversial subjects. We talk about people who die from violence. Next term, I'll talk about sexual assault. So, the mental health and safety aspect is an important thing to remember.

*MM* *That's right, we've lost so many of those social cues. Because of that, it's obviously more important than ever to open up that space where people can speak freely if they need to say something or get something off their chest and just feel a little safer.*

LS Exactly.

*MM* *Well, thank you so much for chatting with us today, Lisa.*

LS Thank you!

REFLECTION

COVID-19, instead of creating an unknown future, is beginning to recede, taking with it the anxieties and concerns we all experienced as educators. This does not mean we are back to the old ways of course delivery. Nor does it mean that we can jettison the teaching and learning practices we once successfully employed. Rather, we now have a unique opportunity to integrate our learnings from the past year into our in-class environment. We can take what works and modify it by making it better. That's what I intend to do as I prepare for Fall 2021.

The interview I gave in December of 2020 speaks of opportunity and change. The pandemic gave me a reason to rethink my approach to teaching and to reflect on best practice. This reflection was done in the online environment, but it applies equally to in-person teaching and learning. In my interview, I explained how I used D2L to create a virtual classroom for the students. D2L became the roadmap for the students' success. I intend to recreate this D2L space for my in-person class this Fall. D2L will not take the place of the classroom but it will support it.

This is what I learned during the year teaching online—that meaningful support matters, be it academic or personal. In my interview, I expressed concern about my ability to bridge the digital gap and build a strong relationship with my students. To my surprise, I found I could do so by creating a supportive atmosphere built on trust and respect. In some ways, I feel I know my students even better than when I taught in person. Yes, the social cues I spoke of in the interview are different online but in place of those cues I became more intentional in my learning and teaching practices. Being intentional requires me to acknowledge the communication gaps and embrace them by finding alternative ways to engage with my students.

The pandemic, instead of pushing people apart, pulled us in the same direction. I became acutely aware of EDI practices online and this awareness will now be implemented in my in-class space. Mental health concerns were at the forefront online and will continue to be so offline as well. The pandemic taught me that support makes us stronger and is not a sign of weakness. Showing support may be as simple as a word of encouragement or extra help after class. Support may also be the directing influence I use to decide on course objectives, assignments, and assessment. Sometimes a little bit of humanity goes a long way.

## ABOUT

**Lisa Silver** is a proud Calgarian, lawyer, educator, and avid blogger. She holds a BA in Economics (UWO, 1984), an LL.B. (Osgoode, 1987), and an LL.M. (Calgary, 2001). She is a member of the Bars of Ontario (1989) and Alberta (1998). As a criminal lawyer, Lisa has appeared in all levels of Court, including in the Supreme Court of Canada. Presently, Lisa is an associate professor at the University of Calgary in the Faculty of Law, where she teaches criminal law and evidence and is the course director for the 3L Advocacy program. She writes about and researches an extensive range of topics including sentencing, judicial decision making and the admissibility of expert and digital evidence. She is the author of the forthcoming *Criminal Law Defences*, 5th Edition with Pat Knoll, QC. Lisa maintains her own award-winning law blog at www.ideablawg.ca and regularly contributes to the Faculty's ABlawg website. She was awarded the Faculty of Law's Howard Tidswell Memorial Award for Teaching Excellence in 2016–2017. Her educational interests go beyond the classroom through her involvement in judicial education. Lisa sits on many committees and is currently on the Board of Calgary Legal Guidance.

# Thomas Keenan

Professor, School of Architecture, Planning and Landscape,
University of Calgary, Canada

Interviewed December 2020 by *Mac McGinn*

MM *Tom, let's start off with you telling a little bit about yourself. I understand you have a little bit of a story to introduce as well.*

TK I was born in New York City. I went to Columbia University and wound up getting a wide range of degrees there, everything from engineering to philosophy to education. I came to Calgary in 1972 to take a job in the Computer Services Department of the University of Calgary and I've been with the University ever since. I have been a professor of computer science, a professor of continuing education, dean of the Faculty of Continuing Education, and now I have the honour of being both a professor in the School of Architecture, Planning and Landscape (SAPL) and an adjunct professor in the Department of Computer Science. My lifelong interest has been cybersecurity. It's a subject that's never going to let us down. There's always something surprising and it teaches me a lot of great lessons. When COVID-19 came along, one thing that I learned is that it's always a good idea, educationally, to give your message right out front in case people tune out. So, I'm going to tell you in the next ninety seconds or so, the key message I want to get across with a little story.

It starts out soon after COVID. I went into a food store and there was a big, long line to get through the checkout. I saw a sign saying something like "first responders and medical personnel—we honour and thank you—please come to the front of the line." Now, I have a doctorate from Columbia University, but I'm not a medical doctor. But hey, I do have a white lab coat. Of course, lots of people have a lab coat, so that might not be convincing enough. But then it occurred to me that I had something else, an old medical ID card. I was an actor in a movie that was shot at the Calgary General Hospital. I played a doctor named Dr. Joseph Bullock. As we were about to shoot a scene, the assistant director said "Hey, that doc doesn't have an ID badge." So, I was marched down to human resources where they took my photo and laminated up a badge in my character's name. I still have it in a souvenir box.

And here's the point. Just because I could have used this ID card and my lab coat to get to the front of the line, I didn't do it. My key message about teaching with technology is that just because you can do it doesn't mean that you should. For example, you can probably spy on your students in whole new ways and find things out about them, but don't do it. Make sure that every use of technology is intelligent. In fact, I teach a course on intelligent communities and that's a key message of that course: just because you can do something doesn't mean that you should.

MM *Going forward into online education and having to do remote learning, that brings up some interesting aspects for educators and instructors. What does your teaching look like now in 2020, considering the adjustments we've had to make with COVID?*

TK One part of my teaching has not changed, and that's the EVDS 401, which is now called ARCH 400, the overview course of our SAPL disciplines that anybody at the university can take. We had as many as 120 students sign up in the Spring semester, and that was because they didn't have summer jobs so they thought they might take courses instead. That course has been completely online for nine years now.

We designed it right from scratch to be a totally asynchronous, virtual experience for the students. It's very popular, I have to say, and it often has a long waiting list. Each week I get one of our professors to speak about something really interesting in their field of expertise. I cut that lecture down and I build a week around that. There's a week on urban planning, there's a week on industrial design, there's a couple of weeks on different aspects of architecture, residential architecture and so on. That course did not need to change at all to adapt to COVID-19 since it was designed to be completely online.

My other teaching has moved to **Zoom**. That's different, and there are pluses and minuses. One of the things is that when I have a room of maybe thirty students, I say go form a group and work together, and they go with their friends. Well, now Zoom assigns them randomly and they get to meet everybody else. So, in this aspect, the switch to Zoom has been a plus.

However, I do see more people getting very stressed. Some students are just disoriented; people that I have known and who I think should be fine but are not. I had one young lady e-mail me this morning, saying my computer crashed and I have lost my final paper. What am I to do? The computer security guy said, I hope you had a backup, but I gave her extra time. I am seeing a lot more of the human side where people are suffering. I had one guy who said, I can't really go to look at a neighbourhood in Calgary for EVDS 401. I have never been to Calgary. I'm in Nairobi, Kenya, and I'm a first-year student. So, I said, well, do a neighbourhood walk in Nairobi, that's fine. But I also thought how weird it must be to be a first-year student at a university when you've never even set foot in the country where it's located.

*MM* *I think this is the first time in this interview series that I've had somebody say that their course hasn't changed. It's great to hear that you were already set up beforehand.*

TK Well, let me tell you another story. We're going back to the 1970s, early 1980s when I taught some courses by audio teleconference. We didn't have Zoom, nor did we have the ability to do video conferencing. I would go into a place similar to a radio studio. I had people taking this course from all over the province and we were studying computers. There were computers then, but they were hard to come by. You could actually buy a Timex Sinclair computer for about $100. So, I called up the Timex Canada people, and I said, can you give me a university deal? They were very abrupt, and they said, we're not in computers, we're a watch company. I said, I have an ad here that says you sell computers. And they said, yeah, that was a bad mistake. Do you have some? Unfortunately, yes, they said, we have 755 of them. I said if we can set a good price, I will buy them all. I think we got them for about $30 each and I had them shipped to Calgary. For several years on that course we gave away one of these computers. It was a big thing—a $100 course that included a free computer.

So, we were doing the course via audio teleconferencing and back then you had to store your programs on a cassette deck. I had a student in Peace River, and he couldn't get his cassette deck to record his programs. I couldn't see him of course, and I finally said, look, Carl, would you please describe your cassette player? And he said, well, it's pink and it says My Little Pony on the side. I said, I think you have your daughter's cassette player. Go buy one that's a Sony or Sanyo. The point of this is that I have also learned the limitations of technology. That very day I swore we would never do another course by audio teleconferencing where we really needed to see the people.

MM *Interesting. That leads us into the next question as well. What are the opportunities that you see being created by digital education?*

TK Brilliant ones. I chair the board of the Information and Communications Technology (ICTC) Council of Canada. We normally go to Ottawa three times a year where we have a dinner with the CEO and a board meeting. It became very clear that we were not going to be able to do that for this last board meeting and we were all disappointed. We like to see each other. But I talked to my son about it and I said, do you have any ideas? And he said, why don't you turn it into an opportunity and go out there and find somebody that you normally wouldn't be able to bring to the meeting? So, we found a member of the German government who was able to give us their perspective. Before the switch to remote meetings, we would not have asked this person to fly to Ottawa for a forty-five-minute presentation. I know that in the architecture program, they're bringing in people as guest speakers that normally would not want to come to the university, wouldn't have the time, or who live in a different place.

It's a good thing and a bad thing. It means that the whole world is on the list of guest lecturers. The flip side is what I call the astronaut problem. I happen to know people at NASA, and they said we have this awful issue when the astronauts talk to grade three students. And I said, why is that awful? And they said, well, there's only so many hours in the day and the astronauts are busy. We have a list of 14,000 teachers who want their kids to talk to the astronauts. We're going to get into that situation where some of the best guest speakers from around the world are going to get Zoom fatigue and maybe start telling us no.

MM *Zoom fatigue is a quite real aspect. I have also seen in my courses that we've had a lot of international guest lectures coming in and providing different perspectives that I wouldn't have otherwise been able to see or access. So, on the flip side of that, what challenges do you think are experienced more through this online, remote education?*

TK I think there's the mental challenge. I mean, as you said, there is Zoom fatigue and there are also students who are attending university in a country that they haven't even been to yet. I think it's taking a toll on peoples' psyche. Many may be cooped up, particularly if they're in an environment where they don't have a space of their own, maybe in a multigenerational family household. I'm certainly seeing students struggling with that. The problem is that, in person, I can look a student in the face and see that they're not doing okay. On Zoom you can hide that. A lot of students turn off their camera, even when we encourage them to leave it on. I might go through an entire class without ever looking somebody in the eye, and I am worried that they're going to miss something important.

Then there are obviously questions of academic integrity. There are worries such as, if we can't see the student, how do we know it really is that student taking the test, and things like that. But I think that this is actually an opportunity. I have a doctorate in education, and I think that the idea of putting students in the gym for three hours with a proctor walking around to invigilate a timed exam is not always the best way to test if they've learned something. So, in my classes I've come up with ways where we don't have final exams, but I get a pretty good idea about whether or not they know the material.

*MM* *Interesting, if you could elaborate a little bit more I'd like to hear about how you're testing and going through those new processes.*

TK Well, the course that I have coming up in the Winter term is a course that anyone can take. It's called EVDS 402—Design, Digital Technology and the Built Environment. It's based on my own research and a book that I wrote called *Technocreep: The Surrender of Privacy and the Capitalization of Intimacy*. This is the textbook for the course—I don't feel too bad about requiring it because it's less than $20, and you can use the e-book. So, for EVDS 402, we have three-hour classes, and that's a little unusual for an undergraduate course. I give a lecture for about the first hour, and then I give the students a problem and they go off into groups with their classmates. Then they come back in the third hour and make their presentations. The result is that their presentation skills become extremely good, there's no question about that. When it comes to grading, those presentations are their micro-grades. Each one of them is worth maybe four or five percent of their final grade. I grade all of the presentations and if there are, let's say, ten of these presentations in the course, I take the five highest grades for each student. So, the reality is that every week they learn something. Every week they share and work together on the presentations with their peers, and every week they show their work to me. If they do a bad job, I let them know. I might say, you got a C on that first presentation and that's not really up to par. But you can still get an A in the course. Here's how you can make it better. By the end of the term, I actually have a really good sense of what they know and can give honest grades.

*MM* *Absolutely. I think that instead of the traditional term project, creating a midterm and a final to be able to test and acknowledge students' work, and assess their progress each week is a great methodology. It would be great to be able to keep students more consistently focused and attentive throughout the whole semester, instead of just having students think, well, all my projects are not due for another three weeks, so I'll put that on the back burner. Then they're panicking the night before.*

TK That never turns out well.

*MM* *Definitely not. So, you did mention that you use Zoom as one of your most frequently used software tools. Is there anything else that you are using as a primary software tool?*

TK So, the global answer to that question is the Internet, but we all know you can spend an awful lot of time on the Internet and just waste your time, so I try to channel students into what are useful resources. I like to use specialized search engines and search databases. So, if the students are going to do something in psychology, I tell them to log on to their Taylor Family Digital Library account and use PsycINFO because that will help to narrow it down. In the course that I teach on smart communities, I'm a big fan of the Intelligent Community Forum (www.intelligentcommunity.org), which names the Intelligent Community of the Year each summer and provides lots of terrific resources.

I always tell the students to go look at their stuff first. Then it may take them off in other directions. So, I don't want to just say the Internet is my primary software tool. It's the Internet, along with guidance, that directs them to things that I think are going to be useful.

MM *I like that you brought up the term "guidance" instead of just saying, go look at this topic, and then have your students sift through so many different avenues and routes. The Internet is so broad. It's good to hear that as an educator, there are ways that you can provide good guidance through those kinds of software and tools. You've talked about directing students to the Taylor Family Digital Library databases to help them narrow down their searches to get the information they need more efficiently, but is that the only way to do it? Or are there more?*

TK It depends on the field of study. As I said, in psychology, which I know pretty well, PsycINFO is a curated database. You're not going to find papers in there on high density lumber or other things like that. You're going to find relevant articles.

The human beings in the library are amazingly good and they're accessible by chat. I hate to tell people this because it'll get really busy there, but the reality is that you can ask them your research questions and at the very least, they'll be able to point you in the right direction. And these are human beings. I think they're pretty much all working from home now. Most of the time when I go to that library info chat line, there's no delay. They get right on it. I see nothing wrong with seeking human assistance to point you in the right direction.

Then there's peer learning. In all of my courses I have discussion boards. They're always a small part of the grade; for example in EVDS 401, students are required to make a post every week and it's worth about ten percent. They are also encouraged to reply to each other's posts, but at the very least, they have to post a resource every week. And guess what? I scoop them all up at the end of the term, thank them for them, and then I build them into next term's class because they find stuff that I didn't know about. Anybody who tells you they know everything about any field is an idiot. Students, when motivated even by this little bit of their grade, will go out there and post stuff that I look at and say, hey, I didn't even know that existed. It really and truly is collaborative learning, and that's one of the big pluses. I mean, because in many courses where you would be face-to-face Monday, Wednesday, Friday from 10: 00–10: 50 AM, there is really no space for this. Now with the switch to remote teaching, we're forced to make space.

MM *Absolutely. I like that the posts each week allow you to progressively accumulate good resources each year. I imagine that also allows you to stay more updated with what's going on in those resources and perhaps it might even save you time from having to go over all of that reading yourself. Maybe it filters it a little bit.*

TK I should mention something about that. You have to also teach students how to tell fake from true. There's a famous professor, T. Mills Kelly, who taught a course on fakery on the Internet called Lying About the Past.[1] In this course students go out there and their assignment is to create something false that will fool people. The most famous one was called, The Last Pirate of Chesapeake Bay. This had people believing that—I think in the 1920s—there was a pirate ship sailing around Maryland and Virginia. It was so well done, with fake *New York Times* articles and clippings from newspapers, that it got picked up by *USA Today*.

On the bright side, in the latest one that they tried, some girl supposedly opened up her grandfather's trunk and found trophies that showed that he was a serial killer; it was debunked on the Internet in 22 minutes. Thinking critically is an important skill that I try to teach everybody.

MM *If you're sitting at home and trying to analyze and gain a perspective on that, nobody really teaches you how to filter out false information. Sometimes we fall into a habit of just taking in the information for what it is, so it's good that you're able to introduce these analytical skills and have them take on the other angle of providing that false information. That's a really interesting strategy. So, we've been chatting about the different resources that you use, but do you have one favourite resource in terms of remote and online teaching and learning?*

TK I've become a pretty big fan of Zoom. I've used it in lots of presentations and what I like about it is that I know all of its features, although I learned just yesterday that, apparently, you can give yourself a virtual beard or a moustache or something like that. So, I haven't tried all of its features, but I like Zoom because I do like to have visual contact with people. I've done conference presentations all over the world on other platforms, and often something goes wrong. I have a conference presentation on video fakery, where I play some Deepfakes, and I would say that one time out of three, the audio doesn't come through properly. So fundamentally, I'm very comfortable with Zoom, but I'm also open to other things.

MM *Zoom seems to be the go-to, especially at the University of Calgary, as it is an approved platform for our school. So final question here, and this is one of my favourites. What do you expect higher education to look like in ten years' time?*

TK We'll still be going back to campus, but maybe not for everything. I don't think someone will stay in Nairobi or Kenya and get their entire degree from the University of Calgary. We have other facilities such as the Open University in the UK and Athabasca University that specialize in distance education. I suspect that most of our students ten years from now will still have a campus presence, but there will be so much more technology in hand. We'll be doing things like we're doing now, where people can be reached anywhere in the world.

Strange and even humorous things will still happen.

1 https://clalliance.org/blog/interview-t-mills-kelly-on-lying-about-the-past-and-media-literacy/

*"I don't think we're ever going back to what I hated when I took calculus at Columbia University— a boring professor who was more interested in his or her research droning on from 8:00 AM to 9:00 AM reading from the textbook. I don't think that students are not going to accept that anymore. They've seen the holy grail of being able to do things better ... "*

THOMAS KEENAN

I taught a University of Calgary course while I was at a conference in Australia. It turned out to be during the noonday sun. It kept getting hotter and hotter, and I had to keep picking up the computer and moving it to get out of the sun. There are always going to be logistical problems, but I think we're going to get beyond that. People now go, yeah, you've got your mute button on, or whatever. I think we're going to get over the logistical problems of using technology and get back to the core of education.

I don't think we're ever going back to what I hated when I took calculus at Columbia University—a boring professor who was more interested in his or her research, droning on from 8: 00 AM to 9: 00 AM simply reading from the textbook. I don't think that students are going to accept that anymore. They've seen the holy grail of being able to do things better, and I don't think that we're ever going to go back.

There are a whole number of things that we can anticipate. Right now I have my students working on augmented reality. I haven't used the new Oculus VR headset, but people who have tried it tell me it's like really being there. Ten years from now, there's going to be stuff that we can't even imagine now.

## REFLECTION

The TALON project has given us a remarkable, and much-needed opportunity to reflect on a major social disruption, COVID-19. This won't be the last cataclysm that "rocks our boat," as we face major challenges from climate change to social equity to ethical issues in science and medicine.

COVID-19 has demonstrated how fragile our lives are and also how connected they are. As some countries are emerging from their pandemic lockdowns, others are just starting to feel the full impact of the disease and its variants, which are almost certain to get worse.

What does this mean for education? Will we ever go back to the world of 2019? I think not. Some evidence can be found in the excellent recent study by Jose Maria Barrero of ITAM (Instituto Tecnológico Autónomo de México) in Mexico and colleagues at Stanford and the University of Chicago called *Why Working from Home Will Stick*.[2] These researchers surveyed 22,500 US workers and executives on their post-pandemic work plans. They learned that during the pandemic, half of all paid works days were done from home, and that the experience was "better than expected for the majority of firms and workers."

Going forward, they predict that most workers will continue to have offices, and go into them, but "that about 22

2 Available at https://nbloom.people.stanford.edu/sites/g/files/sbiybj4746/f/wfh_will_stick_v5.pdf.

percent of all full workdays will be supplied from home after the pandemic ends, compared with just 5 percent before." They suggest that a typical worker might work from home for two days per week, and they predict that they will be happier and more productive and spend less on work-related expenses like commuting.

I see a similar future for education. Since we are social animals, we will want to get back together in face-to-face situations. I chair a board (the Information and Communications Technology Council), which normally meets face-to-face but has been meeting virtually. We get our business done, and it's efficient, but I think most members value those exchanges around the coffee pot outside of the formal meeting agenda. I predict we'll move back to in-person meetings but probably with a hybrid option for those who are unable to attend. In the past, we have sometimes done this by audio teleconference, but it was less than satisfactory. Now we have better technology and are better at using it.

The pandemic has given us new tools and, more importantly, the need and desire to use them. People no longer laugh if you forget to unmute yourself on Zoom. We bring in experts from around the world without worrying about the time and cost of their travel. Most of all, we have learned new ways of teaching, learning, and interacting that, just as Barrero and colleagues found about the workplace, are going to stick in the learning environment.

## ABOUT

**Thomas Keenan** taught Canada's first computer security course in 1977 and has been a systems programmer, computer science professor and expert witness in technology cases. He is also the author of the best-selling book *Technocreep: The Surrender of Privacy and the Capitalization of Intimacy*. He has spoken about the social implications of technology on five continents and appears frequently in the media.

Tom was educated at Columbia University, earning degrees in philosophy, mathematics and engineering, and a doctorate in education. He is currently a professor in the School of Architecture, Planning, and Landscape at the University of Calgary, where he teaches courses on smart communities. He is also an adjunct professor of computer science where he teaches students about computer security and cyberwarfare. He is a fellow of the Canadian Information Processing Society and the Canadian Global Affairs Institute, and board chair of the Information and Communications Technology Council of Canada.

# Rationale for Design

Frances Motta, Graphic Designer

I start design projects with the ultimate goal of revealing the larger themes and ideas within the content I'm designing. In my mind, the work of a designer is to distill ideas to their most potent form and to find ways of expressing those ideas using the tools of graphic design.

This project had many promising ideas to explore. The Teaching and Learning Online Network (TALON) is an online project, and since the goal was to produce a hard copy book, the design challenge was to transform virtual content into a physical form. The content of the project, however, had the opposite intent: how to handle the transition from an in-person to an online learning format. This theme of "pulling in two opposing directions" was what intrigued me, and what I wanted to explore from the outset.

The most eloquent tool in the book designer's arsenal is typography. Typefaces lend a formal voice to the content, and in a book the selection of this voice is one of the most important design decisions to make. I only considered contemporary typefaces released in the past few years for this project because I wanted to capture the voice of this period of societal shift. I defined "contemporary typefaces" as those designed with no intent to faithfully recreate a singular historic style, which is a common trait within type design.

This book is set in GT Alpina, a typeface from the vast serif family designed by Swiss designer Reto Moser and released in 2020 by Grilli Type. We—the TALON team and I—came to this decision after exploring several other options, each with their own narrative context. At first, we experimented with geometric sans serif typefaces, which are the quintessential choices for digital brands and with Signifier, a typeface that formalizes a digital immateriality by drawing on a deeply material past. In the end we settled on GT Alpina, in which the forms of the letters reach into the grab-bag of typographical histories to create an expressive but pragmatic voice untethered from a certain style. Its letters are rooted in classic book typography that require steady rhythm and careful proportions. However, GT Alpina subverts the idea of being a "workhorse" typeface by fully embracing expressive and unexpected forms. In selecting this typeface, I considered its outspoken personality—the letters lend personality to the perspectives of the interviewees, which is a great match for a book of multi-disciplinary interviews.

The largest single influence on the design of this book was the commissioned photography, which was created prior to the layout of the book. The tangible quality and notable lack of digital signifiers within these images largely inspired the direction we took, which was to avoid typographic or graphic plays that reference digital interfaces.

In these photographs, the skewed nature of the interview screenshots was an intriguing effect that I wanted to highlight. The transition of the interviewees' likeness from a three-dimensional person to a two-dimensional screenshot to a three-dimensional presence in a frame, and back to a two-dimensional image in this book is a process that typifies the experimental and iterative nature of the transition from in-person to online learning at the beginning of the COVID-19 pandemic.

The shape of a skewed screen is used throughout the book to represent a window into the interviewees' perspectives. We imagined the cover as the all too familiar grid of a Zoom call, with all twenty-five interviews represented.

In my mind, these skewed screens point to the constant process of transitioning our experience from the physical to the digital and back again. Undoubtedly, these transitions will be ever-present as we shift to a new norm of teaching and learning.

ABOUT

**Frances Motta** is a graphic designer and creative director. She graduated from Alberta University of the Arts in 2015, and has worked and studied in Calgary, Toronto, Philadelphia, and Vancouver. She splits her focus between print, infographics, publication work, and brand identities. She is particularly interested in collaborating on projects with designers in other fields, and is currently involved in ongoing publication designs for Sustainable Calgary, brand identities for design practices Man & Son and MTHARU, and infographics for The Atlas of Furniture Design by the Vitra Design Museum.

# Afterword

Richard Parker, Supporter Richard Parker Initiative

In reading the articles regarding the multitude of ways in which educational institutions and students had to adapt to online learning, I realized that many other organizations must have faced similar situations. One such organization is The Kerby Centre in Calgary (referred to as Kerby hereafter), a very large seniors centre that I am associated with.

Prior to March 2020 Kerby primarily offered a wide range of educational and recreational programs for seniors as in-class activities. With no notice Kerby had to shut its doors on 17 March 2020 and did not know when it would reopen.

One of the things that Kerby prides itself on is providing activities that support vulnerable seniors, many of whom feel isolated, particularly if they live alone. Staff immediately realized that these feelings of isolation would be greatly increased due to the COVID lockdown.

In March 2020 Kerby did not even have a Zoom account, let alone experience of offering classes online. Within three days of closing, they offered their first online course and within weeks were offering a range of programs including Yoga, Zumba, Feldenkrais, Storytelling, Expressive Arts, Tai Chi, Spanish, Men's Shed, Fitness, Indigenous Studies, and Zoom Pals.

From March to September 2020, Kerby offered 280 individual classes for free and had over 600 participants, many of whom took multiple classes. The number of participants and courses has continued to increase since September 2020 and other initiatives Kerby has undertaken include offering lectures on health and personal finance, which have often attracted as many as 200 participants, something that could not have been handled in the building. Kerby has received financial support from companies to enable these to be offered free, plus the programs were recorded and put up on **YouTube** leading to even more viewers.

The success of these efforts is shown by the following comments from participants:

*I never expected online Art Classes to have such a positive impact on a day-to-day basis. From her themes expressed through art it made me realize how much I enjoy hiking in nature (which I am now doing). I have started baking again which I am thoroughly enjoying just to name a few activities that have inspired me from her classes! When people are sharing their drawings at the end of class it is so interesting to see the theme expressed from others as to their perspective. I always feel inspired and joyful at the end of class! You offer so many interesting classes with such well-qualified instructors. I can honestly say classes such as Tai Chi, Core Strength and Balance, and Feldenkrais (to name a few) have made such a difference in my life! I feel very fortunate and grateful that I have had the opportunity to participate in these activities. LB*

*Thank you to the Kerby Centre for the innovation you have undertaken in this time of isolation. The use of Zoom to bring us activities such as exercise classes and storytelling is keeping us healthy in mind and body. Prior to March 2020 we came to Kerby every Wednesday morning and did a range of things. The at home Zoom classes now take the place of our Wednesdays at Kerby—though sadly we miss the tasty breakfast and lunch. We look forward to the classes. Our Mom is enjoying them. At 96 she is to learning Tai Chi and chair Yoga. As shopping is curtailed for her and activities are limited to going for a walk or pottering in a garden these classes/events are very important. (A 96-year-old mother and her daughters, 71 and 68)*

As Kerby starts to open up the Centre again it is proposing to continue offering both in-class and online programs and is even rethinking its name because it is no longer just a seniors centre but is now providing services to seniors both in the building and wherever they live and have access to the web. This change would have probably occurred gradually over the next five years but COVID caused it to occur literally in days.

In conclusion I would like to acknowledge the efforts TALON, the Teaching and Learning Online Network, which undertook to facilitate the discussion about online learning. These efforts have led to the creation of an international network that helps to advance and enhance the digital classroom. The voices of some of those at the forefront of this new virtual practice have been included in this book, which is a record of the start of a process. I look forward to watching how the lessons learned and ideas shared continue to spread and help in our new hybrid and HyFlex future.

## ABOUT

**Richard Parker** is a Fellow of the Canadian Institute of Planners with over fifty years of experience in Land Use Planning in the United Kingdom and Canada. Richard retired from the City of Calgary in October 2003 following a 29-year career that included 15 years as Head of the Planning Department.

During his time with the City, Richard was involved with a wide range of planning issues, including Calgary's overall Land Use and Transportation Plans, Downtown Planning, and innovative projects such as Garrison Woods and Mackenzie Town.

Since retiring from the City, Richard has provided consulting services to Municipalities and non-profit groups in Alberta on a range of planning topics. In addition, as a partner in The Real Estate Development Institute, he has designed and delivered education programs related to real estate and planning to numerous groups, including the University of Calgary Real Estate Certificate Program.

Richard has been a member of the Board of Directors of the Kerby Centre in Calgary since 2015 and is currently Chair of the Board.

An adjunct professor in SAPL, he enjoys participating in courses and student projects and mentoring young planners.

# TALON Manifesto

TALON is committed to and advocates for ...

- Inclusive and equitable online education
- Open and positive learning environments
- Interactive and engaging pedagogy
- Transformative and imaginative design curricula
- Empowering virtual classrooms
- Collaborative learning and design teaching
- Software and tools enabling meaningful learning experiences
- Respect and care for all students and instructors
- Connectivity, creativity, and co-creation

# TALON Glossary

What do we mean when we say ...

**Asynchronous Learning:** Learning that takes place through content available online for students to access when it best suits their schedules.

**Blended Learning:** Course delivery that uses in-person and online methods to engage students.

**Classroom:** A space for teaching and learning. A classroom can be both a physical room and a shared digital learning space.

**Digital Disparity:** Differences in individuals' access to digital information and relevant technologies for learning due to geographic location and/or socioeconomic factors such as income level, race, gender, etc.

**Digital Literacy:** An individual's ability to use digital information and relevant technologies for learning.

**Distance Education:** Students study at their own pace without face-to-face contact with an instructor.

**Emergency Instruction:** An alternate teaching delivery model implemented in times of crisis—a temporary solution in a serious, unexpected, and dangerous situation that requires immediate action.

**Experiential Learning:** Learning that takes place through experience, action, and critical reflection, i.e., learning-by-doing.

**Higher Education:** Tertiary (or postsecondary) education leading to the award of an academic degree.

**Inclusive Practice:** The possibility for all students to participate and succeed.

**Interactive:** Activities that invite students to participate and contribute.

**Netiquette:** Accepted social behaviours for ethical conduct, and politeness in online communication, and digital teaching, and learning.

**Online:** Connected to another computer or to a digital network (the Internet).

**Online Education:** Any kind of learning that takes place online, via computer/the Internet.

**Pedagogy:** The method and practice of teaching or, more generally, the knowledge and skills utilized in a classroom context.

**Physical Distancing:** The requirement for students to maintain a safe distance (6 feet, 2 metres) to avoid catching or spreading COVID-19.

**Remote Learning:** Scheduled instruction whereby the activities happen away from the physical site of a provider. Usually, students use digital means to engage with program content. Transition to remote delivery is often done in response to crises, as happened with the COVID-19 pandemic.

**SAPL:** The School of Architecture, Planning and Landscape at the University of Calgary, Canada. The "home" of TALON.

**Synchronous Learning:** Learning that takes place with students engaging with tasks/materials in real time.

**Tools:** Software, apps and online platforms that help keep the online classroom engaging, inclusive, and interactive.

**Virtual Classroom:** A learning environment in which students engage with course materials online, both synchronous and asynchronous.

# TALON Team

EDITORS

**Sandra Abegglen** (editor and interviewer) is a researcher in the School of Architecture, Planning and Landscape at the University of Calgary where she explores learning and teaching in the design disciplines as the project lead of TALON, the Teaching and Learning Online Network. Sandra has an MSc in social research and an MA in learning and teaching in higher education. She has over eight years' experience as a senior lecturer in education studies. Her research interests are online education, creative learning and teaching, mentoring, visual narratives, identity and qualitative research methods. She has published widely on emancipatory learning and teaching practice, and playful pedagogy. Sandra is a certified practitioner for learning development and a fellow of Advance HE. She has been awarded the Team Teaching Award 2020 by the University of Calgary.

**Fabian Neuhaus, PhD** (editor) is an associate professor at the University of Calgary with the School of Architecture, Planning and Landscape. He is the research lead for the Richard Parker Initiative (RPI) and the principal investigator for TALON and NEXTCalgary. His research interests are the temporal aspects of the urban environment, focusing on the topics of habitus, type, and ornament in terms of activity, technology, and memory. He has worked with architecture and urban design practices in the UK and Switzerland as well as on research projects at universities in Switzerland, Germany, and the UK. He is passionate about learning and teaching, and design pedagogy.

**Kylie Wilson** (editor) is a graduate student in the master of architecture program at the School of Architecture, Planning, and Landscape, University of Calgary. In the 2020–2021 academic year, she completed the foundation year. Before pursuing architecture, she graduated with a bachelor of arts in communications, minoring in political science, also from the University of Calgary. She joined the TALON team as graduate assistant researcher in May 2021 and works actively on the project's audiovisual content collection, newsletters and TALON publications. She is passionate about storytelling and knowledge sharing through media and built form and empowering users through placemaking in architecture.

## INTERVIEWERS

**Martina MacFarlane** (interviewer) is a community planner, researcher, and artist living on Treaty 7 territory. She was born in Vancouver, lived and learned in a number of Canadian cities, and came to call Alberta home where she completed a bachelor of fine arts at the University of Alberta in Edmonton and later her master of planning from the University of Calgary. Martina brings a unique background to her planning practice from art, design, and visual communications to interests in social inclusion, equity, and belonging. She takes a hands-on and iterative approach and has worked in community art initiatives and instruction, as well as on social innovation and research projects in inclusive and affordable housing, community safety, and sustainable urban design.

During the second term of her graduate studies, the COVID-19 pandemic marked the sudden shift to online courses, communications, and—well, everything. In spring of 2020, Martina joined the TALON project as a graduate assistant researcher, exploring what this shift meant for teaching and learning in the design disciplines and the challenges and opportunities of online collaboration.

**Mac McGinn** (interviewer) is motivated by the power of architecture to be solution driven by shaping how we think and feel about the world and set the stage for social behaviours. Due to rapid and dynamic changes in the political, economic, and social environments we live in, the built environment is uniquely positioned to provide solutions to challenges that our world confronts. Also, Mac's passion lies in the business development and operations within architectural firms to facilitate ongoing growth through B2B and B2C relationships, marketing, and office operations.

Mac is among the 2022 graduating class in the University of Calgary's master of architecture program. He previously completed a bachelor of business administration at Mount Royal University with a minor in international business. He worked in the Calgary business community for five years prior to continuing his education. As a result of his passionate interest in design, he switched gears and pursued a career in architecture. Mac was a graduate assistant researcher working on the Teaching and Learning Online Network project (TALON).